First published 2000 by
Edward Gaskell publishers
6 Grenville Street
Bideford
Devon
EX39 2EA

isbn 1-898546-39-8

The Dawn Stand-to

The Life of I.V.B. (Peter) Mills, QPM, CPM

As told to

Christopher Lawrence Hiscox

Printed and bound by
Lazarus Press
Unit 7 Caddsdown Business Park
Bideford
Devon
EX39 3DX

To the lady companions of my life
and to my very many African friends
who so loyally and selflessly aided and protected me.

9/5/00

To Rob

with best
regards

Pete

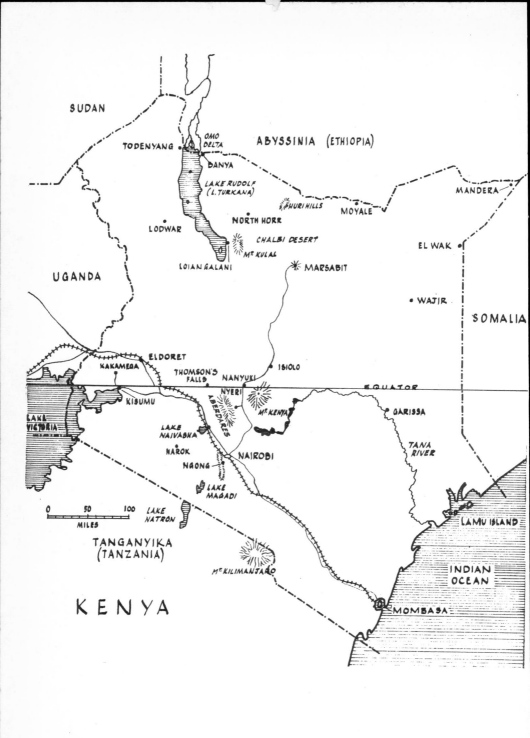

Contents

Preface

There is a stamp on the souls of some men which compels them to sit down and write a book detailing the ideas, the emotions and the events which have shaped their lives. Do these men believe that their story is one of great importance; that what they have done or achieved in their lives is somehow of historical significance or will hold a fascination for those who read it?

These questions, I admit, had on rare occasions crossed my mind, but never in regard to my own life. Some I have met along the way have been involved in momentous events, some have achieved fame and some notoriety, they all had a tale to tell which was worth the listening – but I? No! I have simply done my job to the best of my ability, followed my guiding star and enjoyed every single minute of it. The few incidents in which I have been involved seemed to me at the time to be not in the least bit unusual or out of the ordinary and surely of little interest to anyone else, so the idea of writing it down never entered my head.

I had been retired some fifteen years and long settled back in my native Norfolk before any such ideas came to me. I was a regular customer of the village pub and spent many hours in the company of others, discussing the usual pub topics – weather, women and the pursuit of justice, which talk was interspersed with anecdotes and reminiscences of times long past. To my surprise, my stories were often met with the comment, "You know Peter, you really ought to write a book."

So often in fact, was this said that I became encouraged and told my wife that I might just consider doing so. She, however, lost no time in telling me that if I did, she would leave me. Her reasons were, I think, not unconnected with the fact that, as my second wife, she had not been part of my earlier life and so considered that it would be unseemly, not to say embarrassing, for me to publicise some of the less savoury details of the behaviour of colonial officers in those times.

Out of my profound love and respect for her, I bowed to her wishes and forgot the idea. However, as time went by and friends and acquaintances continued to urge me to "Write that book", my wife's objections began to fade and eventually she too joined the chorus of persuasion.

The decision, eventually to tell my story brought me immediately face to face with my biggest problem – I am no great hand with words. Hitherto, my experience has been confined to the compilation of reports to my Police superiors on the activities and conditions of the units under my command, and of notes for the prosecution of suspected criminals. So now, I called upon an old friend who was an experienced writer and also one of those who, for years, had been urging me to tell my story. To him I said, "OK, let's do it," and we did. My story is related in a forthright and purely factual manner with little literary embellishment other than to describe those sights and sounds, those smells and sensations which would enhance the reader's visions of the extraordinary places, people and events to which I have been a witness.

Insofar as it is reasonable to do so, the narrative is confined strictly to the facts, however in certain cases, I have changed names and been imprecise about dates and locations in order to avoid as much as possible, giving offence to those involved who are still alive.

Concerning the ladies of my life, I have, without exception, greatly enjoyed their love and companionship and continue to have the greatest respect for them all. Were it possible, I would like nothing better than to relive each happy moment that I have spent in their company.

I.V.B. (Peter) Mills
Ranworth
Norfolk
1999

Childhood

I was born in November 1918, a week after the signing of the Armistice which ended the Great War, and looking back, I am convinced that my complicated birth and the handicaps it left me with, coupled with my strange upbringing and my family relationships, put a stamp upon my character which was to influence my behaviour, my decisions and in fact the progress of my whole life.

My parents already had four children, two girls and two boys and I arrived unplanned, after a four year gap, so, as my mother constantly made clear to me, I was, as far as she was concerned, totally unwanted. She never showed me any love or consideration and lost no opportunity to scold and humiliate me, while my father remained neutral.

My complicated birth, which ended in a Caesarean Section, left me with two afflictions, at least, I am led to believe that this is how such afflictions can arise; firstly, I was a bed-wetter until the age of seven or eight; and secondly, I had, and still have, a slight st-stammer.

I was christened Ivor Vernon Barfoot Mills, but, from the earliest age was always, and still am, known as Peter and I grew up to be acutely shy and reserved, but oddly, with an excess of self confidence and, as though to make certain that I was something of an eccentric individualist, I experienced three head injuries between the ages of twelve and seventeen.

The first, at the age of twelve, happened when I was watering the garden with a hose-pipe that had a long heavy bronze nozzle. For fun, I started to swing the hosepipe at high speed around my head, sending cascades of water flying all over the place. Unfortunately, and perhaps inevitably, the nozzle came down hard across the back of my head, knocking me to the ground where the gardener found me, lying unconscious, some time later. It was several days before I was back to normal.

At the age of sixteen, I was cycling to work one morning, and while descending a steep hill at my usual reckless speed, the front forks suddenly collapsed and I landed yards down the road on my forehead. Our local greengrocer witnessed the incident and stayed with me for half an hour until I regained consciousness, then he kindly transported the remains of my bicycle home for me, while I continued to work on foot.

Upon my arrival, the boss was so alarmed that he had me taken home immediately. Apparently I was battered and scarred and covered in blood, and, as he put it, 'acting queerly'. I, however, remembered nothing of the incident.

The third accident occurred a year later, after I had acquired a motor-cycle. Our house had a long approach drive which widened out by the front door, either side of which, stood a heavy stone pillar topped with a large plant container. In summer, though the inner door was closed, this front door was always kept open and it was my practice to accelerate violently up the drive, lay the machine hard over, apply the back brake and skid side-ways towards the door-way to see how much gravel from the drive I could shower into the outer hall-way.

One lunch-time when I was practising this art, my foot slipped off the brake and I careered headlong into one of the pillars, hitting it hard with the side of my head. I recovered consciousness the following morning in bed and with a terrible head-ache which throbbed painfully for a good forty-eight hours.

I believe that these three head injuries have, in some way, affected me permanently, leaving me with no sense of taste and an appalling memory for names and faces, and these, as well as the slight stammer, have caused me much embarrassment over the years. Later, in my official life, I developed a dread of public functions and of occasions when I was obliged to read out documents in court. In everyday speech, however, I quickly learned to exchange one word for another, when the first became suddenly stuck and wouldn't come out, and with practice, I did become very skilled. Few people, even those close to me, ever knew, or even suspected, my afflictions. I mention these handicaps and my mother's lack of affection for me, not as excuses, but as a possible explanation of my personal motivation and my, sometimes strange, activities in later life.

My father, Doctor Lawrence Hitchin Barfoot Mills, was a General Practitioner. He was born in 1874, one of five, four boys and one girl. His Father, born in 1820, owned a number of maltings scattered throughout Norfolk, which produced malted barley for the brewing industry, and as a side-line, he owned a small fleet of ships operating out of Suffolk ports.

Grandfather, must have been quite wealthy since he was able to educate his children to a reasonably high standard - two of his sons became doctors, one a Solicitor who founded the largest firm of Solicitors in Norwich, another an auctioneer and estate agent who married a brewery heiress and his daughter became an opera singer who, before the 1914/18 war, married a millionaire German shoe manufacturer. She lived to fly the Atlantic in one of the earliest piston- engined aircraft, on a visit to her son, who had settled in America, and himself become a millionaire. She was then aged ninety-two and it was her first flight.

My father, the youngest, who had been a Major in the RAMC during the 1914/18 war, and his oldest brother, also a doctor, practised together in Norwich for forty-four years until they eventually decided that they didn't get on very well together and dissolved the partnership. From then, my father practised on his own until his retirement in 1939 when war broke out, but even then he continued to treat anyone who came to him seeking medical aid.

My uncle, who was born in 1860, was, by all accounts, a real medical 'character'. He was one of the last doctors to qualify at twenty-one years of age, by apprenticeship, rather than by examinations, and had led a colourful life. He had been, amongst other things, an Army Surgeon to the Forces fighting the Mad Mullah in the Sudan and the Ships Surgeon on the vessel that took the first rubber plants to Malaya, the profits from which have financed Malaya ever since. During the years he practised in Norwich, he was in many ways a pioneer, he was the first local doctor to use X-rays and every year, he spent two months in Germany learning their medical techniques, which were, at the time, way ahead of those in the U.K.

He was a bachelor for over sixty years and always travelled in a bright yellow 1927 American Oldsmobile car which had the family crest on each rear door and was driven by a lady Chauffeur. He would be seen travelling about the city, sitting in the middle of the back seat with his two Labrador dogs bolt-upright on the seat, one either side of him.

Eventually, he married his house-keeper, a really delightful young woman, who was forty-two years his junior and by whom he had a daughter. He lived to see his grandson reach the age of four and was still practising when he died at the age of ninety-four.

After his death, my Aunt found a box which he had kept by him all his married life. She had often seen it before, but its contents were a mystery to her and when she opened it, she found scores of love letters which he had received wherever he had been in the world in the years before their marriage. She, my aunt, was ninety-three when she died and that was only three years ago.

Mother, who was six years younger than my father, was an extremely beautiful lady originally from Nottingham, and one of those elegant Edwardian beauties who, up to her death at the age of only seventy-three, still retained her figure and her elegance.

One of her two sisters, as beautiful as herself, married a local Solicitor. The other, of quite different looks and personality, became a state registered nurse and never married. Instead, she became totally obsessed with a High Church Priest and spent endless hours at his Church during the later years of her life, just to be near him.

How times have changed - and quite naturally. In 1918, when I was born, Norwich was largely controlled by a tight-knit community of top business and professional families who met, entertained and inter-married in what amounted to a 'closed shop', and since the city had few doctors, my father and my uncle were called upon to attended many of this wealthy fraternity.

Father therefore, on only his general practitioner earnings, was able to maintain a large city house, two cars, a chauffeur, a resident cook, two house-maids, a nanny and also a large country home which the family occupied at week-ends and during school holidays and where he employed a full-time gardener to attend the grounds and take care of the house.

In the season, he spent two days a week shooting and, at week-ends, he competed in sailing races in a succession of successful yachts. He was able to afford to put four children through public schools up to the age of eighteen and take sea cruising holidays with all his family. Over Christmas and New Year the whole family were taken away to stay in a hotel for a period of ten to fourteen days. What general practitioner, I wonder, could afford to do all this on his income today?

I was born at 35 All Saints Green Norwich, but almost immediately we moved one hundred yards away to an elegant Georgian house at No. 39 Surrey Street, which, though it was in the centre of the city, had a very large garden, complete with pond and croquet lawn. The house has since been bought by the Norwich Union Insurance group and the garden is now a part of Norwich's main bus station.

The house had a basement, a ground floor and three other floors, all with large well appointed rooms. Above these, was a spacious attic, and from the basement to the attic, there was a lift which was operated by continuous pull-ropes. Since our dining room was on the 3rd floor, and all food, cutlery and dishes had to be put into the lift in the basement kitchens and then hoisted all the way up to the delivery level - a considerable task for a family as large as ours.

I think I was about four years old when we moved again to another big house about a quarter of a mile away. It was called 'The Wilderness' and stood behind the old city wall built in the Middle Ages to protect the city. A one hundred yard stretch of the wall was in the garden and two ancient defence towers, one called the Black Tower, were in the garden of the adjoining house.

I remember the large garden with its three ponds, a large summer house, many pear and apple trees, an abundance of lime and oak, two stables and along its borders some two acres of woodland, sloping steeply down to an area of terraced houses way below. Altogether I had some three acres of land and three ponds to entertain me.

No house directly overlooked either the house or the garden and our nearest neighbour was old John Colman of Colman's Mustard who had so large a garden that he employed two gardeners to take care of it. Although there was a ten foot high wall separating our two properties, I still managed to cause our neighbour considerable anguish when in one of my more mischievous moods.

Mr Colman was extremely proud of his garden with its gorgeous flower beds, rare trees and fruit of all kinds. For a city garden it was truly extra-ordinary and, as a boy I would climb onto the high wall which divided our two gardens and watch open-mouthed as he showed friends and dignitaries around his horticultural paradise.

One day, the devil in me got the upper hand and with my newly acquired air rifle, I fired a slug into each of the apples on Mr Colman's rarest and favourite tree. The following afternoon, I peeped over the wall just in time to see him pointing out the tree to a group of admiring friends. Suddenly, a look of amazement spread over his face.

"Good heavens," he exclaimed. "A beetle or a disease or something must have got into the apples." And he dashed off to berate his gardeners.

12

I slid silently to the ground, disappeared into the shrubbery and didn't show my face outdoors for a week or more.

As a small child, I seldom saw my parents. Nanny, or as we children knew her, Nurse Betts, kept me well out of their way except to say good-morning and good-night, and as I grew older, I spent almost my entire time with the servants, finding their company much more fun than that of my brothers or sisters or parents.

I lived for the outside, where I had endless interests, the two main ones being shooting and keeping garden pets such as rabbits, pigeons, bantams, wild ducks, pheasants, jackdaws and an limitless succession of other creatures. I taught my jackdaw to speak, which he did far better than most parrots do. I made all my own cages and pens and dug out a large fourth pond for my ducks which would fly in and out over the city, often bringing wild duck back with them.

Although we were close to the city centre the houses of the area mostly had large gardens inter-spaced with patches of woodland, and these stretched right as far as the open county-side. Through this link, pheasants and other wild creatures frequently reached our garden, to my great delight. The garden was for me a paradise, filled with endless interest and fascination.

Shortly after my birth Father built a new and much larger holiday home on land owned by the family in the tiny village of Ranworth on the Norfolk Broads. This house had five double bedrooms, a large lounge and dining room divided by folding doors which, when opened, created one huge room with an old-fashioned recessed fireplace at each end. My mother had designed the house on the back of an envelope which she then handed over for development to our Architect, Robert Bond, a professional friend. Robert Bond was a member of the family which founded Bonds, the large department store in Norwich, and it was to his son that my nearest sister had almost become engaged.

My present house, which I built some twenty-three years ago on old family land purchased from an Aunt and a cousin many years before my return from Kenya, is situated only about two hundred yards away from my parent's old holiday home.

We five children, and our parents, complete with nanny, cook and two house-maids, were transported to the country house each week-end and for the duration of the school holidays, during which period, my Father commuted each day by car to Norwich.

Since my Father was a keen shooting man, it seems only natural that I should follow in his foot-steps and, at the age of about three or four, I did. I clearly remember my first 'gun', it was a little break-back pop gun that fired a cork held captive by two or three feet of string and my first shooting experience took place at our holiday home in Ranworth.

On arrival, at week-ends or school holidays, I was given the job of going round the house shooting mosquitoes off the walls until I had rid the place of them. Since the house was situated close to water where mosquitoes bred, I was always kept pretty busy with my quota of insects. After this, I progressed rapidly in the shooting world and it was only some fourteen years later that I shot my first buffalo, quickly followed by my first elephant, using, not the pop gun, but a massive .577 double barrelled rifle which weighed 15lbs and packed some two and a half tons of striking energy derived from a 100 grains cordite charge behind a 750 grain bullet - and this at an age when most boys would still be wondering whether it was time they changed from a little .410 shot gun to a 12 bore to shoot rabbits.

I was given another task, considered suitable for a small boy of my temperament, this was to scoop the drowned mice out of the well in the garden from which we drew water for the house.

Adjoining the country house were some four acres of gardens, a cottage, a complex of malt-house buildings, a long water frontage on one bank of the lake known as Malthouse Broad, some seven acres of the Broad itself and twenty odd acres of rough marsh-land which stretched from the far bank of the Broad to the River Bure some distance beyond. All of this property, which, as I have said, I later bought from an aunt and a cousin, was owned then in shares by my father, an uncle and two cousins, having been bequeathed to them by my Grandfather.

Originally, the site of one of my Grandfather's malting businesses it had once been the scene of bustling enterprise, turning barley into malt for the brewing industry. Carts brought barley from the local farms, steam rose constantly from the malthouse, and wherries, (Norfolk Broads sailing barges), moored at the staithe to load up and ship the malt to the breweries.

There was always plenty to do; our garden had a nice lawn tennis court to keep us children occupied, we had rowing boats, a sailing dinghy and a motor cruiser. The rough marsh-lands and the water produced excellent duck shooting, not to mention a few pheasants and rabbits. To a boy of my inclinations, left to roam free, this was heaven - my second paradise.

Adjoining our garden was a three acre field that belonged to the Church Commissioners from whom my father rented it, and this proved to be quite a productive area. We grew all types of vegetables and fruit, a few mangolds for the small flock of black sheep kept there by my uncle and we kept a few pigs which were sold to offset the gardener's wages.

All things considered, I was very fortunate in having ample space, both in Norwich and in the country, in which to follow my various pursuits. I remember going through the bow and arrow and catapult phases until, whilst I was still very young, Father gave me a small air rifle and pretty soon afterwards, replaced it with a more powerful BSA .22. I was seldom without it and soon became a crack shot.

I grew to be self sufficient and saw little need for friends of my own age. The house maids, chauffeur and gardeners gave me any company I needed, and from them, I learned a great deal, far more than ever I learned from my parents. I hated being indoors almost as much as I hated being cooped up in school, where, being a solitary child, not keen on team games, I often managed to dodge football and cricket so that I had more time to myself. I did, however, enjoy tennis and swimming at which I even excelled, to the extent that, I twice won the school diving cup.

I never excelled in academic subjects, and, because of my many outside interests, I invariably ended up scribbling down my homework five minutes before the morning bell, or cribbing the efforts of those who were academically stronger, but physically weaker, than myself. At best, I can claim to have achieved only 'fair' results in the only two subjects in which I had any interest, English and Maths. These interested me because, to my way of thinking, what more would I need in life but to make myself understood, to understand others and to figure out the profits from my dealings. I always carried home my end-of-term reports in a state of quaking apprehension.

One thing for which I owe my parents a debt of gratitude is their attention to diet. Being a doctor, my father would tolerate only the healthiest regime. Our food contained few fats, plenty of vegetables, wholemeal bread etc, augmented by calcium tablets, iron and Virol so that we all grew up healthy, well formed, and with good physiques, a state none of us, his children, ever lost.

From the start, I resented school because it denied me the free time I longed for. My first school was the Notre Dame Convent, only a few yards from our house in the centre of Norwich. Discipline was strict and the Nuns allowed no nonsense, so I was quickly in trouble, and at the end of my second term, Mother Superior sent for my father and told him she would not have me back because I was too rough with the little girls. I, of course, denied this, though I do recall pushing over one little blonde girl because she teased me unmercifully, and some time later, swinging her round by her hair for the same reason. Naturally, on each occasion she screamed the place down.

Next term I was sent to Norwich Grammar School, as it was then called. This ancient seat of learning is situated in the Close, with its entrance right alongside the magnificent west end of the Cathedral and at a considerable distance from our house, which stood on the far side of the city. Still only a small boy, I walked this distance, winter and summer, alone - though I must admit, that on occasions when it was very wet, I would be driven there in the morning and collected in the evening, by our kindly chauffeur.

I don't remember much about the Grammar School, because, in fact, I wasn't there for very long, due to an unfortunate incident which occurred soon after my arrival. One summer day, when a section of the playground was being re-surfaced with tar and chippings, a fellow pupil set about me for some reason best known to himself, and in the ensuing scuffle, I knocked him against a half full barrel of tar. The barrel promptly rolled over, disgorging its sticky black contents all over my unfortunate adversary.

His screaming soon brought masters scurrying onto the scene and seeing the state the poor chap was in, they immediately laid the blame upon me and I was duly expelled.

In truth, I think that my father was told by the headmaster, politely in deference to my his civic standing, that a different school would possibly be of greater advantage to me.

Next, I was sent to Bracondale School, a small private school taking both boarders and day pupils, and which was situated only about a hundred yards from our house, and over-looked by it. Bracondale was a good school catering for all social levels, and I was sorry to read recently that it was being forced to close due to a lack of pupils.

Since the school and its grounds ran alongside our house, the head and the masters soon became acquainted with my garden activities, and particularly from whence came the air gun pellets that often broke lights and windows on that side of the school. But they were quite tolerant and I managed to remain there until I was just sixteen.

In those days, one usually took two examinations, first the Junior Cambridge and then the Senior Cambridge. Some stayed on to take matriculation levels a year later. I sat the Junior Cambridge exam at nearly fifteen - and passed it. This came as a great surprise to everyone since, despite cheating by every means possible, I had never yet managed to obtain good marks.

I sat the Senior Cambridge examination a year later and failed it. As I recall, we were required to pass each of six different papers, including one foreign language paper. For a while, we had been taught both Latin and French until five of us - deemed to be holding back the rest - were removed from the Latin class and made to take double French instead. Even with this extra tuition, I don't think I learnt ten words, so I failed the French paper, and with it, the Senior Cambridge exam.

I suppose I was ill-equipped to be a good scholar. I was pre-occupied, ill-disciplined and rougher than my potentially genteel upbringing should have made me and I was often in trouble with my tutors.

Once, when kept in by a Master who had left me to do an hour's lines, I took the class marks book from his desk drawer and altered my 1's to 9's, 3's to 8's and a few 0's to 10's. In the event, this attempt to improve my academic standing was never discovered, or if it was, nobody mentioned the fact to me, but I spent weeks in abject terror in case my cheating should come to light.

I'm proud to say that, throughout my school career, I was caned only once, (though I'm sure I deserved it more), and that was for a crime I didn't commit.

A two gallon jug of milk had been left to stand on a staircase leading from the cloak-room and someone, not I, had knocked it over, but since I happened to be the closest to it when the deputy head passed by a few moments later, it was me he grabbed and to whom gave six of the best. To my surprise, however, the punishment didn't hurt, and who it was who knocked it over, I never did discover.

Whenever rough behaviour broke out in school, I was usually the one called to the head-master's study, and on one such occasion, towards the end of my school career, he said to me, that since I was near to leaving school, instead of caning me, he would give me some advice. He told me that I ought to adopt a more responsible attitude, to study seriously and to stop thinking that I could make a living with my gun. Little did he know, as you will discover later - that was precisely what I did do.

Here, my schooling ended and I went forth into the world, unqualified and unrepentant.

Higher Education

I was not yet sixteen when I left Bracondale School and, with little academic achievement to my name, the prospects were not rosy. I doubt that my parents entertained any hope of me achieving a worthwhile position in life as my brothers had done, but they could, at least, be content that they had instilled into me a few basic social accomplishments. I spoke reasonable English, I knew how to behave under most circumstances, I had become a competent player of both auction and contract bridge, whist, chess, draughts, mah-jong, roulette, which my parents played with their guests after dinner parties, and pretty well every other gambling game. I was also able to stand my own at billiards and snooker on full size tables, and even knew how to hold a lady while dancing, though not yet how to keep in step or off her feet.

Immediately upon leaving school, I started work in the export department of Coleman and Company - makers of a popular tonic wine, and since taken over by Colmans the mustard people - at a starting pay of 2/6d per week. After two months, this doubled to five shillings per week - 25p in modern money - and seemed to me to be quite a generous wage. I had, however, other sources of income.

During my school days, my parents had never given me regular pocket money - my father used to say, 'ask if you want money', and Mother went a little further saying 'take what you want'. She always kept a little in a handbag in her bureau. In retrospect, I think this was wrong, since it led me to borrowing from any 'handy' source and so, causing considerable upset among the household.

However, the lack of a regular supply of pocket money caused me to seek other ways of obtaining funds and thereby, learning the value of money and the folly of wasting it.

My earliest trading was when I commenced school at Brackondale. Four hundred yards away from the school stood a cake shop which sold, amongst other things, doughnuts, and when the bell sounded for mid-morning break, I would race to the shop, grab the bag they always had ready for me, then race back to school again. The deal I had with the shop was, fifteen doughnuts for one shilling, and I would sell these to the other pupils for 1 penny each, so I made three pence a day, or 1/3d a week.

Then I bred rabbits which I sold to our local butcher. I kept pigeons and always left a few hen birds free to sit on the house roof. These would attract male feral birds from all over the city, which I shot and sold to the game dealer for eight pence each along with pheasants and ducks from my menagerie. I had chickens and bantams, and sold their eggs to my mother. I used to collect swallow-tail butterfly caterpillars which, in those days were abundant, for sale to a taxidermist. Also I collected coot, waterhen and plovers eggs which my parents bought.

During the summer months, the Norfolk Broads were visited by holidaymakers just as they are today, but then, mostly in sailing boats. Our Broad, at Ranworth, had not been dredged and had only a narrow deep-water channel running through, flanked on either side by shallow water, barely covering sticky mud-banks. Yachts heading for the village would often sail innocently into the shallows and get well and truly stuck. I would lie in wait until the crew had worn themselves out trying to pole themselves off the mud, then I would take father's cruiser and offer to tow them off - for a fee, of course. Having agreed the fee, I would drag out the operation, making a great show of getting stronger ropes and tackle and pulling and pushing, on only about quarter throttle, until finally, with a flourish, I completed the exercise. By this time, my customers were usually so grateful that they were more than willing to pay me a little extra on top of the agreed fee.

Frequently I would pocket a few of my father's cartridges and visit local farms where I was known, to shoot hares, rabbits and pigeons which, of course, I sold. Hare shooting in the Spring when corn was around twelve inches high was fun and particularly profitable. From the edge of a field not a hare would be seen, but after I'd fired a shot in the air, half a dozen heads would pop up, only to disappear again. Noting their positions

I would then walk them up and shoot them one after another, for sale, of course.

During the migration season for greenfinch and goldfinch, I trapped them, (now of course, illegal), and after a period of rehabilitation, sold them to collectors of cage-birds.

Despite my enthusiasm for earning extra cash, there was one ruse, used by our gardener at Ranworth, that I never did pluck up enough courage to attempt. He was in his mid fifties and apart from the 1914/1918 war, was employed all his life by my father. Throughout the holiday season he was to be found most lunch times and evenings, sitting in his "personal" corner of the local pub wearing two large poke hats, one on top of the other. Holiday makers inevitably asked him, why the two hats, to which he would reply, 'Because everyone who asks me that buys me a pint'. They usually did and he often ended up drunk.

While he went about his work, the gardener always chewed tobacco and, on his head, instead of the two hats he wore in the pub, he wore a flat cap. At intervals, he would remove his cap and spit the chewed tobacco into it for use later, then replace the cap upon his head. This practice resulted in channels of brown juice running in continual streams down his face.

He was also the Church grave-digger and on one hot summer's day, when he was about six feet down he felt suddenly sleepy from his exertions and lay down in the bottom of the grave to sleep. Some while later, an elderly couple who were visiting the grave-yard, happened to pass by, and seeing the prone figure of the gardener lying at the bottom of the grave, thought he was dead. Panic ensued; the old gentleman swooned and his wife passed out in a dead faint so the vicar had to be called to go and fetch my father to attend to her.

In those years at Ranworth our gardener taught me a lot; how to bab for eels and how to set night lines for them, how to snare pike in the drainage dykes, how to castrate pigs and a host of old country lore. He was a very patient and understanding man, but died comparatively young and lies buried in my family's line of graves in the village church yard.

My parents seldom went to church in Norwich, but regularly attended Sunday services while staying at Ranworth, and I was usually pressed into pumping the organ. I quickly discovered that if I pumped really hard, I could over-pressurise the air bag, which would release the safety valve. This would create several amusing effects, the valve would emit a loud whistle, clouds of dust would be showered onto the heads of the congregation and flocks of bats would be disturbed from their roost in the church roof and fly about the church terrifying the female worshippers. I saw to it that this happened as frequently as I dared.

I did, however, perform one useful service for the church. The vicar had a large plot of land, between the church-yard and my father's land, upon which he used to grow vegetables for the vicarage kitchens. To his great annoyance, it was plagued by a vast army of rabbits which did considerable damage around the graveyard and always managed to harvest more of his crop than he did. With his blessing, I was allowed to climb the church tower and shoot them from above with a .410 shot-gun and this seemed to compensate for my misbehaviour at other times.

One day, when I returned home to our house in Norwich and went down the garden to inspect my menagerie, I came across a funny little man sitting in a deck chair in the large lower section of the garden. He was puffing a pipe filled with tobacco flavoured with foul smelling herbs.

Standing by him was a tall, ponderous police sergeant who was examining an elevated pigeon loft I had recently constructed on the edge of a three-hundred foot slope overlooking the city so that it would be visible from a great distance. The policeman was investigating a report of the loss of a quantity of 1" x 1" and 2" x 1" timber from a nearby building site, and, upon my arrival, began to question me. I was a bit disconcerted because, even though I had managed to convince myself that the timber was abandoned, I had indeed, recently spent three evenings pilfering it for my pigeon loft.

Fortunately for me, the sergeant gradually realised who it was he was questioning. My father and my uncle, in addition to the private practices, were surgeons to the Norfolk County Police Force and Norwich City Police Force, respectively. In fact, Father held the post for more than twenty years, and my uncle, for some sixty years and between them, they medically examined for entry and for discharge, every policeman for generations. The sergeant, being a discrete officer, decided that the wood was unidentifiable and having no witnesses, departed, no doubt closing the case on grounds of insufficient evidence. This left the little fellow, whose eyes had been popping out of his head, in a very agitated state at my narrow escape. We soon became good friends.

He was, I guessed, aged about forty, but looked a lot older. He was small, frail, hump backed, pigeon-breasted and wheezed pitifully. It transpired that the poor fellow was under Father's medical care for asthma, and, because of it, could not work.

21

He lived in a minute one up one down terraced house in a back alley off the main road a quarter of a mile from our house. His house had no garden and was hemmed in by large buildings. He existed on 50p (ten old shillings) a week which paid his rent, enough electricity to power an old wireless he had been given, for food and for a few bits of coal for his fire when temperatures dropped below freezing. Father had given him permission to use our garden when he wished, to enjoy some fresh air and, during the years of our companionship, I never once heard him complain or bemoan his lot.

His name was McPherson, Mac of course to me. He had a great sense of humour and, together for three years, we engaged in endless escapades, though at times, he found it difficult to keep pace with me. He took over the care and up-keep of all the birds and animals that I kept in the Norwich garden, and relieved our chauffeur of these chores when we were away at our country house. Given new interests, his health began to improved a little and his life did, I think, become more tolerable.

Mac had another friend, a spinster, who worked in a factory close by his home. She used to keep an eye on him and would buy him little treats now and then and tend to him during bad asthma attacks. She was about Mac's age and quite attractive, and though she never associated with other men, Mac told me that their relationship was strictly platonic.

After the war she bought a little bungalow on the Norfolk coast close to the beach and they lived there happily together until he died in around 1950. She wrote to tell me of his death and, at the same time, thanked me for having given him what she described as 'his three wonderful years'. She said that, to his death, he never ceased to chatter and laugh about our exploits together.

By the time I started work, both my sisters had married and left home and my eldest brother was married and living in London, leaving only my youngest brother, Raymond, eight years older than me, and myself at home. My parents decided that it was time to economise, so the household staff was reduced to a cook and just one maid.

The only three boys of my age with whom I was friendly had similar family backgrounds to myself but to my mind, all three lacked initiative and a sense of adventure. Their idea of amusement was a weekly visit to the cinema, followed by coffee in a city cafe. One of them did play games, another's only interest was in motor magazines and cars, and the third seemed to have no particular interests at all.

To me they were an uninspiring set of characters, somewhat timid and too well behaved for my taste, which tended more towards the active, outdoor type; for example, an older friend of mine who was a game-keeper on a large estate six miles outside Norwich. He taught me keepering, ferreting and night long-netting for rabbits, trapping and believe it or not, poaching.

Upon turning sixteen, life for me began to speed up - literally in one aspect, since I bought myself a motor bike. It cost me two pounds ten shillings and was an ancient belt driven, square tank 640 cc Norton. I kept it out of my parent's sight but after a couple of weeks, Father came across it and, to my surprise, said, 'If you must have a motor-bike, I'll get you a safe one', and he bought me, for thirty-eight pounds, a new, 350 cc side valve BSA, complete with leg-guards and pillion seat. I had the leg guards off it on the second day, since, in my view, they were unmanly.

Some weeks prior to this, while I was cycling through a nearby shopping centre, I began to notice a girl who seemed regularly to follow the same route. She was aged about twenty-two, blonde and rather plump. I suppose she would be considered dowdy but, to me, she was quite pretty.

I was too shy to make any advances but, each day, as we passed each other, she often caught me looking at her, though she made no response. Passing her one day on my motor bike, I smiled at her, and, to my delight, she smiled back and waved. The following week, I plucked up the courage to stop her and strike up a conversation and to my surprise, it was as if we had known each other for ten years.

She was extremely blunt and out-spoken, in fact, on occasions, quite coarse, and she spoke with a rather unpleasant Norwich accent. This worried me at first, but since, at Ranworth, I had learned to speak broad rural Norfolk, I always did so when I was with her, so as not to embarrass her. But I needn't have worried, she couldn't have cared less.

It appeared that she looked after and elderly couple and that her name was Sheila. Although she never did tell me her surname and I never found out where she lived, I presumed it was in one of the many back-street terraced houses which abounded on the edges of the city. I told her I was called Peter, and that was all she ever knew of me. She never enquired where I lived or what I did for a living. If ever there were two opposites, it was myself and Sheila..

We soon started taking trips on my motor bike and these led, in turn, to petting sessions down by the river. If we were in the mood for each other's company, we would arrange a place and time to find each other, and off we would go.

Despite being shy, I was by this time not entirely ignorant of sexual behaviour - our house-maids had seen to that - and though with them, it never got as far as full intercourse, it went pretty well far enough.

The maids shared a bedroom on the top floor of the house and, to get to it, they had to pass by my bedroom door which was also on the top floor. Since there was no television and few radios in those days, they were in the habit of going to bed at about 9.30 pm, Cook having retired earlier.

One of the maids, sometimes both, took to coming into my room and sitting, one on the side of my bed, to talk; as I have said, I had always spent far more time with the servants, preferring their company to any others.

One night, I would be about fourteen at the time, they came into my room and sat down as usual, and I noticed that they were rather quiet but tittering to each other at some private joke. Suddenly, one of them slipped her hand under the blankets and, to her surprise, her fumbling was met by an instant rigid response which made them scurry back to their room in a fit of giggles.

Once, when I was much younger, my mother left me naked in front of her bedroom gas fire while she went to fetch my pyjamas. By the time she returned it was waving about like a branch in a gale. I, of course, had no idea of the why's and wherefore's, but Mother, in a fit of rage, smacked me hard across the face and called me a filthy little toad. Sex, to her, was something dirty, never to be spoken of, even in a whisper and, as for educating her children in the matter, she wouldn't hear of it.

Children in that era grew up in total ignorance of sex, especially the girls, so that most were shaken rigid by the occurrences of their wedding night. Yet, throughout the Victorian and Edwardian eras, male pillars of society apparently spent much of their time procuring girls of fourteen and fifteen years of age to satisfy their lust.

These two maids were replaced by a new single maid who also proved to be good fun, but whilst willing to continue night time chats, she would tolerate from me, no undue impropriety. However, she did indicate to me quite clearly, some of the pleasures that might lie ahead for me. These sessions took place while my parents were out at the theatre or one of the dinner parties they frequently attended. So we had the house to ourselves until we heard their car return.

24

This replacement maid was a pretty country girl, only about seventeen years old and far less inhibited than city girls of her age. She hadn't been with us very long when she astounded me one day by washing her hair in the scullery sink - stripped to the waist. I had never seen a girl topless before but the sight delighted and inspired me.

One evening when Sheila and I had taken one of our accustomed trips down to the river bank and were deep into a heavy petting session, she suddenly asked,

"Have you got one of those things?" meaning, I assumed, a condom. Well, of course, I hadn't, since in those days, they were by no means as easy to come by as they are today. Several evenings later, at the same spot by the river-side, she asked again,

"Well! Have you got one?" This time, I'd come prepared, so in her perfectly natural way, she said,

"Don't hang about then, use it".

This was my introduction to full sexual intercourse. She wasn't, I quickly discovered, a virgin, but neither was she a tart.

We continued to meet once or twice a week right up to the time that I left England at the age of eighteen and as I have said, I never did know anything about her, nor she anything about me.

When I was seventeen I passed my driving test and bought my first car, a 1926, 7.5 Citroen Clover Leaf coupe and I paid three pounds ten shillings for it. It had a wide front seat and behind that, a single seat ending in an elevated point. It had no self starter and, as I recall, only rear wheel brakes. Sheila and I, of course, made the most of it.

One night we parked up on a wooded slope and, in the somewhat cramped conditions, had just managed to bring ourselves to the most passionate part of the exercise, then she managed to dislodge the brake with her foot. The car rolled backwards, gathering speed as it went until it was suddenly brought sharply to a halt by a tree. The resulting violent jolt seriously upset my rhythm, causing her to utter a string of swear-words worthy of a wounded trooper. This was the only time I ever heard her swear.

We never went anywhere together other than on these love-making sessions and looking back, I believe that Sheila was probably the safety valve that helped to prevent me from ruining my life.

It wasn't long after that the Citroen developed crank shaft problems and started to seize up without warning, but luckily, I sold it for four pounds ten shillings and that made me very happy.

I still had my motor bike and when an occasions demanded it, I was able to borrow my Mothers car and on rare occasions, Father even lent me his, though mostly for shooting trips since he would not have approved of foot-prints on the windows and on the dashboard - upside-down.

At seventeen, I acquired a 'Fol-Boat' which was a folding, two-seater kayak type of canoe, constructed of rubberised canvas stretched over folding wooden frames and it almost became the instrument of my demise.

I kept it in a boathouse on the Colman family estate, two miles down river from our house and, that Easter I planned a great adventure. I decided that I'd try to canoe all the way from the boathouse to our country property at Ranworth. This entails a journey down the River Yare to Great Yarmouth, across a large stretch of open water known as Breydon Water, then at Yarmouth, turning into the River Bure and negotiating upstream as far as Ranworth. This is a distance of forty miles or so and normally, a nine or ten hour trip by motor cruiser.

I didn't reveal the plan to my parents, since they were apt to disapprove of such exploits, instead, I intended to telephone them on arrival at my destination.

I left home at 3.30a.m., taking with me a huge hamper of food that Cook had made up for me, and travelled to the boat-house by bicycle, which I intended to leave there for the duration of the journey.

A bitterly cold wind was blowing, bringing with it, sleet and snow but, undaunted, I loaded the canoe and paddled off into the darkness hoping that with the dawn, would come better weather.

I pressed on down the River Bure, but as dawn broke, the foul weather continued. Spray flew over the bow and I was soon soaking wet. After seven or eight hours hard paddling, I reached Breydon Water, having already consumed all the food and in a state of near exhaustion.

Breydon Water is some three miles long and a mile wide with a deep-water channel, flanked by mud banks which flood with the incoming tide. The wind and tide were both against me, producing two to three foot waves and very, very foolishly, I decided to cross it. By the time I had struggled a mile, fighting the adverse conditions all the way, I was at that point of physical exhaustion when the muscles can no longer obey the mind and I was in a state of near panic.

The boat was rapidly filling with water which came in each time the bow dipped into an on-coming wave and its increasing weight delayed the bows rising, so admitting more water. When eventually, it did struggle up, the water rushed to the stern and held that down.

With ever more water being taken in, I became really frightened and desperately wanted to turn back but I feared that if I turned broad-side to the waves, the boat would certainly be swamped and I would drown.

At that moment of panic, inspiration arrived to save me. I got the bright idea that I could simply turn round in the cock-pit, and use the stern as the bow. With some difficulty I managed to struggle round without losing control and up-ending the flimsy craft, then started paddling like hell.

The following sea sped me along, almost surfing at times, and although I took in yet more water, I cleared Breydon and got back onto the River Yare in next to no time. I landed, tipped the water from the canoe, and promptly decided that my great adventure was at an end so after a brief rest, I started the long haul back upstream.

It was nearly 1.00 p.m. when I reached the boat-house two miles from home and my bicycle was missing - stolen, I assumed - so I had to trudge the two miles back home. When eventually, I dragged my exhausted body to our doorstep, I found the house locked and in complete darkness so I had to spend the night, cold and wet, in the summer-house. My parents were not impressed by my activities.

The next morning I went to the Police Station to report my missing bicycle.

"Ah!" said the desk sergeant, "It's yours, is it?" Apparently a constable had seen it at the boat-house at dawn and again after dark, and had assumed it was yet another suicide, a frequent occurrence on this stretch of the river, and had taken possession of it.

Not long after this adventure, I set off on another, which nearly caused my parents to have heart attacks.

I was on holiday from work and decided to see a bit of England on my motor-cycle. I chose Lands End as the first stop, and setting off early one morning, I reached it comfortably by evening. On arrival, I telephoned home to let my Mother know I was okay. "Where are you?" She asked.

"Lands End". I replied.

"And where are you going tomorrow?"

"I think I'll head north into Wales", and this, I fully intended to do. However, after an uncomfortable night in a bed-and-breakfast house, I changed my mind and decided to return to Norwich.

I set off early and reached Norwich about eight in the evening but, instead of going straight home, I called in at the house of the elderly bachelor accountant with whom I often played chess and billiards, and who happened to live right next door. I hadn't been there long when I got the notion that it would be a great wheeze to give my parents a big surprise, so I rang them and told Mother that I had arrived in Wales and intended to travel further North the next day.

Half an hour later, I let myself into our house and walked boldly into the drawing room where Father and Mother were sitting, listening to the wireless. I can still see the looks of profound shock that spread across their faces when they saw me. Mother half fainted and Father, leaping to his feet too quickly, fell over and hit the floor with a resounding crash. After that incident, I tried hard to be more considerate towards them.

A Doldrum Period

I worked in Norwich for Coleman and Co Ltd. for a total of two and a half years and hated every moment of it. At first I worked in the export department and after a short time, I moved to the advertising department as one of three assistants under the department manager. They were all nice people, but I resented the regular hours and being cooped up indoors when all my interests were outside. I think I spent more time in the company of the factory workers than with the office staff, at least, every moment I thought I wouldn't be missed.

Strangely, though I lived a masculine kind of life, I have always preferred the company of females to that of males, and having associated exclusively with people much older than myself, it was, perhaps, not surprising that I should fall in love with a typist seven years older than myself.

Claire, as she was called, was blonde, petite and very pretty, and was always fresh and lively. She had a slight cast in one eye, which strangely, enhanced her attraction for me, rather than diminished it, and I was besotted with her.

Whilst I was with exports, I didn't see as much of her as I would have wished, but at the time I moved downstairs to the advertising department, she had been given responsibility for wages and mail and moved, with another girl, into an adjoining office. To my delight, I discovered that she also took shorthand on a relief basis and so I was able to dictate to her, the few letters I had to deal with. Yet again, shyness intervened and, for a long time, prevented me from disclosing my feelings. But then, fate stepped in to rescue me.

The firm worked a five-day week but, every Saturday, two members of staff were detailed to come in to handle anything urgent. One Saturday morning, nearly a year after I'd first seen her, she and I were the two asked to come in and were the only people in the building.

I sat at my desk trying to concentrate on the pile of papers which lay before me, yet fully conscious of Claire's presence only a few feet away. Suddenly, the door opened she came into my office.

"I've got something in my eye," she said, leaning over the desk. "Please get it out for me."

I stood up and, as I examined the eye, she leaned closer and closer until she was pressing against me, making my heart race with anticipation. After a while I told her I couldn't find anything, but then, instead of drawing apart as I feared we must, she kissed me, and very passionately.

It was the start of a happy two year relationship during which, we went for countless motor-cycle, car and canoe trips together and for many long, romantic walks. Only one thing disappointed me, we never made love. I think she would have liked to, judging from the petting and kissing we indulged in, and once, she asked me, rather pointedly, what I would like to do more than anything else in the world. Somehow, my respect for her inhibited me from giving the obvious reply; there was something very special about our relationship. Anyway I was still secretly enjoying nature with Sheila.

After leaving England, I never saw her again, but I heard that she had married and had a number of children. I suppose she'd be about eighty-three now, and, to this day, I am still not certain whether I am pleased or sorry that we never consummated our relationship. But, in any case, standards then were different from those of today.

When I was about seventeen and a half I saw, at the local cinema, a film shot in East Africa. A silent film, as I remember, which was, in fact, little more than a continuous series of pictures of every type of game animal in Africa. I can't be certain, but I believe it was called 'Africa Speaks' and considering the primitive camera equipment of those days, it was an astonishing movie.

It had an instant effect on me - darkest Africa, wide open spaces, thousands upon thousands of genuinely wild animals, not the tourist tamed spectacle of modern times - and by the time it ended, I had decided that was where I would go, to East Africa.

This decision did not fade away during the night, nor in the following weeks and I began to search frantically, first, through Boys Own Annual, then through the library, for any mention I could find of Africa and over the next few months I acquired a mountain of publications relating to the area. From Jarrold's department store, I managed to obtained a Swahili grammar and an English Swahili dictionary and started to learn the Lingua Franca of East Africa. Being interested, I progressed well, unlike my meagre efforts with French or Latin.

Eventually, I picked on Kenya, Britain's youngest colony, and in those days, very much darkest Africa, penetrated only in the 1890's and then, only by hunters and explorers.

My researches soon told me that Kenya had a population of 5,000 Europeans, 2,000 Asians and about 2,000,000 Africans. Over 70 main tribes were included in the population, all with entirely different languages. A vast territory, it largely comprised unoccupied wilderness, teeming with game and it sounded to me like paradise.

Farm land was cheap. The so called White Highlands had been surveyed into large farms but many had never been occupied and so, pretty good land could be had as little as 10 shillings (50p) an acre, and, in some areas, even as low as one shilling (10p) an acre. The whole country boasted only thirty-seven miles of surfaced road, all in townships.

After the 1914/18 war, the Government granted free, or almost free, acreages, to demobilised soldiers in the hope that they would start to produce crops and thereby, begin a process of economic development. However, the European depression of the late 20's and early 30's had worked its way out there, and that, combined with attacks on their produce by disease, vermin, locusts, floods, droughts, tsetse fly and white ants left most Settlers near to bankruptcy.

If , by chance, a farmer were to succeed in producing a reasonable crop, he was hard pressed to sell it because no viable market existed. Coffee, tea and sisal did, with a struggle, create a small export market, but many settlers couldn't afford so much as a car, or even a tractor so virtually all cultivation had to be executed by work oxen.

Doctors, hospitals and schools were few. Malaria, dysentery, black water fever, and even yellow fever, were a constant hazard and the grave-yards were full of head-stones depicting the early death of white settlers, also of those saying, 'Killed by buffalo', 'Killed by lion', etc etc. There was no income tax, nobody licensed a vehicle and few insured them, since it wasn't then mandatory.

The results of my researches left me with vivid impressions of the whole of East Africa - Kenya, Tanganyika, Uganda and Zanzibar - as a glorious land of adventure and opportunity, where my destiny must lie.

I saw no future in working with the firm in Norwich; after two and a half years, I was earning only one pound five shillings per week, and, as far as I had observed, no employee got promoted until they were fifty-five or sixty.

By this time, Father had sold our country house, though we still had access to the rest of the property. I remember the last time that I visited the house, I went into every room and looked at the view from each window, vowing to return one day and buy back the property.

My father was, by now, becoming concerned about my wild and unconventional activities, even so, he was not keen on the idea of me emigrating. Instead, he kept muttering that he must buy me a Norfolk farm (which, then, could be picked up for as little as thirty or thirty-five pounds an acre). Mother, however, supported me, for two reasons I think. Firstly, she feared that I would get the maids or some other girl pregnant, and secondly, of course, she never really liked me anyway and welcomed the opportunity to get me off her hands.

The winds of fortune blew kindly for me. By chance, two years earlier, an elderly brother and sister, who were Kenya pioneer settlers, were on a visit to England, and were staying in Norwich, when the brother fell ill. Father was called in to treat him and, as a result, came to know them quite well. The old boy was so pleased with Father's success at curing him that, after he returned to Kenya, he wrote a thank-you letter. This letter, which contained their address, had somehow survived and I told my parents that going to Kenya would present no problems since we already knew these people out there. I would have gone anyway. In the end, Father submitted and preparations for my departure began.

It was 1936, and to give Father his due, he fitted me out very well. First, we obtained two regulation size 50lb metal suitcases - 50lb was the accepted head load for an African carrier - with rubber sealed lids. Clothing included a double terrai, red lined, wide brimmed hat, khaki shorts and shirts which had detachable spine pads fitted because, in those days Europeans visitors to the tropics feared sun stroke. I was given a new dinner jacket, tails, boiled shirts, stiff collars, pointed patent leather shoes, a silk scarf and white gloves. The tails were only discarded a few years ago and unless my wife has disposed of it recently, the dinner jacket still survives.

Of more interest to me was my 12 bore shotgun, a 9mm Webley automatic pistol, donated by a Solicitor friend and an 8.56mm Manklicher Schoenar Revolving Magazine rifle given to me by C S Rosson the Norwich gun-maker, who was my brother's Godfather. Father gave me the field glasses he had possessed most of his life, I still have them now, and, by God, they've seen some scenes.

Fearing Malaria, Father gave me a supply of Quinine tablets, but he needn't have worried, because on arrival in Kenya, I found that, with Malaria so rife, the Government gave away Quinine, free of charge.

For two months everyone I met gave me their advice, but what they thought they knew, God only knows because, in those days, if an acquaintance went as far away as Paris, you never expected to see them again and Kenya was virtually unknown. Only a very few of them knew that it was somewhere in darkest Africa.

I disposed of my menagerie and also sold all the runs and cages. I said farewell to my friends, including Sheila, and Mac, and finally, before leaving home, I was invited to their house, by my brother Raymond and his wife for, what turned out to be, a very lively evening.

We had just finished our meal and the three of us were sitting around the table beside the fire, listening to the wireless. Outside, it was blowing a gale. The area had recently been troubled by a peeping tom, and so, they were both a bit on edge. All at once, there was an almighty crash outside and Raymond leapt up shouting, "That's him".

He and I rushed outside to investigate, only to find that the wireless aerial had blown down in the gale.

In those days, aerials were very long and he started to pull on the wire to drag it towards him. Immediately, piercing screams came from within the house.

"The swine's got into the house", he yelled, and we dashed in-doors to find my sister-in-law white as a sheet and shaking like a leaf. Apparently, in pulling the aerial wire, he had dragged the wireless set across the table, frightening the poor girl half to death.

Intending to effect a temporary repair, he went outside again and into the shed to get some tools, but seconds later, he staggered out again, holding his head in both hands and moaning,

"He's got me, he's got me, get him quick". It transpired that, what he'd done in the dark, was to stand on an upright rake, which flipped up and smacked him smartly across the face, causing him considerable pain and no small amount of bleeding.

This was my last night at home and I lay awake for some hours contemplating the totality of the break with my family, my friends and my home that tomorrow would bring. From then on, I would be on my own, entirely reliant on my few skills and my native wit, and I have to confess that, in the blackness of that night, I did wonder whether this great adventure might not turn out to be like my canoe trip down the river, a disaster. For a few moments, a dreadful vision drifted through my crowded mind, of my return home in a few month's time, shame-faced and defeated, but soon these fears were dispelled by the thrill of anticipation, and I slept.

No Regrets, No Homesickness

On November the 24th. 1936, my eighteenth birthday, my mother and I were driven to the docks at Tilbury by our Chauffeur, Percy Thrower. It was a slow, faltering journey, hampered all the way by thick fog and we arrived an hour and a half after my ship, the Llandaff Castle, had been due to sail. But we needn't have worried, as we approached, she loomed out of the mists, still moored at her berth.

As I boarded and said goodbye, Mother was in tears, but I was more distressed to say farewell to Percy than I was to my mother. He, like our gardener, had come to work for my father at the age of sixteen, and, apart from a break for war service, had been with him ever since.

From the earliest days of my childhood, Percy and I had always been close and he had undoubtedly helped to shape my character. His tales of adventure as a machine-gunner for the four years of the 1914/18 war, during which he had been involved in most of the disastrous campaigns, including Gallipoli, the Somme and Ypres, had always excited me. Now, on the brink of my own great adventure, I felt a particularly strong affinity for him. As I waved a last farewell to them both, below me on the dockside, my heart was heavy and I think I saw Percy brush a tear from his face with his course leather gauntlet.

As the ship pulled away from the dock and Percy and my mother disappeared into the fog, I shrugged of sentiment and turned my mind to the voyage ahead. My father, god bless him, had provided me with a first class ticket and had given me fifty pounds, so I considered myself well set up for the passage to Mombasa.

The Llandaff Castle was a 9,500 ton Union Castle passenger/freight ship plying the round-Africa circuit, and, at the time, I thought she was huge, but as a cruise-ship she did lack one or two refinements. She was propelled by coal-fired engines that gave her little speed, and 'though she didn't carry many passengers, her cabins were small with no air conditioning, no intercom and only sea-water in which to wash and bathe. None of these shortcomings bothered me in the least. I was young and fit and used to a rigorous existence so I would have been happy even to travel on the meanest scow, as long as I got there.

My cabin, which I shared with a chap going to East Africa to work for the Shell Oil Company, was two doors away from that occupied by Lord and Lady Baden-Powell. On the opposite side of the passageway was Raymond Hook, a pioneer Kenya settler/hunter who had taken half a dozen cheetahs to England in a venture to race them against greyhounds. He had managed to arrange a few races but since cheetahs were about 15 miles an hour faster and not averse to downing a greyhound instead of the hare, his venture was not a great success. He had them onboard ship with him on his way back to Kenya.

Also on board was Gerald Brookes of Brooke Bond Tea, accompanied by his wife and their daughter, Geraldine who was the only other passenger of my own age. Gerald was on his way to inspect the company's tea estates in East Africa and then, proceed to India to inspect estates there before returning to England via South Africa.

Geraldine, who was very attractive and mature for her age, soon took me under her wing and we became close companions for the duration of the voyage, however, in a very proper manner. Gerald and Mrs Brookes were strict Quakers and very protective of their daughter, but later, Geraldine wrote to me and told me that on the final stretch of their long voyage, she had fallen in love with one of the ship's officers and was now married to him.

As we made our way down the Thames, I spent some time taking stock of myself and my assets; I was quite tall, well built, fit and strong and was, or so I had been informed on more than one occasion, quite good-looking. I had my guns and most of the other equipment I might require and my finances were in reasonable order. I concluded that I was well provided for and therefore, happy with my circumstances.

This last item, finances, consisted of £38 of my own savings and a letter of credit for £50 provided by my father with which I was to open a Bank account in Kenya. Father had also put up a Bond for £50 with the

Kenya Government which they would use to repatriate me if I became a "destitute British subject" and without which, an immigrant was not allowed to land. In those days, many wayward sons of wealthy parents were sent to the Colonies and paid an allowance for as long as they didn't return to the U.K., so I was only half a remittance man. In the event, the voyage to Kenya took thirty-two days, and in that time I spent less than three pounds.

Apart from the first and last nights of the voyage, gentlemen were obliged to wear a dinner jacket for the evening meal and in hotter regions like the Red Sea, on a ship with no air conditioning, the likelihood of heat-stroke with its possibly fatal results, was greatly feared, particularly by the elderly. Since custom wouldn't allow the removal of even the jacket, and light-weight ones were unheard of, many ships, over the years, had suffered casualties among their passengers. In fact, if humidity rose above a certain level, ships would avoid putting into Red Sea ports.

Through the channel and the Bay of Biscay the weather was cold and rough, but, after lunch on the second day out, I braved the elements, and went up to the boat deck where I bumped into another, equally hardy individual. We had a long chat and, as he seemed to accepted me as an adult - even as an equal - I took to him instantly. It transpired that he was Lord Baden-Powell and after that first meeting, we met there every day after lunch for a stroll and a chat. He proved to be a fascinating man and, in the most diplomatic of ways, gave me much useful advice acquired during his varied and adventurous life.

When we reached warmer weather, he and I played chess on the boat deck each afternoon that we were at sea and, at times, I had him racking his brains, in fact on more than one occasion, I actually beat him: although I suspected that sometimes, he let me win.

They settled in Kenya and I never saw them again together, but, some twenty-five years later, long after her husband's death, Lady Baden-Powell attended a Guide's jamboree in the Lake Province, of which I was by then, the Police Commander. I provided her with Police transport and escorts and, at the main function, sat beside her in the stadium. I reminded her of our voyage together in the Llandaff Castle and we had a long and interesting chat. I found her to be, just like her husband, a delightful character and a great personality.

The Llandaff Castle zigzagged lazily through the Mediterranean, put in at every European and North African port and never seemed to be in a hurry to leave them.

Early in the voyage, I had made the acquaintance of a very plum-voiced, university educated, landed gentry type of fellow of about thirty-five years of age. He was accompanied by a lady of about his own age who was quite good looking, with a nice figure, always immaculately dressed and who spoke fairly good English, but with an unusually attractive foreign accent. At first I thought she was his wife, then after a few days, I began to suspect that, maybe, she was his mistress. They were on board for the round-Africa trip, proceeding down the East coast of Africa, round the Cape and up the West coast back to the U.K. Although I never knew for certain, I gathered that she had originated in Switzerland, but, I did ascertain that she was Jewish.

We three got on famously, in fact, participating together in the ship's fancy dress competition, we went as Hit, Muss and Rot, "the never lasting triangle", and won first prize. I was Muss, he was Hit and she was the Japanese Rot. I must say we all looked the part, and as talk of war was in the air, the skit upon our potential enemies proved very popular.

The ship docked early one morning at Genoa and many passengers disembarked for tours ashore, but since I couldn't afford such luxuries, I stayed on board. After a while, I wandered up to the boat deck and there I met the Swiss/Jewish lady also taking a stroll.

"All alone?" I asked.

"Yes," she said, "I wasn't too keen, so he's gone on his own."

We strolled the decks for a while, then went down for mid-morning coffee and ice-cream together. We chatted gaily for some time then suddenly, after a short silence, she turned to me and said quietly, "I go to my cabin, come with me." Being a bit naive, I thought that she was perhaps feeling unwell and wanted me to escort her there. On reaching her cabin, she let us in and it was then that I discovered that she and her escort were not even sharing the same cabin. I noticed also, that there were suddenly, none of the signs of ill-health that I'd expected.

She went over to the mirror to put her hair straight and then, turning slowly to me, she took my hand and said,

"Come, we make love."

I didn't need telling twice and we were soon in bed together, and, for a delightful hour, managed to rock the ship a little at her moorings. During the rest of the voyage, to my enjoyment, and her's I hope, we found frequent opportunities to make love.

One observation that I made about her which stuck in my mind, was the fact that, around her nipples was a ring of small black hairs. Later, I compared this with two other Jewesses with whom I became associated, and found them to be both similarly endowed. Ever since, I have asked myself, do all Jewesses have them, and though I have been acquainted with many over the years, I have never had courage enough to ask them this ticklish question.

For meals I sat at a table with an elderly couple who were doing the round-Africa trip, and a captain on his way to Kenya to visit his brother. He told me that, after the 1914/18 war, he had joined a firm in Burma which exported teak and which had been very successful, and though, to me, he looked about seventy, he kept telling me, 'I have just retired young man, you see to it that you do so when you're young like me.' In the end, I heeded his advice, but when I retired, I was only forty-four years old.

After thirty-two days on board ship, putting in at so many ports, and seeing so many different countries and peoples, made me feel, on reaching my destination, that I had really arrived on a different planet. I said goodbye to my ship-board companions, promising as one always does, to write or to look them up if ever, etc. etc..., and so I landed at Mombasa in darkest Africa. This was Kenya, Britain's youngest colony, where, it was said, the trees have no shade, the rivers no water and the women no virtue.

Once ashore, I booked myself and my luggage into a small hotel and set off for a quick tour of the town. The heat, the smells, the noise, the people all thrilled me and I wandered past the docks, the railway station and through the bustling street markets in a trance. And this was just the gateway to adventures I had, so far, only dreamed of. I soon located the British Consulate and the bank where I would deposit Father's letter of credit and open my account and then returned to the hotel to dress for dinner.

The thought briefly crossed my mind that I was friendless in this strange and distant place. Not that the thought worried me but, as a mere youth of eighteen with no set plan of action, I realised that friends would certainly be useful to me. I fell lucky.

That evening, before dinner, I strolled into the hotel bar and immediately fell into conversation with a family from up-country who were there on a coastal holiday. They were Will Blain and his brother, and Will's two daughters, Dar and Sue who were both about my own age. They realised that I was new to the colony and was alone so they invited me to dine with them and, very quickly, I learned something of their life and their family history.

They were pioneer settlers and farmed a large cattle ranch at an altitude of over 9,500 feet, close to the peak of Mount Satima in the Aberdare Mountains. Adjoining their ranch was a similar one, owned by Will's brother- in-law, a third, by another brother-in-law and, between them was yet another occupied by a sister-in-law. They were a large family and the total acreage they ranched was vast.

They were all classic examples of Kenya pioneer settlers, and they dressed, spoke and acted the part. Will even had an unmarried sister-in-law who drank two bottles of gin a day, which was, she said, 'to prevent malaria'.

Will was an Englishman, who had been a civil service engineer in India, and then in Kenya, where he had married into a family who had emigrated there before 1900. Having fought the Germans in East Africa during the 1914/18 world war, the family had taken up the Government's offer to ex-soldiers, of unoccupied settlement farms, and 'though they claimed to be of Argentinean descent, they all spoke and behaved like typical English gentry.

Thus started a new phase of my life and it was to be nine years before I would next see Britain.

I stayed on the coast with Will and his family for a month, and in that time, they took me under their wing and I began to feel almost like one of the family. Before they left to return to their ranch, Will took me on one side and told me that, if ever I was in trouble and needed a friend, I was to contact him immediately and, in any case, I must visit them soon on the ranch and stay with them for as long as I wished. The Blains departed, leaving me alone to take stock of my situation and make some decisions concerning my future. I decided that first, I would like to see some more of Kenya and set off to wander the country. And what a country!

From the steamy equatorial coastline to the permanent glaciers on the 17,000 foot Mount Kenya, the southern border with Tanganyika, running from the Indian Ocean to the top of Mount Kilimanjaro 19,000 feet, the whole area was totally underpopulated with vast areas inhabited only by game of every type. In the plains country you could climb any of the sugar loaf hills that rose at intervals, probably a thousand yards wide at base and up to 300 feet high, and see huge herds of Topi, Kongoni, Thomson's Gazelle, Branch Gazelle, Impalla, Eland, Zebra, Wildebeest and often Buffalo, Lion, Rhino and Elephants, not to mention odd Reedbuck, Leopard and Wild Dogs.

These animals were totally wild and knew nothing of humans or of civilisation. There were no game-parks or game reserves, quite the reverse, the animals roamed free, unrestricted by any fences or boundaries and bred so profusely that vast areas were overrun with them, obliging Government Control Officers to cull them in an attempt to assert a measure of control. I simply couldn't wait to get stuck into them myself.

This situation was, over subsequent years, to change dramatically. In 1960, just before we handed Kenya, Tanganyika and Uganda over to independent black Governments, game-rangers were killing seven thousand elephants a year, just to keep the numbers down so that the huge herds didn't starve by destroying all the trees upon which they fed. Now the entire area holds probably only seven thousand survivors, and this has come about largely because of the irresponsible attitudes and actions of the post-independence Governments.

By 1960, the Kenya Game Department had divided all the game areas into hunting zones, and hunting parties in these zones were allowed to kill only male animals beyond breeding age, and only then in such numbers as befitted the ability of the zone to support that species. Thus, no species was threatened and hunters prevented areas from becoming overpopulated to the detriment of the environment.

One of the earliest measures enacted by independent Kenya's first president, Jomo Kenyatta, was to grant his wife the proceeds from all ivory sold or exported, and, at the same time, he issued a decree, banning all professional hunting. As soon as hunting was banned the poachers moved in, slaughtering the Elephant and Rhino towards virtual extinction. The few African game wardens, Police and even Army Personnel in the game areas, jumped on the band wagon, and shot everything in sight, just for a few pounds in their pockets.

Had Kenya allowed professional hunting to continue, and given the professional hunters Government backing and limited legal powers, this would never have happened as they would have detected and controlled the poachers.

Now, years later, several African ex-colonies are finally beginning to authorise controlled hunting, only to preserve the few animals left in order attract the tourists.

Herein, lies a lesson for the U.K. do-gooders who seek to ban shooting, fishing and hunting. Should they succeed, Britain will be emptied of most of its game and birds within twenty years, leaving nothing but carrion-eating jays, magpies, grey squirrels, stoats, foxes and crows to survive.

The hunter is the only serious and effective conservationist, he farms for the future.

East Africa possesses one great advantage over Britain in all this, the tsetse fly. It greatly aids the wild animals since they are immune to its bite which otherwise kills all domestic animals, leaving vast game areas with no human population, because they are unsuitable for farming.

After visiting many areas of the country, I finished up, a couple of months later with my friends, Will Blain, his wife May and their daughters, on their ranch, high in the Aberdare Mountains. By then, I had £20 left and they agreed to put me up for £5 a month. They were generosity itself, but I suspect that they also had another motive, to marry off one of their daughters to me. What other chance would the girls have, in such a remote area, of finding a mate?

I arrived one Friday morning at Thomson's Falls, a rail-head and their nearest trading centre, where they had arranged to meet me. After a thirty-five mile journey over deeply rutted, barely passable earth tracks, we reached their home, a cedar-wood house, constructed in true pioneer fashion from timber felled in the forests on their own property, but spacious and, apart from outside loos, remarkably comfortable. It was the highest ranch on the mountainside with the house standing at 9,500 feet, and the land running up to 10,500 feet and, although it was situated just twenty miles north of the Equator, after dark, if the sky was cloudless, the temperature would plummet and a heavy white frost set in; so, day and night, a roaring fire would be kept burning in a huge fireplace in the lounge.

After taking possession, Will had first engaged pit sawyers to cut cedar planks, and masons to mine and shape soft stone for the construction of the house. He took on other Africans to train and drive work oxen, and had taken in a few African 'squatters' to provide labour on the ranch.

The house started as simply, one room, but, year by year, more rooms were added as they became necessary, until, by the time I arrived, it had grown into a substantial settler's house, quite picturesque under its cedar-shingle roof.

In the grounds were a tennis court, stables, servants quarters, a workshop and auxiliary buildings. Water had to be hauled in by oxen, and there was no electricity, telephone or other communications. The last 10 miles from the nearest road-head was a two-wheel, earth track, virtually impassable to vehicles during the extensive rainy seasons. The nearest neighbours, his in-laws, were seven or more miles away.

The ranch was situated in beautiful country, with rolling grass-land, forested valleys, and higher up, belts of cedar and hard-wood forest, which, at around 10,000 feet gave way to dense bamboo; not our garden type, but 30 and 40 footers, 8 or 9 inches diameter at the base. Above this, was open moorland, wet, soggy and dotted with giant lobelias. Unoccupied by humans and inaccessible other than by game tracks, the whole area abounded with big game - buffalo, elephant, rhino, you name it - they were all there.

They had tried to grow wheat but the heavy rain-fall at that altitude caused the virus infection known as 'Rust', so they abandoned the idea, and instead, had gone into ranching and producing milk for conversion into rancid ghee for use by Asians in their cooking.

The morning after my arrival, Will took me for a three-hour walk across rolling, grass-covered hill-sides and through forested valleys. He carried a .318 Westley Richards rifle and pointed out to me elephant, rhino and lion tracks, and, in the distance, but still on his land, vast herds of plains game. My trigger finger itched.

That evening - a Friday - at about 7.00pm, just as we were going in to the evening meal, Will put his hand on my shoulder,

"By the way," he said, confidentially. "On Saturdays, we dress for dinner. Yes! Dinner jacket"

This was thirty-five miles from the rail-head, twenty miles from any Government maintained car track and seven miles from their nearest neighbours, but still, they were determined to keep up certain standards of dress and behaviour. Accordingly, every Saturday night, we all, the daughters included, dressed for dinner. There must be a moral there, somewhere.

Most mornings, at dawn, just after 6.00am, Will and his two daughters would mount up on horses and, taking with them, ten or so dogs of indeterminate breed, set out to ride and hunt. Will asked me if I rode and unwisely, I said, "Oh! Yes, of course." The truth was, that I had ridden a few plodding cart-horses, and on occasions, the odd saddle-horse, but, by no stretch of the imagination, could I be considered a competent horseman.

The next morning they provided me with a mount, a sturdy gelding who seemed quiet enough, and off we went. Will carrying his .318 rifle, the dogs racing eagerly ahead and the horses following at what I considered was an acceptable pace, left me feeling, if not completely happy, at least, reasonably comfortable.

Suddenly, about half a mile ahead of us, the dogs picked up a scent and started to bay, giving an instant signal to Will and his daughters to whip their horses into a flat-out gallop and take off across the rough country in pursuit of their prey. My horse knew the signal, and to my absolute horror, leapt into action and galloped after them in hot pursuit. No amount of pulling on the reins had any affect and shortly, I found myself hanging on, fighting desperately and barely succeeding just to stay in the saddle.

The baying of the dogs took us along a game trail and through a wooded valley, and now, some way behind the others, and my horse going full tilt to catch up, I came to a sharp, muddy bend in the track. To the left, the wooded hill-side sloped steeply down and I foresaw that the beast would be hard pressed to keep its footing. Sure enough, down it went, and off I came, flying about thirty feet through the air and landing, with a thud, much bruised and shaken, but thankful that I had been lucky enough not to hit the trees.

When both the wretched horse and I had sufficiently recovered, I remounted gingerly and slowly caught up with the others.

As I arrived, I found that Will had shot the water buck that the dogs had been coursing and had bayed, and it lay in a mountain stream where it widened into a deep pool. Will wanted to collect the buck for dog meat, and I was talked into stripping and diving into the pool to drag the animal up by one foot and anchor it to the edge from where it could be recovered. At 10,000 feet above sea level, the water was icy cold and as I emerged, after successfully accomplishing the task, it was apparent that my manhood had shrivelled and the girls were mesmerised. The following morning, I woke up stiff and bruised and ended up doing very little for three days, but Will and the girls considered that, all in all, the morning's hunting had been a hilarious success.

On these hunts, I quickly learned the necessity of killing the animal with the first shot. Until that shot was fired, the nondescript pack of dogs would encircle the animal and every time it lunged at one of them, a dog from the opposite side of the circle would dash in and attack its rump. Swinging like lightning, the animal would slash and lunge with its horns or tusks - from pig to small bush buck, buffalo or rhino, all would do the same. Then, the instant a shot was fired, the whole pack would leap on the animal which, if it had not been killed by the shot, would kill or injure several of the dogs. In thick bush or dense forest it could be doubly difficult to obtain a certain killing shot.

These morning hunts could become very exciting, more so even than fox hunting in the UK, (in which, incidentally I have never indulged), particularly when the dogs picked up the scent of buffalo, rhino or even elephant. Once the dogs commenced baying the horse's ears pricked forward and off they went at full gallop with no regard for how large or dangerous an animal was at the end of the chase.

There was no way that I could stop my horse, and he was not in the least bit fussy about the rough terrain over which he galloped. Will's daughters would whip and spur their horses to ever greater speeds, while I tried desperately to slow mine down and remain in the saddle. In the end it taught me one thing - I would rather hunt on foot than on horseback.

The terrain was rather like the Scottish highlands. Below the forest edge, vast rolling plains separated by streams and verdant valleys, stretched down the lower slopes for perhaps fifteen miles, eventually to blend into the endless flat-plains country. The valleys were heavily forested, passable only along the well-trodden big-game tracks.

In the early days of the British occupation of Kenya, a Sunday morning pastime amongst some of the more hardy and adventurous young men, was to 'Ride the Lion'. This sport involved them riding on horseback across the open plains to the south of Nairobi, armed only with revolvers or .45 automatics and sweeping the plains until they found lion. In those days, there were plenty, and indeed there still are, though the area is now the Nairobi Game Park. Having spotted lion they would give chase at full gallop and, when near enough, they would open fire, still going flat out. They did kill a number of lion but, as can be read on many a Nairobi tombstone, lion killed just as many of them.

Lion can develop a speed of over 50 miles an hour and are capable of turning in their tracks to attack, flat out, without loosing speed. A horseman, too close behind to swerve to safety, stood little chance of survival. This pastime eventually died a natural death.

Speaking of lion, I was advised during my early days in Kenya, that if I were suddenly to be confronted by a lion while unarmed, to look it straight in the eyes and never, under any circumstances, take my eyes off its eyes. I'm glad the circumstance never arose, for I have yet to meet anyone who followed this advice and survived.

I don't want to bore you, the reader, with endless descriptions of how I saw East Africa's geography, vegetation and climate, so I'll give you a rough guide now and then keep quiet.

The first and perhaps most noticeable feature of the area is its variety. Virtually all regions have widely differing environments, each being influenced by altitude and rainfall.

This huge area extends from the palm fringed, equatorial coast on the Indian Ocean to permanently, ice and snow capped mountains; Mt. Kilimanjaro at nineteen thousand feet, Mt. Kenya at seventeen thousand and the Ruwenzori range in Uganda, even higher. As one leaves the coast and travels west towards the Congo and beyond, one climbs steadily, and, as the altitude changes, so does the vegetation.

Coconut palms extended for thirty odd miles inland from the coast together with fairly lush vegetation fed by the monsoon rains, then, gradually, dryer, more arid regions take over. Some four fifths of Kenya is either true sand desert, low-lying semi-desert of sparse or dense thorn bush, or grassy plains, though at intervals, hills, and even mountains, add to the variety with, of course, a range of different trees, animals and plant life.

For three hundred miles inland from the coast, little water is available apart from a few rivers, the odd open water hole like Mzima Springs fed by Mt. Kilimanjaro's glaciers, and some flooded areas that hold water for short periods after heavy rain. Further inland still the ground level rises steadily to the snow lines.

There are several large mountain masses peaking at ten to twelve thousand feet whose lower slopes - from six to seven thousand feet - could be mistaken for Welsh hill country.

The whole of Kenya, Tanganyika and Uganda had, at the turn of the century, a population of only about seven million souls, and inland, there are still low-lying areas which were, and still are, very sparsely populated, comprising near-waterless terrain amongst overlapping belts of open plains, light thorn bush, dense thorn bush, sand, lava rock and as always, at wide intervals, odd mountains, their upper reaches having good rainfall and consequently, lush vegetation and forest cover.

Flora and fauna was as varied as the climate and the terrain, and wild-life abounded, remaining virtually undisturbed since the beginning of mankind.

The highlands have a near perfect climate and looking around you would think you were in England in the midst of summer. Even in the two rainy seasons, the morning would be bright and sunny, then, sometime after mid-day, the rain set in and usually continued until around midnight. Above seven and a half thousand feet, clear nights produced frost and even ice, so houses all had fire places. No one lived above ten and a half thousand feet because, if they was not completely acclimatised, their hearts laboured, they suffered from panting and altitude sickness and life was thoroughly uncomfortable.

Travelling in this region is fraught with danger for the unprepared. In mountainous terrain, one is forced to climb and descend through every variety of climate in a distance of only a few miles, and, caught out in minimum clothing, one could experience severe exposure which led in the early days, to a high incidence of pneumonia.

In the transition period between nakedness, or the wearing of only animal skins, and modern clothing, many Africans, caught out in violent rain or hail storms, died from exposure through wearing skimpy European clothing which, in failing to provide protection, when drying out, acted like a charcoal fridge. Missionaries who persuaded them to abandon skins and nakedness in favour of a more modest form of dress, were responsible for many deaths.

Until recently, because all roads were simply earth tracks, cars were obliged to carry mud (snow) chains and it was wise to travel only between dawn and mid-day for fear of being caught in the afternoon rains. Human nature being what it is, when running into bad road conditions, instead of taking immediate action to fit your chains, one usually delayed just a little bit too long and ended up having to jack the wheels up out of deep mud, getting completely covered with it in the process.

In hot, sandy country, one carried short strips of heavy wire netting to lay under the wheels to enable them to climb out of the holes they had dug themselves into in the loose hot sand. Because of these and other possible hazards one might meet on the way, a journey was measured, not in the distance travelled, but in the time taken to complete it.

Travel, for the unwary, was open to a variety of other discomforts and you could take nothing for granted. In some areas there were trees that shed a virulent powder that showered down on you as you walked underneath them, and this powder caused unbearable itching for some time afterwards. In other parts, a type of thorn tree, known as the stink thorn, emitted a most foul smell very similar to hydrogen sulphide, to the discomfort of those foolish enough to go near it. Knowledge of such matters kept you always on your toes.

While staying with the Blains, I found that, despite being fit and strong, the altitude posed certain problems for me. The air was rarefied, and exertions like playing tennis could sometimes make me very dizzy or even pass out so that I would suddenly sit down gasping for breath. The Blain's daughters, Dar and Sue found this highly amusing and would tease me mercilessly. In fact, to them, who were a pair of real backwoods tomboys, I was, with my tame English rural ways, a constant source of fun.

The first time I appeared, dressed in the tropical kit I had brought from England, double terrai hat, long, narrow shorts and spine padded shirt, they fell silent, looked hard at me, then at each other and after a gallant attempt at silence, collapsed into hysterics. The first visit after that, to the trading centre at Thomson's Falls, saw me kitted out by an Asian tailor with wide shorts and shirts without spine pads, all for about 55p.

Both of the girls were attractive, the elder one, Dar was dark and slender, and Sue, blonde plumpish and pretty. They could ride, safari, shoot big game using heavy rifles and play polo like back-woodsmen. I liked them both and took rather a fancy to the older, darker one, Dar.

The trading centre, Thomson's Falls, which was named after an early British explorer, was sited beside a magnificent waterfall which, when it was in flood, was a spectacular sight. At times, hippo from the swamps that fed it, would be swept over, and killed at the bottom. The centre was also the rail-head and comprised a hotel, a collection of corrugated iron trading shops and an area Police headquarters station, commanded by a British Inspector.

Eighteen months before I arrived, the Inspector, known as Potty, had led a party of his African police into heavy forest to track down a gang of Africans who had murdered two Asian traders. Neither he nor his men had worn uniform but Potty had blackened his face, arms and legs to disguise himself as an African. After forty-eight hours, they managed to make contact, only to be instantly attacked by the gang. In the fight that followed, two of the gang were shot but the rest escaped and were never seen again. However, in the melee, Potty's head got sliced open by a Panga, (a Machete), and he was lucky to survive. He was carried back to Thomson's Falls and patched up but, ever since that day it was rumoured that, at times, he went 'peculiar'.

Had he not disguised himself, the gang would probably have surrendered on contact, for the elite Kenya police were highly respected and feared by both blacks and whites. Their thin blue, (khaki), line of eighty British, and one thousand eight hundred black police, controlled an area almost three times the size of Great Britain and, like the Mounties, nothing daunted them and they would stop at nothing to get their man.

In the dry seasons, at fortnightly intervals, the Blain girls would visit the centre to play polo, having sent their horses down in advance, ridden by their African grooms. Watching them play I had little doubt that their male opponents were terrified of them, they rode like demons and swore with the best.

Will Blain and his wife did, I think, entertain hopes that I would marry one of their daughters, but, in fact, though I found them both attractive, I never once made advances to either of them and our relationship remained close, but purely platonic. Somehow, their hospitality, their personalities, the terrain, the wild-life, just were not conducive to romance, which would have changed our whole relationship.

I never did know how many head of cattle Will and his in-laws owned between them, and I don't think that they knew themselves, since the stock was herded by their squatters. Squatters were native Africans who were given a contract which permitted them to settle on the ranch, to put up huts, keep a prescribed number of cattle, sheep and goats and to cultivate limited areas. In return, they had to provide essential labour for the ranch and, in effect, became the children of the settlers, who, with very few exceptions, looked after them and protected them with unlimited patience and sympathy.

In different areas of the colony, tea, coffee, sisal, wheat, maize, fruit and other crops and, of course, cattle were cultivated.

Thus, were some of Kenya's vast areas 'tamed' by the few pioneer settlers, and in just over fifty years, converted into a land of milk and honey, and good order.

The whole country under this system of early penetration was eventually freed from inter-tribal friction, famine, crop and stock diseases. Malaria was brought very largely under control, Black Water Fever became unheard of, good schools and hospitals were provided for both blacks and whites, and corruption was virtually eradicated.

It took just twenty years of 'independence' for Kenya and her sister colonies to sink to the depths of famine, disease, bankruptcy, tribal warfare, mal-administration, total corruption and the begging bowl. The productive white farms were fragmented into little more than allotments and settlers houses broken up for fire-wood. The new black bureaucracies had their Mercedes and often, their bank accounts full of pilfered grant-aid money and companies' bribes, and were seemingly, disinterested in the plight of the general populace.

I used the Blains' ranch as a base from which to explore some more of Kenya and I liked everything I saw but while I was there, I was never idle and helped Will to construct a large cattle shed and to lay a piped water supply to the farm from a forest spring a mile distant.

We laid a one inch galvanised pipe in a straight line through the forest to the ranch house and, in places this supply pipe was suspended twenty feet above the bottom of the valleys it crossed.

At the spring we installed a ram, first concreting in a small catchment area around the spring. From there, we fed a two inch pipe eighty-five feet down a one in four, continuous slope where it was connected to the ram which somewhat resembled an oxy-acetylene bottle. The one inch delivery pipe was then connected to the outlet of the ram.

Pressure from the water in the two inch feed pipe activated a valve in the base of the ram which sucked noisily up and down at two second intervals, forcing water through the outlet, the spare water gushing from its base. How pleased we were when it functioned in almost perpetual motion.

At last the ranch house had constant running water, though the delivery pipe, where it passed through the forest, did suffer quite frequent damage from Elephant and other big game. It would surprise me if it took longer than a couple of days for incoming African 'Independents', to destroy it.

Deciding to replace his wooden stables by stone ones, Will engaged a couple of stone-masons and commenced gathering suitable material for the job by blasting soft stone outcrops which were scattered around the farm.

The method used for blasting was for the African labourers to punch a two-inch diameter hole, some 3 or 4 feet deep, into an outcrop using a crow-bar. Then, Will would carefully measure out half a four-ounce tobacco tin of black powder, which he poured down the hole. He then inserted a fuse wire down into the powder, filled the hole up with earth and tamped it well and truly down with a crow-bar. He would then sit down beside it and light the fuse.

The first time I saw him do this, I panicked and ran back to a safe distance. Will laughed, and while waiting for the explosion, he just sat there beside the hole, happily rolling a cigarette. After twenty seconds there was a dull thud followed by a wisp of smoke escaping through cracks that had opened up in the outcrop. These, the masons would widen with a crow-bar until they freed blocks which could be shaped by hammer and chisel.

Every few days we would walk or ride the 4 miles to a particular outcrop, to blast a new supply and, one day I was given the job of filling and priming the hole. This time, as a practical joke, instead of the usual half a tin, I put in one and a half tins of powder. I lit the fuse, and Will, as usual, sat back to roll a cigarette while I, as I had done the first time, backed well away. Will turned, smiling, and said,

"You know, you don't have to stand so far away." I smiled back.

"But, Will," I said. "I put one and a half tins of powder in the hole." Never had I seen him move so fast.

"What!" He screamed and, discarding his tobacco tin and cigarette papers, he leaped to his feet and ran like hell. It was just as well he did, for suddenly, there was an almighty 'whoof' and rock fragments flew in showers for forty feet in every direction. The Africans turned white, Will began to shake and he was so upset that he wouldn't allow me near the holes again. Worse, the explosion had so shattered this particular outcrop that it had to be abandoned and another one found. Eventually, though, he forgave me.

Very early on in my stay with the Blains, I was given the job of supplying the household servants and the dogs with meat, and it was an every-other-day job. The first time that Will detailed me, he looked at my 8mm rifle.

"It's a bit light," he said. "You'd better take my Westley Richard .318. You never know what you may bump into." The .318 was a classic. A light to medium bore, it delivered a penetrating bullet that tended not to break up while imparting heavy shocking power. Will also had a heavy Gibbs .505 three-shot magazine rifle which he used for the big stuff. Few bores were classic, reliable game killers and East Africa was the world's great testing ground for such weapons.

I quickly learned that animals (and humans) suffered great nervous shock when the first bullet struck them but, if only wounded, often appeared not to feel subsequent bullets. The first might knock them down, but after that, it was a case of kill or disable, or get the hell out of it.

Handing me the .318, Will also gave me one round of soft nose ammunition and four hard nosed solid rounds, with orders not to fire the latter unless I was in real danger. He allowed me only one round to ensure I didn't start blasting away at obscure targets. Soft nose dumdums are best for soft-skinned, plains-type animals, hard nose for thick skinned, dangerous animals, which required deep penetration on an undiverted course to stop them.

51

Ideally, a soft nose bullet should expand and penetrate some two-thirds of the animal's body, while the solid should reach the outer skin on the far side, but fail to leave the body. This way, maximum shocking power is obtained.

"Also", he told me, "Never fire until you know exactly what you are firing at and never, until you are certain of killing the animal. Always count to ten between deciding to fire and doing so - that is, of course, if circumstances permit. A charging animal would be the exception to the last rule."

In the fading light of late afternoon, Bush-buck, Reed-buck, Water-buck, Stein-buck and Duiker would emerge from the edges of the forest to graze, and at this time, off I would go, accompanied by a couple of Africans to butcher what I killed and carry the meat back.

I soon reverted to using my 8mm Mannlicher, with which I proved deadly accurate on both stationary and fast moving targets. It was beautifully sighted with fore, rear and aperture sights and was perfectly balanced.

Later on, I was allowed to take the Gibbs which I had one of the Africans carry, keeping close behind me. I told him to stay especially close when we were in forested areas smelling of fresh buffalo, elephant or rhino and be ready to hand it to me at the slightest hint of danger. To my regret the opportunity of using it never arose.

Using my own 8mm, I felt at liberty to shoot, not only for meat. One evening I hit a bush pig, but seeing that it wasn't dead, and loath to waste a round of precious ammunition, I pulled out my hunting knife. This was the fine German knife with a nine inch folding blade which my father had given to me and which I was justly proud. I stabbed the pig, as I thought, through the heart, but instead of expiring, as I expected, the pig leapt to its feet and fled. Though I followed the tracks and blood trail till dark and next morning hunted the area with dogs, I never saw it or my knife again.

This taught me a very sharp lesson, never to approach a wounded animal unless ready to instantly kill it. Many hunters were killed by going up to wounded animals, even non-dangerous antelope or buck, unprepared, only to be met by a lightening-quick lunge and horns through their stomachs.

I was, in years to come, to do a great deal of hunting, for both meat for my men and for sport. In fact, I spent every available moment at it, mostly in Government time and largely at Government expense, but it was some years before I hunted with professionals such as George Adamson of

"Born Free" fame, Eric Rungren, a sadistic killer employed by the game department, who by then had shot over 1,200 elephant, Miles Turner, a game warden and later warden of a Tanzania tourist game park, Tom Salmon of the Kenya game department, who often shot elephant when mounted on a donkey because he tended to be stout and disliked walking, and many others. By the time I could benefit from their experience I had already learnt much the hard way and I was accepted by them as a professional when, in times of danger, it was an every-man-for-himself situation.

During my last week at the ranch I helped Will to survey, by Theodolite, a valley which he intended to dam and flood, and with little work, form, a twenty acre stretch of water. Whether he ever finished, or for that matter, even started the work, I do not know. Many ranches created dams in those days using work-oxen to drag scoopfuls of earth to create a dam wall. With teams of oxen criss-crossing from each side, compacting the deposited earth with their feet as they went, a solid dam wall could be quickly constructed.

Another lesson I learned at the ranch was taught to me by their tame monkey. He was tethered, by a collar and lead, to a long wire strung between two trees and, up one of the trees, a wooden box was fixed as his shelter. Each morning the girls would feed the monkey and gave him some milk, but one evening, as a joke, we offered him a cup of whisky, which he promptly drank. Obviously a bit tipsy, the monkey performed all sorts of antics and acrobatics and chattered away fifteen to the dozen. The next morning, however, the poor creature lay quiet in his box all hunched up, holding his head in his hands and feeling very sorry for himself. The girls, instead of offering him his usual milk, gave him some more whisky. He smelt it, looked at us in disgust and then hurled the can a good twenty yards away!

I had been with the Blains for nearly four months and for the past two, I had become increasingly concerned about my future. I was earning nothing and my finances were dwindling. After what I had learned from the Blains about the poor state of farming in Kenya, I saw no future in getting work as a farm manager or the like, nor, in fact, in East African farming at all. I couldn't bring myself to ask my parents for more money, they had done enough and besides, Father was hoping to retire soon and I knew he had no great capital, having largely earned and spent. My prospects looked dismal and I was becoming desperate.

One day, on a visit to Thomson's Falls, I had to wait while the Blain family visited friends at Barry's Hotel, so during their absence, I walked over to the Police Station and introduced myself to the British Inspector, (Potty) and told him of my problem. I don't know what I expected him to do for me but I hoped that he might be able to suggest some profession that I could follow or, at least, introduce me to someone who could. Secretly I suspect that I was giving in and placing myself at his mercy with the depressing expectation that he would send me home to the UK.

We had a long chat and he took me on a tour of his head-quarters, then, returning to his office, instead of invoking the dreaded Repatriation Bond, as I had expected him to do, he told me that he had heard that H.Q. was seeking two or three British recruits.

"Why don't you join the force?" he said. The idea had never crossed my mind and I was stunned. A policeman! The very idea was against all I had planned; cooped up in an office somewhere, my freedom curtailed; pinned to a desk or to a routine of work, which would be almost as soul destroying as my job in England had been. But what choice did I have? It would bring temporary relief to my precarious financial position and, for a while at least, I would still be here in the country I had come so quickly to love and the chance would remain that I could still find my niche in life here rather than be sent back home with my tail between my legs - a failure.

After 5 minutes careful consideration, I said, yes, I would certainly apply and in due course, I was accepted. I was now a member, albeit the most junior, of the Kenya Police and the time had come for me to move on.

The next couple of weeks passed slowly and I was torn between the desire to be on my way to sample what my new life had to offer and my devotion to the friendship, the freedom and the delightful experiences I had come to cherish on the Blains' ranch. Inept and comical though I must have appeared to them at times, I suppose that I had become as much a part of the Blains' existence as they had of mine, and they too, seemed sad at the prospect of my departure.

On my last night at the ranch, at around midnight, a great commotion arose as the stables were invaded by a colony of Siafu, (Safari ants), which smothered their six horses and commenced to bite. Siafu are crafty, walking through grass or under-growth, you could be half covered with them before you know that there's one on you. Then suddenly, as if by a signal, all of them would start to bite you at once. It was not unusual to see someone, male or female, start ripping off their clothes, dancing about like dervishes, slapping themselves all over and yelling for help.

The horses covered by the Siafu had gone frantic; neighing, whinnying and attempting to kick down the stables. What a night! We all turned out; house staff, grooms, squatters, everyone in hearing distance of the uproar; even a travelling Asian Artisan who had arrived seeking work.

With only hurricane lamps for illumination and with the horses literally going mad, we all got battered and bashed about, but by dawn we managed to get things under control.

The following day, I said goodbye to May Blain and the girls and Will drove me and my possessions the thirty-five miles to Thomson's Falls. As we shook hands and I thanked him for all his kindness to me, he slowly nodded his head. I think he was as doubtful as I was about the prospects that my new life in the Kenya Police held in store for me.

Fertile Ground

I arrived at the Police Station in Thomson's Falls in the searing heat of mid-day and, determined to make a good and lasting impression on my first day in the force, I took a deep breath, squared my shoulders and marched smartly into Potty's Office.

"Ah, Mills," he said, apparently surprised to see me. "The train's leaving for Nairobi at one, but don't worry..." He quickly scribbled a note and detailed a prisoner to deliver it to the Station Master. "I've told him not to let it go until you're safely on board." Then bidding me to sit, he opened a drawer, pulled out a bottle and two glasses and poured us each a rather large glass of whisky. Whisky was a beverage I disliked then and have always disliked since, but who was I, a raw recruit on my first day, to argue with a senior officer. I sipped while he drank.

For the next couple of hours, Potty rambled on about life in the force, reaching over the desk at frequent intervals to replenish my glass. As time went on, I began to fret in case the driver should become impatient and decide to depart without me but it was evident that I was stuck there until Potty decided otherwise. Eventually, he handed me an introductory note addressed to the police headquarters in Nairobi and, somewhat the worse for the vast quantity of drink we'd consumed, we left for the station.

We arrived at the station at 3.00pm and, to my great relief, found the train still waiting there, patiently puffing clouds of steam into the still afternoon air. Slowly, I scanned the length of the train looking for the carriage in which I would travel to Nairobi but, to my astonishment, there wasn't one. The whole train from engine to brake van was goods wagons.

Suddenly the Asian driver came towards us waving his arms and calling excitedly. In broken English he conveyed to us that there were no passengers booked on the train, furthermore, during the extended wait, the African brake-man had decided he'd had enough of the job and disappeared.

"No problem." Potty volunteered waving his hand in my direction. "My friend here will travel in the brake-van." And with the problem apparently solved, he bid me farewell and departed, leaving me no time to object to the proposal. I stood open-mouthed while the driver explained the braking mechanism to me.

"Wind the wheel round and down to apply the brake then round and up to release it. And don't forget, each time we get into a bend and the wheels screech under you, you must apply the brake" It all sounded simple enough to me so, ever ready for a new experience, I took up my position ready to leave.

That blasted train took eight hours to reach Nairobi and, being a highland track, it was continuous bends and screeching wheels all the way. I was forced to spend the whole journey, apart from a brief stop to take on wood and water, ferociously cranking the brake wheel up and down in a desperate attempt to prevent the train from running out of control and leaping off the track. Next time I was forced to travel that way, I decided, I would be the driver.

The following morning, Saturday, I strolled over to the headquarters of the Kenya Police and, locating the C.I.D. Superintendent, as Potty had instructed me to, I handed him my introductory note. He read it in silence, looked me up and down then, leading me to the office of the Commissioner's Staff Officer he handed him the note saying, "Here, sign him on."

The Staff Officer was rather more formal and sat me down at a table. "First," he said. "I'd like you to fill in this form." This was the application form and it was brief.; name, age, nationality, etc... I filled them all in. Then came the statement that the minimum entry qualification was the Senior Cambridge examination which, unfortunately, I had not passed. For just a moment I hesitated, then quickly entered 'Cambridge' and handed back the form. The Staff Officer glanced at the form then gave me a long, fixed stare as if questioning my fitness for duty. "You'll have to produce references you know..." he said at last. "And have a medical examination."

"Yes, sir," I replied. And with that, he seemed satisfied.

"Right then," he continued, pushing another document towards me. "Sign that." It was a contract of service and it too was brief. It contained little except a statement of the terms of service which were; twenty-four hours a day, three hundred and sixty-five days a year; if on leave, you were subject to instant recall from anywhere in the world; you had to pass three examinations on Swahili, two on law, one on criminal procedures, one on the Penal code, one on the Evidence Act and one on Standing Orders; you would be on probation for two years at a salary of £240 per annum and might hope for an annual increment of £20 thereafter. Finally it stated, 'You are, for any reason whatsoever, liable to instant dismissal.' I signed it and thus officially became an Assistant Inspector of the Kenya Police.

"All right," said the Staff Officer, smiling for the first time. "Report straight away to the Police training depot. I'll ring the depot commander and say you're on your way."

The depot lay on the outskirts of Nairobi, on the edge of the Embakasi Plains and it accommodated up to three British and sixty native African trainees. Soon after arriving, I was introduced to the two other British recruits who were under training at that time. The older, Ted Robinson, was tall and spare with a nervous habit of stroking his large, hooked nose. He had come up to Nairobi from Mombasa where his father, a drunken Scotsman, ran the office of a small shipping line. Determined to succeed where his father had failed, Ted was set on making as much money as he could in the shortest time possible and was full of questionable schemes for getting rich quick. Mike Bradley, on the other hand, was a handsome idealist. Brought up in a Birmingham suburb, he had arrived in Kenya with little more than the clothes he wore and a romantic notion of life in the colonies. Both of them, I suspected, had joined the Kenya Police for lack of a more promising opportunity.

Soon after settling in, I quickly penned a letter to my parents requesting the references that the Commissioner's Staff Officer had warned me would be required. As I posted the letter, I crossed my fingers in the hope that, considering my questionable record back home, they would find someone with a good word to say for me. I needn't have worried. When, a few weeks later, the reply came, it contained five references which, had I been arrogant enough to believe half of what they said about me, would have sent me scurrying back to England to claim my just reward. One was from the Lord Mayor of Norwich who seemed to be of the opinion that I should commence my police service as

Commissioner. The second was from the Chief Constable of Norfolk, whom I don't recall ever having met, said that I was of unquestionable integrity and impeccable character. Another, from a regular army Major, said that I was a damned good fellow and an excellent shot. The fourth was from the Manager at my former employer, Coleman & Co. which implied that, if I hadn't left them when I did, I would have been Managing Director in a matter of weeks. Finally, one from the Chief Constable of Norwich who wondered why on earth I should need references at all. Father had indeed excelled himself on my behalf and I was pleased, though quite relieved that the writers were far enough away so as not to be questioned further in the matter.

Our day at the training depot commenced with riding lessons conducted by the Depot Commander who held the rank of Superintendent. He was a fanatical horseman and was determined that every recruit under his tutelage would leave the depot as an accomplished and confident rider. Each morning at dawn, we would mount up, sometimes with a saddle and sometimes bareback, and he would bellow, 'Follow me!' Off we would go galloping madly across the Athi plains on the outskirts of Nairobi. We galloped across rough terrain, swerving this way and that, charging down steep hills, across valleys and up the other side. So used to this daily routine were the horses that they would follow him no matter what, and no attempt on our part to control them, slow them down or stop them, was in the least effective so we poor unfortunates were left to hang on as best we could. From this hectic routine I learned just two things; firstly, how to stay on a horse, and secondly, never to ride one again if I could possibly avoid it.

On our return from this early-morning torture, we had to dash to our rooms, quickly change into uniform and present ourselves on the parade ground for square bashing. This part of our training was conducted by an ex-army sergeant who had been specially engaged for the purpose, and he was mean. As the sun rose higher in the sky, he fixed us with his beady eyes and screaming orders at us in a voice that could be heard five miles away, he marched us relentlessly to and fro until we began to resemble the smart body of men he was determined to produce.

Next came bayonet drill and then, thoroughly exhausted, we retired indoors. The rest of the morning was set aside for a lecture on a variety of subjects concerning police activities but it usually degenerated into reminiscences of the lecturer on events and colourful personalities who formed part of the history of the force.

As well as bayonet drill, it was considered appropriate to train us in the use of the old fashioned British infantry square. The Officer Commanding would stand in the centre and order, "In two ranks, form square. Front ranks kneel and fire. Front ranks reload, rear ranks fire. Rear ranks reload, front ranks fire." This supposedly impregnable formation had served the infantry well in many a battle and, I believe, the only force ever to break the square were the Zulu.

After lunch, the afternoon was supposed to be devoted to private study of law and police procedures from the very few books that were available. But things seldom went to plan and the three of us, my two British companions and myself, availed ourselves of considerable quantities of alcohol and got thoroughly pissed instead. We would sleep until dusk then, barely recovered from the afternoon's drinking, we would head off into Nairobi to sample the nightlife until the early hours.

It was on one such evening, just about sun-down as we were stirring from a drunken doze, that an African orderly dashed in with an urgent message from the depot commander. It appeared that Mike Bradley's current girl-friend, a lady of nearly twice his age, had been spotted on a balcony high up on the Torrs Hotel in the centre of town. She was half naked and, to the consternation of passers-by, was threatening to throw herself off. The message ended with a curt 'Can you please sort it out.'

We dressed quickly and dashed into Nairobi and, sure enough, there she was teetering on a high ledge wearing only in a night-dress and threatening suicide. It seemed that the cause of her distress was the fact that Mike had jilted her the night before. Mike took one look at her, fled straight up the stairs and suddenly appeared at a window along-side the ledge.

What he said to her to change her mind, I never found out, but after what seemed like an age, she relented and crawled back in through the window. For the next few weeks Mike was a sight more choosy in the female company he kept - and in the promises he made to them. But he was a strange, fanciful character, always in trouble for his romantic notions, which came to a head two years later when he was dismissed from the force for refusing to investigate the theft of cattle from white settlers on the grounds that, '...they had plenty left anyway.'

My other companion from that time, Ted Robinson, also later fell foul of his superiors and was dismissed from the force. One of his money-making schemes went badly wrong when it was discovered that he had been using the men under his command, together with a group of prisoners, to launder linen for a country hotel which was situated not far from his station.

During my period of training I became involved in a few amorous entanglements. One girl I remember well, not only for her beauty, but also for her boldness, I met just a few weeks after my arrival at the training depot. Our first encounter was at a club in Nairobi on a warm sultry night. Unusual for that hour, I was sober and in a pensive mood as I stood at the bar slowly sipping my Whisky and water. Suddenly, I caught sight of her across the room. She was watching me and as our eyes met, she smiled. That was enough of a signal for me and within a second or two, I was by her side. We talked - mostly, I must admit about me and my entry into the police force - then she invited me to her flat close by. There was no mistaking her intentions and almost as soon as we entered the flat she undressed.

We made love that night and on many occasions afterwards and it seemed to me that we were set for a long and enjoyable relationship. One night, however, as we lay on her bed after making love, she suddenly turned to me and said that it would all have to stop now. I was puzzled. We had been getting on so well together and the thought that we might soon break up had never crossed my mind. When I asked her why, her answer amazed me. Quite calmly, she announced that in a few days time she was getting married and it wouldn't be fair to her husband.

A few years later, I met her again under different circumstances and got the impression that, despite her marriage, or even because of it, she would have been very willing to resume our former intimate relationship.

On a shopping expedition to Nairobi, I met a girl who told me she lived in a local convent. She was neither a nun nor a novice, she said, she just worked there. We arranged to meet and the following evening we spent a pleasant few hours together. Around midnight she said that it was time she went home so we hopped into my old Chrysler coupe and drove across town. As we neared, I noticed that the convent stood on elevated ground approached by a wide sweep of some thirty steep steps, at the top of which was a flat paved area in front of the main entrance.

It was raining hard and I was too considerate an escort to allow her to climb all that way and get soaked into the bargain. So, with hardly a second thought, I jammed my foot hard on the accelerator and, with headlights blazing and engine roaring, I drove straight up the steps to the top.

As my passenger got out, the doors of the convent opened and there stood a nun, her mouth open and a face like thunder. Quickly realising my error of judgement with regard to appropriate behaviour, I shot the car into reverse and clattered, bumpety-bump to the bottom then sped off into the darkness. The girl never went out with me again.

It was during my stay at the training depot that I first saw locusts and the memory of that awesome sight has stayed with me ever since.

One bright afternoon, I noticed that a cloud was gathering on the horizon. At first I though that it heralded a change in the weather but its strange pulsing movement made me stare in amazement. Gradually the cloud darkened and started to travel nearer until, when it was almost overhead, I realised that it wasn't a rain storm as I'd expected, but an enormous cloud of insects - in fact, a much-feared swarm of locusts. They blocked out the sun and it was as dark as night.

When swarming, these large insects fly wing-tip to wing-tip with the lower ones just above ground level and the higher, 1000 feet or more up, the swarm stretching from horizon to horizon.

Years later, while travelling in a lorry with some of my men, I encountered an even larger swarm. It was heading north, at right angles to our route and we drove for eighty miles from first point of contact, constantly bombarded by insects with insufficient airspace to allow them to avoid us, until eventually we emerged into clear air at the other side. Many times the vehicle faltered and we had to halt in order to clear the radiator and the air filter of the carcasses of hundreds of the creatures.

A couple of weeks after I arrived at the police training depot I was ordered to have a medical examination by the Government doctor to ensure that I was physically fit to join the force. The prospect worried me and gave me a few sleepless nights because, from an early age, I had developed varicose veins in my legs and their discovery would certainly mean failure. However, I thought, I'd conned my way past one doctor so surely I could do it again.

Some months earlier, while I was still with the Blains, I had had a fit of patriotism and joined the Voluntary Kenya Regiment, Territorial Army which would entail a few weeks military training each year.

The Regiment was an all white force which aimed to produce a core of British officers who would be ready to command black forces in the event of war, and acceptance into its ranks depended on being passed medically fit. The nearest doctor was some eighty miles away and when I presented myself to him, I discovered that he was the notorious Doctor Searl of the

'Helen of Troy' scandal. Some years earlier, while in general practice in England, he had conducted a torrid and much publicised affair with a lady patient, whom the press had dubbed Helen of Troy. As a result, he was stuck off the medical register and had emigrated to Kenya where morals were much more practical.

At the time, the Colony was very short of qualified medical personnel so, despite his past misbehaviour, he was allowed to practice. As I entered his surgery, he slowly looked me up and down then said, "Well, you look jolly fit." I replied that I was in fine condition so, without more ado, he signed a chit and said,

"Here you are. That'll get you in."

When I presented myself at the Government doctor's surgery for this latest examination, I fervently hoped that I could achieve a repeat of the performance with Doctor Searl. "Oh, by the way," I said. "I've just been declared fit for the regiment." The doctor peered at me over his spectacles for a few seconds.

"Good," he said. "That'll save me a bit of time. Now, on your way and I'll notify the force that your fit." I could hardly contain my delight. Got away with it again, I thought, and skipped down the steps and headed back to the depot.

That afternoon, I lay on my bed and took stock of the situation. Having passed the medical, even by devious means, meant that there was little in the way to stop me from becoming a fully fledged officer of the Kenya Police. With a little application to study, though not sufficient to curtail my social life, I knew that I could pass the examinations and from then, it would be simply a matter of doing the job well, whatever it might entail. I had a job with prospects and I need worry no longer about imposing myself upon my parent's limited financial resources. The awful prospect of being forcibly repatriated began to fade and I decided that I would make a go of it, come what may. I felt more at ease than I had done for a long time.

During my six weeks at the depot, I devoted a portion of my study time to the history of the force and made careful notes for later reference.

At the time I joined, the force was still relatively small and undeveloped. There were some eighty British officers, mostly eccentric individualists, with the lowest rank of Assistant Inspector, and one thousand eight hundred Africans with the highest rank of Sergeant, the rest being Corporals and Constables. Every African who joined saw his recruitment as a tremendous privilege and all ranks, British and Africans alike, were held in the highest esteem by the public at large.

The force had its origins some fifty years earlier. In 1886/7 a small Police force of mainly Asian officers was created in Mombasa with a mandate to police only the port and its immediate locality. The rest of the territory was divided into administrative Districts each controlled by a Government Officer who, from his District headquarters, would recruit Africans to act as armed police, but only able to operate in his particular District. Called Askaris from the Swahili word for soldier, they were dressed in uniforms designed by the Government Officer himself and, since there were few funds available, they were paid mostly in trade goods rather than in cash. These small, local forces acted entirely independently of each other and there was no co-ordination on a territory-wide basis and no overall command.

There were other forces in existence at this period, for example; as the Kenya-Uganda railway extended westwards, a railway Police contingent was formed with British commissioned officers while lower ranks were either Asians, Somalis or Africans. No police training was given and they were more a military force than a police force and a poorly equipped one at that, their main weapon being an early Snider rifle.

In 1897 the foundation stone of what was later to become the Kenya Police was laid by the recruitment of armed guards by the British East Africa Company to man a chain of forts along the old slave caravan routes stretching from Kenya's coastline westwards through Kenya and Uganda. These small parties policed the wild and savage areas around their forts and safeguarded, or at least attempted to safeguard, explorers and traders. Again, they were uncoordinated - each a small private army - but they became the nucleus of what, in 1902, was to become the British East African Police.

From 1905 to 1910 these scattered elements of police were gradually drawn into the British East Africa Police which, by then, had its main headquarters in Nairobi, a main branch headquarters in Mombasa on the east coast and another in Kisumu on Lake Victoria's eastern shore. Not until 1920 when Kenya changed status from Protectorate to Colony was the force renamed the Kenya Police and that was just sixteen years prior to my own recruitment.

In the early days, the British East Africa Police lacked funds and had few British officers, most of the junior officers being Indians. As a result, the main language used by the force, that in which reports were written and records kept, was Urdu. Slowly, the force expanded and larger budgets provided better arms, uniforms and equipment.

British NCO's were seconded from army units to introduced positive training, drill and discipline, although recruits were given no specific training in Police work. Contingents of the force served alongside units of the King's African Rifles and undertook lengthy expeditions into remote and often dangerous areas including the Somali-Abyssinian-Sudanese frontiers. Gradually, what had started out as a few ill-disciplined, uncoordinated bands of ruffians recruited to provide protection for white settlers as they penetrated unadministered areas of East Africa, evolved into a smart, well disciplined and unified force.

Eventually, with strength increased to some nineteen hundred personnel and morale rising, an *esprit de corps* not hitherto seen had developed alongside an unswerving loyalty to the distant Crown and it became a force to be reckoned with. Enrolment into the force came to be considered a great privilege, not only by native Africans but by British officers as well.

Momentum gathered as more European settlers arrived and increasingly penetrated previously unadministered areas. Police and Administrative Officers were sent into these areas to establish good order, discipline and respect for strong Government thus, the gradual civilisation of previously untamed and often hostile areas led to an increase in policing as opposed to para-military activity.

The practical policing of these newly civilised regions was being learned the hard way. Area commanders had little opportunity for communication with their counterparts, even in adjacent areas, and so were forced to act mainly on their own initiative. Being mostly eccentric characters, often with extraordinary experience of remote and savage lands, they rapidly won the respect and admiration of both the early settlers and the indigenous populations. Nothing daunted them and like the Canadian Mounties, getting their man became a matter of great pride in the force.

Pay was low, but in this newly settled colony, life for the adventurous was unrivalled by anything that could be found in all but a very few parts of the Great British Empire.

At this period, short training courses for newly recruited British officers and those on long home leave were conducted in Ireland by the Royal Irish Constabulary. But this policy proved to be a mistake since neither Irish nor UK policing had much in common with that required in

East Africa. As a result, basic training was developed for new recruits at the depot attached to the forces headquarters in Nairobi, though even this was restricted to training in military functions.

Despite the increase over the years in the size of the force, they were still too few in number. Many more districts remained without a locally established police force than those that had, so contingents of police had to safari on foot into neighbouring unpoliced areas to quell any serious disorder, tribal fighting and the like.

The colonisation of East Africa around the turn of the century was a far from peaceful affair. In the Northern desert areas there were constant cross-border attacks by Somali and Abyssinian raiding parties while, in the more heavily occupied Central and Southern tribal areas, rebellion followed rebellion with monotonous regularity. These were put down by combined forces of police and King's African Rifles and were usually followed up by punitive expeditions designed to discourage further armed uprising.

Where they were present, Police had to act as jacks-of-all-trades. They were responsible, not only for policing, but also for prosecutions, corporal punishment, executions by firing squad of those sentenced to death, (when hanging was introduced, they carried those out as well), fire fighting, immigration control, attending the sick and even, when there was no alternative, field surgery. Likewise, in the absence of others more knowledgeable, Police often had to construct roads, build bridges and construct any buildings that the proper conduct of their duties may necessitate.

At this time, the Government was giving away land to white settlers with the condition imposed that certain agricultural developments had to be carried out within strict time limits. It was the responsibility of the police to carry out inspections of these developments and report back to ensure that were properly completed.

Game control was a natural responsibility of the Police. Rogue elephant, aggressive rhino, crop-raiding buffalo, man eating lions, (of which there were many), all had to be dealt with from time to time.

Communication were virtually non-existent; no 'phones, no wireless, no telegraph, no aircraft, just a few deeply rutted tracks which passed for roads but which were hard to negotiate at the best of times and, after even modest rains, were rendered all but impassable. Police units were forced to operate in almost total isolation and rely on their own initiative and ingenuity as the situation demanded.

As late as 1912, the force was still in a primitive stage of development. It had laid down no unified code of regulations, a central training depot had not yet been established, its recruitment policy was rudimentary leading to the enrolment of somewhat unsuitable officers into both its junior and senior ranks, the pay was miserable, no pensions or leave were offered and the equipment with which officers were expected to carry out their duties, was, to say the best of it, inadequate.

The approach of the First World War led to a strengthening of the Force and on its outbreak, all units were placed on active service alongside the King's African Rifles. In its many actions, this combination formed a small, but effective force. Tanganykia, then German East Africa, bordering southern Kenya contained military forces far superior to our own which were intent on defeating and taking over British East Africa. However, they reckoned without the grit and determination of the British. During these actions, one police unit distinguishing itself by being the first in the territory to capture a German flag. This feat was emulated at the start of the second world war when a police unit was the first to capture a light machine gun from the Italians.

Shortly after the outbreak of war, an East African Police Service Battalion was formed by drawing 500 or so men and officers from the Force. In its early days, the Battalion was kept busy putting down a serious rebellion by the Turkana tribes in the extreme north west of Kenya. Later, it was used to attack and punish a powerful Somali force which had ventured into Kenya's Jubaland Province which bordered Abyssinia in the northern district.

Throughout the war the northern territories suffered constant raids by hostile tribesmen from Somaliland, Abyssinia and all along the Kenya-Sudanese frontier so both the military and police units were forced to fight continuous actions against, not only the Germans but also warlike tribes intent on taking advantage of the situation. Expeditions to quell these raids entailed marches of 400 miles and more through unhealthy and hostile territory requiring hundreds of camels and thousands of porters to transport food and equipment.

The period from the end of the Great War until the handover of the Colony to black rule in 1963 saw a steady expansion and development of both white and black settled areas bringing with it all the good and evil that civilisation is heir to. Political and racial unrest was on the increase in the settled regions and vast areas, including the Northern Frontier District, remained only lightly administered ensuring that the Force maintained an active military role alongside that of developing its civil policing functions. Just as well it did, for the last era of colonial rule saw Kenya plunged into civil war and eleven years of Mau Mau atrocities.

From the early days of the British East Africa Police when the inefficient Snider rifle was the principal weapon, steady improvements were made in the Force's armoury. By handover in 1963, all units had available to them not only rifles, revolvers and pump guns but also sub- and light machine guns, grenades, gas, light mortars and armoured cars - not to mention a few unauthorised 'goodies'. There was no question about who could authorise the use of weapons or who was authorised to use them. In practice any policeman, be he Commissioner or Constable, could at his own discretion, carry and use any available weapon he thought his task might necessitate. Yet, despite having to face dangerous and often life-threatening situations, officers at all levels preferred to operate unarmed as far as was prudent. In all my years of service, I can recall no abuse of the freedom to carry arms.

In 1920, what formerly had been the protectorate of British East Africa became Kenya Colony and, as such, the youngest member of the huge British Empire and Commonwealth. The British East Africa Police, now a colonial force was renamed the Kenya Police.

The next ten years saw the arrival in the colony of many white immigrants, a large number of whom took up the offer of farms which had been surveyed out in previously unoccupied areas. This development led to the creation of trading centres to serve the new communities and to the establishment of local administrative headquarters with a consequent build-up of Government officers including police.

Police stations were established where none had been before and each had under its command several outposts to assist in maintaining local contact and control. A station's compliment typically comprised of a European Inspector, an African Sergeant an African Corporal and some eight to twelve African Constables, four of whom could be stationed at outposts. Modern means of communication were unheard of and the only means of transmitting information was by word of mouth. Transport for the Station Commander was either by horse, mule or on foot and even a District Police Commander was lucky if he had an ox or mule-drawn cart.

This era witnessed the influx of all manner of strange and wonderful characters who's behaviour would be considered questionable in any other part of the Empire. They settled all over Kenya's white highlands and at gatherings in trading centres displays of their wild behaviour and rowdyism were not uncommon. Revolvers, rifles and even swords were carried, but underneath the outward show, they were generally loyal, hardworking people who were desperate to 'tame' Africa and to scratch a subsistence.

The depression of the 1920s resulted in a slowing-down of development during the '30s and so, until after the Second World War, much of Kenya and its way of life continued with little change. One legacy of the depression was a reduction in the Force's establishment which did little to help the already beleaguered service. Throughout the early 1930s the total annual Police budget never exceeded £50,000 and had a tendency to shrink rather than grow, despite the relentless encroachment of settlers into unoccupied, hostile areas of the colony.

The troubles in Kenya's Northern Frontier District continued to be a thorn in the flesh of headquarters but was remote enough from white settled areas to arouse little, if any, interest and even less sympathy, towards the meagre handful of Police and Administrative Officers who daily and selflessly risked their lives in its defence. There, without wireless, roads, telephones, aircraft, adequate water, provisions or medical supplies and armed only with 303s and revolvers, they fought off constant attacks by Somalis, Abyssinians, Gelubba and Merile all of whom fielded large, well armed raiding parties.

The Northern Frontier District covered an area the size of France with more than a thousand miles of frontier. The region was hostile and unhealthy consisting of low-lying desert country sparsely populated by nomadic tribes-people.

In the 1930s police strength was about five to seven British officers with around four-hundred Africans. It was customary for both British and African policemen to be transferred from less rigorous down-country districts to experience two or three years service on the frontier. In addition there were half a dozen British Administrative Officers with sixty or seventy tribal police under their command. This was cowboy and Indian territory, wilder than ever America experienced and it continues to be so to this day. The Crown owes much to those few who, in such appalling conditions, both in Kenya and all over the Empire, held the thin red line for so many years.

During the 1930s, Italian colonialist ambition had led them to move large numbers of troops into Italian Somaliland and Ethiopia just north of Kenya's northern frontier. Italy fully expected Hitler to over-run all Europe including Britain and saw that this could provide an opportunity to add East Africa to her colonial empire. So, when again war threatened, Kenya's frontier wilderness attracted the close interest of East Africa's military high command. The Kenya Police strength on the frontier was immediately increased by nine-hundred rank and file and the GOC East Africa ruled that if Italy declared war, Police serving in the Northern Frontier District would be given military rank and placed under military command.

In June 1940 Italy did declare war and immediately, the Frontier Police secured all water-holes and strong points along the thousand miles of frontier to defend them from surprise Italian attack. They suffered aerial machine gunning and bombing but resistance was such that it deterred the Italians from risking an advance into Kenya until eventually they were put into retreat by our own military advance northwards. At the same time, the Police patrolled with, and fought alongside, the military for many months and provided men as interpreters, guides and scouts.

These were not operations by large, heavily armed forces with wireless communications, backup, reinforcements and medical support, but by small parties of Police with four to ten men, and occasionally twenty to thirty, under the command of a British officer. They were scattered thinly along a thousand miles of frontier in hostile, little known, semi-waterless desert and forced to act on their own initiative, their only means of communication being by camel-borne runners.

Often they joined battle when a more orthodox force would have decided upon a prudent, albeit temporary, retreat. Though they suffered many casualties, mostly the outcome of facing and attacking numerically superior enemy forces, they constantly displayed great courage and exceptional qualities of leadership.

Morale within the Force was always high particularly amongst the African ranks. All units lived in barracks with their families and, at these barracks, the Force operated a Boys Brigade which the sons of serving officers could join. We issued them with mini uniforms and they would mimic their fathers, organise parades, select leaders to command them and generally conduct themselves as a secondary force. When the boys reached recruiting age they were interviewed to see if they wished to join the Force. I never met one who didn't. They were all desperately keen to enlist and shook with fear lest they should be turned down.

Often a recruit would be below the minimum required height and when he was measured against a mark on the wall and one shook one's head, his face would be a picture of abject misery. In my case, I would put a book on the floor below the mark and say, "Stand on this." And then enlist him. As it turned out, many of our finest NCOs were below height, a condition which seemed to give them a feeling of inferiority so that when they were given authority, they became dynamos in order to compensate.

Almost the only trouble with native African Policemen was that they aged very abruptly. A first class NCO with an excellent record and nineteen of his twenty years service behind him could suddenly lose the respect of his men and consequently, his control over them. The choice was either to pension him off , which destroyed his trust and self respect, or keep him on until he had to be sacked because he could no longer exercise authority. Here lay some of the hardest decisions I ever had to make.

What Was to Follow

The mid to late forties saw some major changes in the Colony's policing policy. A number of Police Levy units were formed for the maintenance of law and order in areas where inter-tribal conflict was an ever present problem, an auxiliary Police force was created and the responsibility for policing, hitherto unpoliced, native reserve districts was handed over to the regular Police. Later, the Auxiliary Police were disbanded and replaced by volunteer, part-time Special Police.

The formation and command of such organisations placed considerable administrative burdens upon the already hard-pressed regular Police and promoted an underlying fear that, by creating and arming such settler dominated groups, the Colony risked laying the foundation of a settler uprising against its declared policy of granting Independence under African rule. At this time the Police began to suspect, and evidence lead it to accept, that a powerful anti-white, anti-government movement was spreading rapidly throughout the Kikuyu tribe - the Mau Mau.

Judging that an armed special Police force would be a lesser evil than that of chronic undermanning, the Force took what then was a bold decision and virtually doubled its strength through the formation of the Kenya Police Reserve.

The Reserve was designed to provide both part-time and full-time officers in support of the regular Police but its organisation was no sooner under way than government fears of a white uprising re-surfaced. Secret contingency plans were drawn up to disarm the Reserves if the necessity arose. In some instances, personal issue arms were withdrawn on the grounds that they would be 'safer in regular Police armouries'. Soon, however, the rapid spread of the Mau Mau brought government and settlers together to present a solid front against it, and all thoughts of a white settler uprising evaporated.

The years between 1947 and 1952 saw the emergence of two other anti-white religious sects which temporarily diverted Police from their routine duties. One, the Deni ya Jesu Christi, arose amongst the Kikuyu Tribe and its followers were known as 'Skin Men'. its main objective was to get rid of all Europeans and to free Africans from colonial rule and discipline. The other, the Deni ya Msambwa, had similar aims but reared its ugly head amongst the Kitosh tribe of Nyanza, Kenya's Lake Province. Both of these factions were suppressed fairly rapidly after sudden and violent conflicts, but not so the Mau Mau which took ten years to subdue.

The period from 1949 to 1954 proved to be a very difficult one for the Force. Increasingly, intelligence was being gathered by both Police and Administrative Officers regarding the rapid expansion of the Mau Mau and the continual rise in the appalling atrocities perpetrated in its name. However, to the great frustration of the Kenya Police, neither the Kenya Government nor Whitehall chose to believe it. The Force, under Commissioner O'Rorke, foresaw the carnage which was to follow and made urgent representations for, not only an increase in Police strength, but also for adequate military support to be immediately available should open revolt suddenly break out.

Commissioner O'Rorke worked hard to press home his case, and despite enormous resistance, eventually succeeded in obtaining extra funding and an increased establishment.

During this frustrating period he was instrumental in introducing a great deal of long-overdue modernisation. He oversaw the establishment of an up to date Police training school, a Police air wing, a para-military Police Emergency Company, the Kenya Police Reserve, a dog section, an effective Special Branch, modern radio communications, an improved rank structure, better pay and conditions of service, and eventually - and most important of all - he convinced both the Colony's government and the UK government that an unprecedented bloodbath was imminent.

While grudgingly acknowledging his perseverance and foresight, both governments made Commissioner O'Rorke the scapegoat for their own blundering stupidity and retired him in disgrace. This done, Kenya's ungrateful government appointed a successor to whom they gave carte blanche to expand as fast as possible without regard to cost.

In the light of the work already done by his predecessor, this new Commissioner, Colonel A.E.Young CMG, had a simple task. He had only to chase up orders for supplies which were already placed and tell his willing field commanders to proceed full steam ahead with recruitment and modernisation. Unlike Commissioner O'Rorke however, he was utterly unsuited for a Colonial command resulting in a considerable erosion of morale amongst senior officers. This occurred to such an extent that they tended almost to ignore him and tackle their formidable responsibilities with a confidence rooted in their previous experience.

To general amazement, Colonel Young had brought out with him, on secondment as his ADC, a Metropolitan Chief Superintendent. This gentleman appeared to spend a considerable portion of his time snooping behind commander's backs and asking subordinates if they wanted to make any complaints against their senior officers. What he hoped to achieve by this tactic, heaven alone knows, but in the event nobody did make a complaint and he was considered fortunate not to have ended up with a knife in his back. That would have been one crime the Kenya Police failed to solve.

Commissioner Young and his 'side kick' didn't last long. Some eight months after his arrival he was replaced by (later Sir) Richard Catling CMG OBE. Catling had behind him, valuable experience of emergencies in both Palestine and Malaya and he spoke the same 'action' language as his Officers. He thoroughly understood those under him and the awesome tasks they had to face and displayed an unprecedented efficiency of command throughout the remainder of the Mau Mau rebellion. Indeed, he continued to do so up to the granting of independence and then for a period following it in the rank of Inspector General of the Kenya Police.

Of the many things that the Force taught its officers, one in particular stands out - never to worry. Worry is destructive and leads to a breakdown in judgement. The better course of action is simply to act responsibly in the best interests of the majority and not to concern oneself with what others might be thinking or whether they liked or disliked you. Instead it is better to act in a matter which will earn their respect. My experience has taught me that the essential qualities of a good Police officer are a sense of humour, integrity, determination, discretion, compassion, understanding, common sense and a degree of ruthlessness.

Catling made one of his first tasks the expansion of the Reserve Police Airwing which O'Rorke had pioneered. Initially the wing comprised of a miscellany of light aircraft borrowed or hired from companies and settlers who owned them. Pilots were civilians who were given ranks in the Police Reserve.

Eventually, the Police purchased their own aircraft, an Auster but it was grossly under-powered for East Africa's mountainous terrain having an operating ceiling of only 8,000 feet. The Auster proved unsuitable since several planes with much more powerful engines had been forced to crash land by high altitude mountainside down draughts.

Quite quickly, the Airwing grew to include a number of Tripacer aircraft but these also lacked the necessary engine power and were eventually replaced by Cessna 180s, seven in all, and one Chipmunk,

By this time, the aircraft were piloted by full-time regular Police officers assisted by both regular and reserve officer with past flying experience. Most were ex-RAF or ex-Rhodesian RAF pilots who had been highly trained and had considerable flying experience. By mid emergency, the wing had been absorbed into the regular force.

Throughout the emergency, year in, year out, by both day and night, the aircraft provided communication, supply drops to both Police and military forces, transport of personnel and, on the active service front, bombed terrorist gangs and their hide-outs, dropped flares and smoke bombs to identify and pinpoint targets for bombing and machine-gunning by Lincoln and Harvard bombers flying out of Nairobi's RAF airfield.

In the early days of the uprising, before more modern developments were adopted, some enthusiastic police pilots lobbed grenades out of the aircraft windows and fired hand-held Bren guns and sub-machine guns through the open doors. This latter was a very uncomfortable, not to say dangerous practice, considering that a Bren gun spat red-hot .303 cartridge cases in a constant stream all around the confined cockpit.

Prior to the fitting of racks to carry 19lb anti-personnel bombs, some aircrew improvised by making their own bombs from gelignite and heavy steel piping. Just how effective these bombs were, is not recorded but it was certainly a step in the right direction.

In supply sorties, the aircraft dropped hundreds of thousands of pounds of essential supplies and, I believe, up to ten million miles were flown throughout the emergency. Seven Police aircraft were lost and six pilots killed during the emergency and, although aircraft were occasionally hit by gunfire from the ground, the terrorists never succeeded in bringing one down. Their only success was to burn out an aircraft while it stood on the ground.

In many of the operational areas, the weather could be seriously influenced by the high mountains, some reaching up to 17,500 feet. Clouds and storms could rapidly develop and with no prior warning any aircraft caught in these severe conditions was in great danger.

Ground-based navigational aids were primitive and only effective at the colony's three main airfields so pilots, with insufficient fuel to reach any of them in poor weather conditions, were forced to land on one of the many roads, car tracks, football pitches or other flat surface which were in daily use as a make shift runway. These pilots showed great courage in their duty and many were highly decorated for their bravery.

1953 and 1954 saw the heaviest fighting in the emergency. Still undermanned and loosely co-ordinated, regular police, reserve police and Kikuyu home guards fought endless engagements and daily killed many terrorists. In one action alone seventy terrorists were killed. In a three year period, Police and the Military killed over ten-thousand terrorists, captured two-thousand and accepted the surrender of yet another two-thousand. Many other casualties went undiscovered.

This is a brief history of the Kenya Police which, when I joined it, had been in existence, as such, for not quite 18 years. The potential it presented for adventure, excitement and danger was enormous, but I could not know that at the time.

Gaining Experience

Soon after my arrival at the Police Training Depot, I engaged a personal servant called Ajuro. He was a 'townie' who had no experience whatsoever of life and survival in the bush, let alone any experience of hunting - the only wild animals he had ever seen were the stray dogs in the back streets of Nairobi - but, to his initial disgust, he was soon to acquire it.

I quickly decided that, in order to fulfil at least one of my ambitions, I would need a vehicle of some sort and after a few fruitless inspections, I came upon a car which I thought would adequately serve my purpose. It was a 1930 Ford Model 'A', two seater, open tourer which had seen better days but which was priced within my limited means. I bought it, and soon with Ajuro beside me, I was putting my spare time to good use hunting over the plains surrounding Nairobi and returning with enough fresh meat to feed half the Depot.

As passing out day approached, it became clear that I had done well in my training and I felt rather proud of the standard I had achieved, but one morning I was summoned to appear before the Commissioner at Force headquarters.

"I've received a letter from the Secretariat concerning you, Mills, " as he spoke his expression turned grave and he tapped the desk impatiently. "They've instructed me to discharge you." Suddenly my knees turned to jelly and my mind raced trying to find an excuse for every possible misdemeanour I had committed during my short period in the force. "On the grounds," he continued, "that you are under the minimum entrance age." I was stumped for a reply.

"B-but sir," I stammered. "Surely it's a bit unfair. After all, I did enter my correct age on the application form." (it was about the only correct entry I had made on the form). He glared at me for a few moments and as he did so the thought flashed into my mind that the next time I walked out of the Depot gates would be as an unemployed civilian, bound for England on the dreaded repatriation bond.

"Sir. I've an idea." It was the voice of the Staff Officer from the adjoining office. "It's not long now, so why don't we delay replying to the Secretariat until Mills has reached the correct age.

'Brilliant,' I thought, and held my breath awaiting the Commissioner's reaction. He raised his chin and, for a moment eyed me intently. Suddenly he waved his arm in my direction.

"Away you go Mills, back to your duties."

The following week I stood smartly to attention at the head of my platoon, my chin tucked in and my gaze riveted to the front, as the Commissioner inspected the passing out parade. Out of the corner of my eye, I watched him moved slowly down the line towards me, here and there, nodding in approval. Then suddenly in front of me, he stopped and, inclining his head towards me, he said quietly. "I'm pleased to see, Mills, that you're looking older every day." And I heard no more of it.

From the Training Depot in Nairobi, British recruits were usually posted to a divisional headquarters station commanded by an assistant or full Inspector, so that they could gain experience under the guidance of a seasoned officer. But, for reasons I never discovered, I was posted direct to one of the 'out stations' which only ever had one British officer and in this case, that was to be me.

Upon my arrival at Kabete Police Station, I encountered the departing commander sitting outside in his old Buick tourer impatient to be off. "Here sign this," he said, waving the Handover Certificate in my direction. "All the rifles are here and are okay and most of the prisoners entered in the book are about here somewhere."

I briefly read the certificate and signed it. "You needn't worry," he shouted, cramming the car into gear. "Everything's dead quiet and you shouldn't have any trouble." Then off he went in a cloud of dust. He was an Assistant Inspector with two and a half year's experience and, as the battered old car, loaded up to the heavens with all his possessions, disappeared into the shimmering distance, I couldn't help musing on the likelihood of him arriving safely at his next posting. He was heading for

Mandera, six hundred miles away on Kenya's Northern border with Abyssinia. Thus, I was inducted, unceremoniously into my first command.

Kabete Police Station was situated on Nairobi's outskirts and policed a large area of white settlements and Kikuyu native reserves. It was considered to be a fairly important station and I was flattered that I, young and inexperienced as I was, had been entrusted with its command.

I quickly assessed the facilities the station offered; one Sergeant, one Corporal and twelve Constables, a telephone which didn't work - vandalised, I think by my predecessor - and the only means of transport throughout my command, my old Ford model 'A' coupe, for which however, I would be paid so much per mile.

I had just set about the task of unloading the car when the station Corporal marched up. He saluted smartly and, speaking part in English and part in Swahili, my knowledge of which was still rudimentary, he tried to explain that there had been a serious accident nearby. 'All's quiet,' my predecessor had said, and I began to wonder at his haste to be off.

It appeared that an African bus had overturned on a corner at the bottom of a steep hill about a mile away and many had been killed and injured so, lacking in experience of such incidents, I proceeded to the scene of the accident accompanied by the Corporal and a Constable.

We found that the bus, which as was usual, had been carrying twice its safe load of passengers, had run out of control down the hill and upended on the bend at the bottom. Three passengers were dead, many more injured and the scene was surrounded by an excited crowd making a tremendous uproar. The driver, as was normal under these circumstances, had fled. I weighed up the chaos, put on a wise and officious look, said, "Carry on Corporal." and promptly departed.

The next morning, at about 9.00am, the Corporal marched in, saluted and said, "Sir, I've sent the prisoners off, and the witnesses. What time do you wish to leave for court?"

He then handed me about fifteen case files. This was something I hadn't expected so soon after taking over command but I managed to ascertain from him that, on two mornings a week, prisoners and witnesses were escorted on foot to an outlying District Officers Court for trial and that I was expected to attend and to prosecute. I was stunned. I had never before been in a Court House and, apart from a little knowledge I had gleaned from the training depot, I was totally ignorant of procedures.

I quickly scanned the case files for some hint of the role I might be expected to play in the proceedings, but each consisted merely of a blue paper cover containing only a charge sheet and occasionally, a barely legible witness statement. Filled with trepidation, I proceeded to the Court where I found the all prisoners lined up outside, as fearful of their impending fate as I was myself.

I entered the Court Room to present myself to the District Officer and to see if he was willing to instruct me on my part in the affair before the start of proceedings. The room was bare and barrack-like with a table to one side and, set on a podium at the far end, a sort of pulpit where sat the hoary old District Officer, an official with full Magisterial powers. "Good morning, sir," I said. He took off his spectacles and glared at me for a few moments.

"You're new to this, aren't you," he said sharply. I nodded. "Don't worry," he continued. "It's all very straight forward." And reaching for the case files he indicated for me to sit at the table. For a while, he studied the files and then, handed them back to me. "They seem like a rough lot." he commented. "Get the Corporal to bring 'em in one at a time."

The Corporal barked out orders making each prisoner march smartly in and stand before the pulpit, himself enjoying every minute of the power he wielded as a court officer.

"Guilty or not guilty?" asked the Magistrate and, whichever reply they gave, he pronounced, "Guilty." Instantly, he passed sentence, ordered the Corporal to remove them from the Court and bring in the next one. The whole lot were tried and sentenced in less than half an hour.

After the last prisoner had been taken away, the Magistrate told me to sit, and with great patience, and in great detail, he explained Court procedure to me. I left the Court and returned to my command full of wisdom and experience. Not many years later, I was prosecuting capital offences in the High Courts against the most skilled and experienced defence barristers in the land.

Not a great deal happened during my command at Kabete, so in order to introduce a little training and a greater sense of discipline amongst the station's personnel, who had fallen into slovenly habits under the former commander, I instituted drill on two mornings a week. Initially the idea met with some resistance but after I introduced a couple of extra hours pack drill for any defaulters, the resistance faded and once again, good order and discipline were restored.

One incident did occur which caused momentary excitement. Early one morning, my Sergeant came running into the Station to report that a buffalo was on the rampage in a nearby Kikuyu reserve area. It appeared

The Mills family.
Left to Right, Back Row: Robert, Father, Raymond.
Front Row: Helen, Mother, Peter, Betty.

'The Wilderness'
Town Residence, Norwich

Country House, Ranworth

Above: Shipboard Fancy Dress. Peter is seated front row, second from right.

Left: Out hunting, 1938

Left: Just recruited to the Kenya Police

Mounted on a camel

With Smith and Wesson .45 revolver

Right: Greeting a VIP

Below: Investiture.
Being presented with the
Queen's Police Medal for
meritorious service

Opening the Supreme Court, 1959

Inspecting the guard of honour 1958, with Peter at the rear of the inspection party

Early Days. Peter on his motor bike.

Vauxhall 26 hp with front wheel sheared off

'Kenya Bridge'. A winch to haul vehicles across a river

On Safari – Masai. Peter at the wheel of his 1938 Chrysler Straight Eight with Ajuro, his personal servant, travelling on the back

The 'Gun Boat' on Lake Victoria. Note the Bren gun mounted on the mast

that a couple of Africans had been hunting it for meat and had made a mess of the job. The maddened creature was running around with a spear sticking out of it and was charging everyone in sight. This, I thought, was the ideal opportunity to try out the Mauser .404 heavy magazine rifle which I had purchased for £10 while still at the training depot. One shot did the trick, to the great delight of the local Africans, who had it butchered and carried away in minutes.

While at Kabete, I changed my old Ford 'A' coupe for a 1934 American hard-top V8 which had very wide rear wheels and narrow front ones. I felt really pleased with my new vehicle; it had plenty of power and plenty of good features including two spare front wheels and one spare rear wheel. However I soon discovered its major draw-back; owing to the odd sized wheels it tended to develop a vicious wobble and break into an uncontrollable skid when driven at speed on the earth roads so again, I had to change it.

This time I picked up, of all things, an ancient 26 horsepower Vauxhall which, like most Kenya out of town cars, had had its rear end removed and replaced with a box body, (what we now call an estate body). I still had this vehicle when, two months later, I was transferred to an up-country station.

My new posting was to the Divisional Police Headquarters in Eldoret, a small town which lay some two-hundred miles North-west of Nairobi on the main road to the Ugandan capital, Kampala.

An elderly acquaintance, hearing of my imminent transfer, had begged a lift to the town of Nakuru about halfway to my destination, and on the morning appointed for the journey, he appeared at the Police station ready to go.

I formally handed over the command to my successor, telling him, "You needn't worry. All's quiet and you shouldn't have any trouble." (It was almost true), then, with my passenger and I in the front of the Vauxhall and my servant Ajuro, the luggage and cans carrying sufficient fuel for the journey in the back, we set off.

Some way along the route, we were obliged to negotiate the Rift Valley escarpment which descended some 4,000 feet in about 12 miles. The road then was very rough, made up of just earth and rocks, and there was no barrier along the precipitous edge. The road was so steep in parts that, when making the ascent, cars like my old Vauxhall had to turn and continue in reverse gear.

We started the descent and, apart from a few bumps, nothing seemed amiss. Slowly at first, the heavy vehicle gathered speed and I began to apply the brakes but the more I braked, the less effective the brakes became. "Good God," my passenger commented, so I changed down and applied the brakes again. I was beginning to get alarmed because, despite my efforts, the car was moving even faster and bouncing around on the rough surface in imminent danger of leaping over the edge into the abyss.

"Please, please slow down!" pleaded my trembling passenger. "I'll walk to the bottom."

"I can't!" I yelled. "The bloody brakes have faded." We careered on for a few hundred yards and I had visions of the vehicle shooting over the edge and carrying us down to crash in a ball of flames a thousand feet below. Suddenly there was a tortured cry from behind me and I caught a glimpse in the mirror of Ajuro leaping out of the open rear window in an attempt to save himself from certain death.

After what seemed like an age in which I feared that, even if we didn't fly over the edge and be smashed up on the rocks below, the old Vauxhall would certainly be shaken to pieces and disintegrate, the road began to level out for a short stretch. By the means of grinding it into the lowest gear I could get and standing up hard on the brakes, I eventually brought the vehicle to a shuddering halt.

For a few minutes, we sat and shook while, behind us, the bruised and grazed Ajuro stumbled down the road to catch us up. Then, with great caution and at a very slow pace, with my passengers hanging on with white knuckles, I managed to ease the vehicle to the bottom in one piece. We journeyed on in silence and at Nakuru, my passenger alighted, thanked me with a weak smile and, I suspect, vowed that, next time, he would walk.

Eldoret, the District Capital of the Uasingishu Plateau region, was a one-horse, two-street town-ship which boasted a Police station, two hotels, two garages and a fire engine. One street of the town was metalled and had European shops while the second was unmetalled and had Asian shops and artisans. European officials resident in the town included the District Commissioner, three Police Officers, a Veterinary Officer, an Agricultural Officer, a Doctor and a Stipendiary Magistrate. There were also several European business residents.

I was to learn later that the fire engine was officially operated by the Police and was an old Ford model 'A' coupe, just like my old car but painted bright red and fitted with four hand-held fire extinguishers, an axe, and of course, a bell. It was housed in an open-sided corrugated iron shelter with the key in the ignition ready for anyone to use, should the need arise. Also in the shelter was one length of canvas fire hose, but quite how this would be used, no one ever explained since there was no pump to which it could be attached.

The Uasingishu was a Police Divisional area commanded by a Superintendent of Police with its headquarters in Eldoret. There were three out-stations each of which had two or three outposts under it, with each outpost manned by three or four Constables. The headquarters station in Eldoret was commanded by an Inspector with one Assistant Inspector beneath him. This latter post was the one to which I had been appointed.

On my arrival in the town, I reported to the Police station to introduce myself to my superior and to find out what accommodation, if any, was available to me. The station Inspector was kindness itself. He showed me around the Station, made me aware of my duties and warned me of any problems which were likely to occur so that, by the time he had finished, I felt like an old hand. Then, realising that I was exhausted after my journey, he took me to the accommodation which had been allocated to me.

To my surprise, it was a rather nice, two-bedroomed government house which stood in the centre of town just down the main, paved street from the Police station. I showed my appreciation and he left.

The following morning, I presented myself at the Station ready for work and immediately my boss, the Inspector, called me in for further briefing. He told me that, on the outskirts of the town, there was a large area inhabited solely by Africans and it was here that most trouble occurred. Crime in the station area was mostly stock thefts, murders and minor crimes.

The Uasingishu Plateau had been settled many years ago by Afrikaners, known locally as Kaburu, the majority of whom had trekked north by ox wagon all the way from the Transvaal to escape British control after the Boar war.

Quite naturally, they harboured a deep-seated hatred of the British, stemming from their memories of the twenty-thousand women and children who had died, mostly from disease and starvation, in our concentration camps during the Boar War. On their arrival they found, to their dismay, that Kenya had been converted to a British colony but, since return to their homeland was almost impossible, they settled in the area and for the British rule they so much hated.

Despite their hatred of the British, the Afrikaners respected the local government and were kind, courteous, law-abiding people who were invariably hospitable. They were mostly farmers who worked extremely hard, training their own ox teams and growing wheat and maize, and ranching cattle. Surprisingly, they fought alongside the British in two world wars and suffered many casualties in the process.

In the early days, when settlements on the plateau were fewer and more widely scattered, the Afrikaners would occasionally arrange a meeting place to which each family group would travel by ox wagon for a get-together.

They would circle the wagons round in a laager, in the same manner used for defence against attacks by Zulu and Matebele in days gone by, and settle down to some intense socialising. During the course of the celebrations, the single boys and girls would select a partner, conduct a respectful courtship and sometimes even marry, in only the few days that were available to them.

When the daughter of an Afrikaner house was being courted, the procedure was always conducted with the utmost propriety. After a prolonged get-together of both families in which each side had the chance to weigh up the pro's and con's of the match, the girl and her suitor were allowed a little time alone together. During this tryst they were expected to behave with due modesty.

In the room where they were to be alone, a candle was lighted but as soon as the candle burned out the boy was expected to leave. If the girl's family approved of the suitor, the candle was a tall one, however, if they didn't, it was a short one.

Despite their often strange customs, I grew to admire these Afrikaners and counted myself privileged, on many occasions during my term of duty at Eldoret, to enjoy their hospitality.

Speaking of strange customs, I once encountered a large family group of them gathered round an old vehicle by the side of an isolated road. To my astonishment, one male member of the family was standing on the bonnet urinating, with admirable accuracy, into the radiator filler cap. When I enquired the reason, I was told that the engine had boiled and run out of water so each had taken turns in order to fill it - women as well as men. This is a tip well worth remembering if ever a similar problem is encountered on the motor-way.

Not long after my arrival at Eldoret, the Inspector, a wise and experienced officer, warned me never to fall for an Afrikaner girl. They were often beautiful at fourteen or fifteen, he told me. But by the age of nineteen or twenty they would blow up like balloons and ruin their beautiful bodies by giving birth to countless snivelling children. I heeded his warning and, fortunately for me, there was a more elegant female distraction in the offing. I soon settled in to the routine of the station while my servant, Ajuro, got the house ship-shape and comfortable.

One morning, not long after my arrival in Eldoret, I saw a rather startling and, for this backwoods town, incongruous sight. Walking purposefully past the house was a woman of European origin, aged about thirty, with dark hair, a slender, attractive figure and immaculately dressed in the latest Paris fashion. I shook my head in disbelief and thought, 'there's a lady I'd like to meet'.

A few days later, she appeared again, and again, I followed her with my gaze until she was out of sight. She made such a pleasant and unusual sight that I found myself waiting each morning just for the shear joy of watching her pass by.

One day, not long after her first appearance, I popped into the chemist's shop to stock up on some medical supplies and there she was. It turned out that she lived in the same hotel as the chemist and his wife and they had become particular friends. They introduced us. Her name was Josephine, she was the proprietoress of 'Josie's', a ladies fashion shop in the main street and she was even more attractive close to than at a distance. I was smitten.

Frequently, over the next couple of weeks, I found excuses to visit Josie's Fashion Shop but I couldn't pluck up the nerve to try to advance our relationship. Any suggestion on my part would, I thought, be presumptuous; after all, she was thirty-six and I a mere twenty-year-old. I began to lose hope of any closer acquaintanceship with the lady when I received an invitation from the chemist and his wife to accompany them and Josephine on a picnic to the Kerio escarpment. I leaped at the opportunity.

This was my first trip to the escarpment and what a sight it presented. We arrived at the top and started to descend the three to four thousand feet down a narrow, rock -strewn track. Every few hundred yards there was a hairpin bend, some so acute that there was no room to turn round and the next stretch had to be negotiated in reverse gear. In places the track was so narrow and the face of the escarpment so steep that rocks dislodged by the car wheels could be seen cascading down the almost vertical slope to the bottom.

Eventually we emerged into the burning desert below and spent a few hours picnicking and in idle chatter, some of which was lost on me since I was concentrating rather too hard on the stunning Josephine with her lovely figure and her funny accent.

On the return journey, Josie and I sat in the back and after it grew dark, I felt her edge a little closer to me. Soon, she put her arm around my shoulders - for support, I thought, since the car was bouncing around rather a lot on the rough road.

We had travelled less than half a mile when I felt her other hand on my thigh and she began to caress me in a spot rather more sensitive than my shoulders. Suddenly, I was convinced that she was attracted to me also and I was thrilled. For the rest of the journey, we exchanged sneaky kisses.

Whether the chemist and his wife knew what was going on behind them, or whether they had even colluded in bringing us together, I never knew, but that was the start of a long and torrid affair.

A few days later as I was walking to the station I met her in the street. She placed her elegant fingers on my arm and whispered, "I stop at your house when I leave the shop this afternoon." All morning, I sweated in anticipation and by mid afternoon, I was at my window, bathed and shaved and eagerly awaiting her appearance down the street.

From the moment of her arrival, she displayed no sign of shyness and made it perfectly plain what she required of me. In return, I made a point of showing her that I was more than willing to cater for her every need.

Over the coming months, Josie's visits became more frequent and on many of these occasions she would stay all night. We became close companions and lovers, and the more we were together, the more she revealed about her past.

She was born of Jewish parents in Vienna and had lived quietly enough with them and an older sister until news reached them that Hitler was about to invade. She promptly fled Austria and headed for Palestine, from whence she made her way to Mombasa. There she had met and married a Jewish refugee from Russia and in company with other Jewish refugee couples, had moved inland and ended up on the Uasingishu Plateau.

The attraction of the region probably stemmed from the fact that, at the turn of the century, the whole of the Uasingishu region was offered to international Jews as the new promised land upon which they could found a Jewish state. The offer was declined on the grounds that the area was "prowled by dangerous savages", but by the end of the thirties, they possibly considered that there were less "dangerous savages" there than would be prowling Nazi dominated Europe.

Josephine's husband worked as a salesman for a chain of garages but had been moved to their branch in Kisumu, seventy miles to the south-west on the shores of Lake Victoria. He lived in a hotel there and only occasionally visited his wife in Eldoret. It seems that, not long after their marriage, they had discovered that they were incompatible and had abandoned sex along with all but the most infrequent contact. Not long after we first met, she and her husband divorced.

Josephine and I, on the other hand, found ourselves to be entirely matched, despite the differences in our ages and our origins. Sex between us was always vigorous and entirely uninhibited. She was well versed in all the positions and techniques of love-making and, occasionally she liked to indulge in a little 'kinkiness' by asking me to wear her night-dress or sometimes an item of her underwear. If I resisted the suggestion, she would punish me with a sound spanking and, at times, just to please her, I would resist.

During that amorous encounter at my house, when I first had the pleasure of seeing her beautiful naked body, I noticed one remarkable thing, Josephine, just like the Jewish lady I met on board the Llandaff Castle, also had small black hairs around her nipples.

Our association lasted for seven wonderful years, in fact, right until my first marriage after which she and my wife became firm friends and continued to be so until, fifteen years later, Josephine died of a heart complaint.

There was just one thing which annoyed me about Josephine - her earrings. She was in the habit of wearing one pair or another which were very ornate and extremely large. I hated the things and begged her not to wear them but she refused to comply with my request and every time we met, she would be sporting yet another enormous pair. She always remembered my annoyance and, in her will, she bequeathed the whole damned collection to me.

During this period, her fashion business became quite successful and, for a while, I became a financial partner in a shop she bought in Mombasa. This shop, called Daphne Seagars, still trades under that same name to the present day.

A few months after my arrival in Eldoret, when my boss, the station Inspector had decided that he had taught me enough about the area and how to police it. I was summoned before the District Superintendent, who ordered me to take over command of the division's largest out-station, known then as Farm 35. This was promotion and a demonstration of the regard in which I was held by my superiors. I jumped at the chance.

Crime in the area followed a regular pattern; lots of murders, stock thefts, which involved night raids and ambushes on the routes taken by rustlers, occasional tribal confrontations to break up; it all became a fairly routine matter.

All the while, the threat of war in Europe moved ever closer and I felt that, when it did arrive, I would prefer to be in on the action, so I made out an application to join the Kenya regiment. A couple of weeks later, I received a reply, dated 19th July 1938, from the staff officer at the Nairobi headquarters of Local Forces, Kenya and Uganda. It said that the 1st Battalion, Kenya Regiment had been recruited up to full strength and it would be necessary for me to wait for a vacancy. In the meanwhile I was to be transferred to the Special Reserve so that I could remain on the waiting list. Naturally, I was disappointed, but I could wait.

Josie and all the other Jewish refugees in the area were terrified. Hitler was rampaging across Europe and they were convinced that it was only a matter of time before he overran Britain and all her Empire. Their fate, they believed, would be sealed then, as surely as if they were in Germany itself.

These fears were not alleviated by the attitude of German settlers in the region. These Germans had moved from Tanganyika which, before the end of the 1914/18 war, had been German East Africa and, as Hitler moved from success to success, they became increasingly arrogant. Some of them would seize every opportunity to remind people of Germany's military might and boast that, very shortly, East Africa would be entirely under their control with the inevitable consequences.

At 3.30pm on Sunday the ninth of September 1939 a Police Constable arrived at my house with a note from my Divisional Superintendent. It said simply that war had broken out between Britain and Germany and I was to 'pick up all Germans'. My orders had been that, if war was declared, I was to pick up and detain all hostile aliens, taking the men to a tented holding area while personally looking after the women and children until they could be moved to a more permanent holding camp. The exercise filled me with distaste, but those were my orders.

Immediately, I commandeered a wing of one of the hotels and set out in a Police pick-up truck, with just two Constables to assist me in the operation. I hated the idea of arriving at, say a farm house, and announcing, "You have thirty minutes to pack, and only two suitcases each."

A few of them were angry and spat at us, hissing, "You wait. A few weeks and we'll have you all locked up instead of us." But the majority just couldn't believe it and it pained me to see the distress the women were put to at the prospect of being forced out of their homes and into a very uncertain future. I took into custody about thirty women and moved them into the hotel where I placed a standing guard on the wing in which they were quartered and detailed sentries to patrol outside.

Apart from the windows, which were covered by the sentries, there was only one way in or out of the requisitioned wing and that was a narrow passageway connecting it to the main body of the hotel. At night I had a camp bed placed across the entrance to the passageway and there I slept each night for the three weeks that the women were in my custody.

The Government had instituted a Unit called 'The Custodian of Enemy Property' which was given the task of protecting the property of interned aliens and ensuring that their farms and businesses were safe and continued to function. This provision did not wholly satisfy the more domestic concerns of my charges and, each morning, some of them, (they had formed a committee for the purpose), came to me with a string of more personal requests. 'Please see that my dog is all right', 'In the top drawer in my bedroom I left.... this, that or the other. Could you please get it for me?' 'I use a certain medicine. The chemist knows it', 'The cook's wife is ill. Please see that she gets treatment'. Each morning there was an endless list of requests each of which I carefully noted then spent the rest of the day travelling around fulfilling them. By evening I returned with all the bits and pieces they required and was able to report that all was well and reassure them regarding the welfare of the dependants they had been forced to leave behind.

Eventually, the Government directed that they were to be moved to a main detention centre near Nairobi so, one evening, I and my men escorted them to the railway station to board them on the 8.00pm down-country mail train.

As we approached the station, I thought about their predicament and felt very sympathetic towards them. What, I wondered, would be the fate of British women should they ever be in the hands of the Germans in a similar situation. On the platform, they all lined up and one stepped forward towards me. "Please accept this," she said, smiling and handing me a small, carefully wrapped parcel. "As a token of our appreciation your kind treatment of us." I was touched by the gesture and somewhat embarrassed, but I accepted, and as the train pulled away I opened the parcel. It contained a neck-tie. I have it to this day.

That night I couldn't sleep. The sight of those poor women quietly boarding the train to be taken away from their homes and their families for no good reason and for how long, nobody could tell, disturbed me greatly. This Hitler and his murderous crew, the cause of all this misery and god knows how much more to come, had to be stamped on hard and without delay. I knew that there was a part for me to play in the coming battle and I was filled with a desperate urge to take my place at the very heart of the action. Early next morning I went to the District Officer's headquarters to sign up for military service.

I was convinced that, by now, the Kenya Regiment would be eager to sign up any man who was fit enough and ready to join, and I, as a member of the Special Reserve would, no doubt, receive priority. I was wrong. "Police service has been declared a reserve occupation," I was told, and I was rejected. I returned to the station angry and upset at the thought that I had been refused the chance that others less able than myself had been offered without question.

For a few days, I boiled with frustration but eventually convinced myself that my role here was an important one and resigned myself to doing the best I could even at this distance from the centres of conflict. In the event, I saw much active service in the next twenty years and probably more 'action' than most members of the armed forces ever experienced.

Routine

Farm 35 was an out-station of the headquarters at Eldoret and covered a large area bordering on the Nandi and Elgeyo tribal reserves and on vast areas of forest. Here, I had the opportunity to run the whole show myself and put into practice some of the techniques of policing that I had learned from my boss at headquarters and to try a few ideas of my own. The crime again followed a fairly regular pattern; murder, cattle theft, arson and night raids on Asian trading centres.

These trading centres were usually wooden framed, corrugated iron structures and were prime targets for Africans on the prowl for an easy theft. The Asian owners however developed a technique which they hoped would discourage such raiders. They would sit up all night, and the moment they heard a suspicious noise outside, would open up wholesale with shotguns, firing through the walls in the hope of hitting their attackers. As a consequence, the walls of their trading posts were riddled with holes from the shotgun blasts.

Murders ran at about one a week, as often as not the result of fights which broke out at drunken parties. Periodically, the reserve Africans were in the habit of holding a get together for which the women would brew large tubs of beer. The beer, which was made in quantities of forty gallons or more at a time, took ages to mature but then, it became very potent especially when honey was available as an ingredient. Some of the women were noted far and wide for their brewing expertise and when word got about that a brew was ready for consumption, a gathering would be arranged.

Only male elders were allowed, the younger men being barred from the event because they were considered too riotous, and usually about twenty of them would attend. They would arrive at the venue each carrying his drinking 'straw' which was in fact, a ten to twelve foot lengths of a vine-like branch from which the soft pith core had been removed. The beer, in a large tub, would be placed in the centre of the meeting hut and the elders, with their women in attendance, would sit in a circle around the tub with the ends of their straws in the beer. Rapidly, the elders would become drunk and pass out, only to waken some while later and start the process all over again.

These parties would often last for days and only ended when all the beer had been consumed and the elders had sufficiently recovered from their drunken stupor to be able to stagger away.

Whether or not the native beer possessed powerful aphrodisiac qualities, I never really knew, but these parties were always an occasion for vigorous wife swapping. Fired up by the beer, the men would leap on any woman they fancied and have sex with her as often as he wanted. Women present, especially the more attractive ones, usually got screwed wholesale.

This inevitably led to arguments and fights which often ended with one or other of the protagonists being knifed, slashed with a Simi, (a Machete-like weapon with a thin blade, broader towards the end and honed to razor sharpness on both edges), or skewered on the end of a spear.

These murders were always difficult to investigate and prosecute. Even if a witness was willing to testify, which wasn't often, his memory of events would be hazy at best, due to the drunken state he was in at the time of the killing. Not all fights ended in death however, and frequently, even though he was badly injured, the victim would survive.

One such case occurred about a year after I had taken over command of the out-station, Farm 35. I returned home one rainy evening at about 8.00pm having spent a fruitless day tracking some elusive cattle thieves. I was frustrated, wet and chilled to the marrow, (the station was at an altitude of seven thousand six hundred feet and cold at night).

As I approached the house, my spirits were lifted to see Josie's Chevrolet Coupe parked outside. Suddenly, I was rejuvenated. I shot into the house, greeted her warmly then dived into the shower and prepared myself for an evening of romance. Josie looked as alluring as ever I had seen her in a flimsy, pale blue silk night-dress which clung here and there to her delightful curves. We sat down to a candle-lit supper and afterwards, settled in front of a blazing fire, with two glasses and a bottle of decent red wine while Kenya LO, Nairobi's radio station, played romantic dance music, just audible on my old battery-operated set beside us. I was inspired.

We were just about to retire to the bedroom when suddenly, a commotion started outside. I could pick out the voices of my Sergeant and my cook amongst the hubbub so, reluctantly, I opened the front door. It was dark and still raining hard but in the glow of a hurricane lamp, stood the Sergeant, the cook, Ajuro, my Personal Servant and my Police Orderly. Between them, they supported an elderly, shrivelled African with a blood-soaked sheet draped across one shoulder. His chest and back were covered in blood and the poor man was obviously in great pain.

Questioning revealed that, in an argument over a woman, he had been slashed in the chest with a Simi and upon lifting the sheet I noticed that, every time he spoke, something dark and balloon-like popped out of the gaping wound in his side. It was a lung and every time he breathed out, it shot back inside his chest again. It was a horrible sight so I turned to tell Josie not to look. But too late, she was already beside me and had seen the old man and his predicament. Promptly, she spun round and fled through the house to the veranda at the back where I could hear her being profoundly sick.

The condition of the old man urgently demanded skilled first aid so I took off his sheet, folded it, wrapped it twice round his chest and secured it tightly with several strands of rope. This measure seemed to stem the bleeding and also stop the lung popping in and out every time he breathed, so I despatched him with my driver to the nearest hospital thirty-five miles away.

The panic over, I returned inside, expecting to resume where I had left off, but one look at Josie soon told me that the romantic bubble had burst. Her face was a pale green colour and she was quick to point out that in no way was she in a fit state to make love that night. However, she stayed over, and next day all was well again, so we made up for lost time.

The Inspector from whom I had taken over the Farm 35 out-station was a man twenty years my senior who was a dedicated drinker. During the week we spent in the hand-over process, he would call out to me at dawn, "Join me in a whisky". I knew that, even at that time of day, he was pissed, and each time, I refused. I had seen the state to which some of the old hands had been reduced by drinking spirits and I vowed that would never happen to me. I kept my vow and have never in my life drunk whisky or, for that matter, any other spirits since.

Despite his habit, he had achieved an enviable reputation with the top brass as a very successful stock theft specialist with an exceptionally high number of successful cases. He had developed a wide-spread network of informers which accounted for some of his achievement but I soon found another - he cooked the records. If, for example three accused were sentenced for stock theft, he would enter it as three separate cases successfully concluded. When eventually he departed, I was left with a formidable reputation to live up to.

Early in my service, I realised that I was personally not very competent at the mundane task of persuading prisoners of the wisdom of confessing their own sins and revealing the names of others who had likewise behaved in a criminal manner. As a result, I evolved a policy of 'delegate, inspect and encourage'. This policy I applied to the execution of the three solutions which, after considerable thought, I had devised to help solve the problem of cattle theft.

The out-station was a timber framed affair with corrugated iron on the outside and wooden boards lining the inside. The cavity between contained the nests of several swarms of African bees, commonly referred to as 'killer bees'. Under the cool conditions of night and early morning these bees were usually very docile but as the sun rose higher and day became hotter, they started to get a bit lively. Even so, they were no great danger - unless provoked.

My first ploy was to place detainees, suspected of having carried out cattle theft or at least having useful information about them, in the cells of the station. At mid-day, when the bees were at their most lively, I would order my men to beat the outer corrugated iron with sticks. The bees would go mad and, pretty soon, the occupants of the cells would be screaming blue murder and begging to give up any information they had.

A second method was to send my men out to arrest several native elders who had, no doubt, been cattle thieves in their younger days, but who had quite possibly not been so for ten years or more. Even though we probably had none, I would tell them that we held evidence against them and that they would go down for at lest five years. Being elders, this would have caused them to loose face amongst their tribe and besides, five years is a long time to an old man so they were quick to cry, "We wouldn't have minded when we were younger, but we are old men. Please, please don't lock us up now." Then they would freely give us the information we needed just to secure their release.

The third method was to offer each of the cattle thieves we arrested, freedom from prosecution if he would inform on two other cases.

Finally, I put pressure on my young Constables on such occasions as when they were called to take possession of a recently circumcised girl who had been sold to them by her parents as a wife. Often, the Constable would have no leave due and if he didn't answer the call and take possession immediately, the girl would be sold to someone else. "OK." I would say. "You have no leave due but I'll give you two weeks off providing you return with information that will lead to the clearing up of three cattle thefts."

These methods worked well and soon I was recording better overall results than my predecessor without having to resort to 'cooking' the records.

I spent a great deal of time, in company with my men, tracking stock thieves and following their trails through all types of country, in all kinds of weather and at all hours of the day and night. Often we would be soaking wet, often frozen stiff, especially while tracking at high altitude or lying low ready to ambush rustlers, when white frost would settle during the night.

Frequently during such raids we captured suspected stolen cattle which were held as evidence or until they could be claimed by their rightful owners. They were kept on the 1200 acres of land attached to the Farm 35 out-station and, to economise on Police manpower, I would make those who were found in possession of the cattle responsible for looking after them. Many were never claimed and became an excellent source of meat for station personnel and their families.

The forest reserve areas held large stocks of big game including buffalo, bongo and giant forest hog and it was rumoured that these forests also contained a strange and, as yet, unrecorded animal which had been named 'the Nandi Bear'.

The creature was greatly feared by local Africans who believed that it was very large, half human and half cat and uttered an unearthly call starting as a low howl and ending in a high pitched shriek. It would rear on its hind legs then pounce on any human it encountered in the forest, tear them apart and completely devour them.

Many years previously, the Daily Express had offered a reward of £5,000, an enormous sum in those days, which would have set me up for life, for the first of these animals to be shot or captured. Naturally - though I didn't really believe it existed - I hunted it whenever the opportunity presented itself and quite frequently diverted from following stolen cattle whenever I saw animal tracks I didn't recognise.

I never killed a specimen nor, to my knowledge, ever got near to one and eventually concluded that it was probably one of the rare striped Hyenas a much larger beast than the more common spotted variety. I don't think the Daily Express ever, to this present day, withdrew their offer.

One day, about a year after I had taken command of the out-station at Farm 35, information came in of a double murder at a remote native settlement some thirty miles away. I detailed a Constable to accompany me and called for my driver to take us there in the station's Ford fifteen hundredweight pick-up.

For the first twenty or so miles we travelled on roads and dusty tracks but the last seven miles took us across rough, rock-strewn country which bounced the truck around, testing it almost to its limits.

At the settlement, I discovered that a jealous male, determined to reek vengeance for his mistress's infidelity, had trapped her two children, aged about eight and ten, in a mud hut, wired the door shut and then set fire to it. Their poor little bodies were burned beyond recognition and the distress amongst the friends and neighbours was harrowing. A few questions to the witnesses soon told me where the culprit was hiding just a few miles away, so we set out to arrest him.

About midnight we returned to the settlement with the prisoner securely under lock and key, then placed the charred corpses under cover in the rear of the pick-up and started back to base.

The return journey was worse even than the outward one as we lurched and bounced our way across virgin country in the dark. Eventually, just before dawn, we arrived back at the station and snatched a couple of hours sleep before setting out to the nearest township where I knew there would be a European doctor to perform the post-mortems.

At the doctor's surgery we removed the cover ready to carry the charred remains inside for examination, and I got the shock of my life - there was only one body in the back of the pick-up instead of two. Presumably, the other had bounced out somewhere on the journey.

I panicked. Oh god, I thought; after all the hard work and trouble I'd put myself through to establish myself as a good and effective Police officer and now I could be tripped up by a simple, silly piece of misfortune like this. What's more, I'd be a laughing stock back at headquarters. The thought nearly drove me mad, so immediately, I set off to back-track the route and try to find the second body.

For hours I drove through trackless bush desperate to locate our route of the night before, but it had been dark and the terrain extremely rough and I failed to find even a single sign that we had ever been there, let alone the body I sought. I scanned the sky on the chance that circling vultures might indicate the location of the corpse, but the sky was empty and I was driven to the conclusion that Hyenas must have cleared up any remains before dawn.

It was hopeless, so eventually, I turned for home filled with apprehension about what the circuit High Court Judge was going to say in open court when I disclosed the loss of a piece of material evidence as important in a murder trial as a corpse. In the end, I charged the accused with the murder of only one of the victims. He was convicted and hung and that - fortunately for me - was that.

By this time, my household at Farm 35 had grown somewhat. I now had a Cook, a child as Cook's Assistant, a House-Boy, a Dorobo tracker, a Gun Bearer and a Gardener and the place ticked over very sweetly.

In addition, I had appointed one of my Constables as my Police Orderly whose duty it was to act in a capacity similar to that of an army officer's batman. He laundered my uniforms, cleaned my car and looked after my weapons but, foremost amongst his responsibilities was to be my 'minder'. His job was to accompany me wherever I went and be on constant alert for any danger to my person that may present itself. It was considered to be a very prestigious role and I had to make certain that he was never left out of proceedings because this would lead to the very serious matter of him loosing face amongst his brother officers.

Each servant has his place in the household and was proud of his role and the status it gave him but principal amongst them was The Cook. He was the major domo who controlled the household, oversaw all the domestic activities and did all the necessary shopping.

My House-boy was Ajuro, the first servant I had taken on while still at the Police Training Depot in Nairobi and who was to remain with me for many years. The tracker, Juma, was of the Dorobo people who inhabited the high forests. The Dorobo had no villages or communities but roamed the dense heart of the forests in isolated family groups avoiding, as much as possible, contact with other groups or with the outside world. They kept a few cattle, lived mainly on milk, wild honey and forest game. Crime, particularly cattle stealing, was virtually unknown amongst them. They were wonderful trackers and could follow the least signs of any animal, human or otherwise, in even the most difficult terrain giving a running commentary on the quarry and its activities in a barely audible whisper. Gradually, as you got close to the quarry, the whisper would dissolve into a series of silent gestures. The Dorobo were an admirable people commanding great respect - probably because, due to their isolated life, the missionaries had never been able to get to them.

Most of the servants had wives and children who had to be accommodated within reasonable distance of the house. The routine here was to detail some of the prisoners to build 'rondavels', circular huts constructed of wattle and mud in which, as soon as they had dried out enough, the families would take up residence.

Of course, the servants and their families had to be fed. Fortunately they were all lovers of meat and I made sure they always had plenty, either by supplying them with the abundant game which we shot on hunting expeditions, or by instructing my men to slaughter one of the many cattle which were held as exhibits to the crime of cattle theft on the station's 1200 acres. The meat, together with maize meal which I also supplied, formed their staple diet and they never went short. The total cost of my servants was £1. 1s. 0p per month (£1.05p in today's money).

Apart from the occasional murder, and other local disturbances, the main preoccupation of the station was with cattle theft which involved countless excursions into wild country, burning by day and freezing by night. It was slow, boring work with little reward, but it was necessary. Almost daily, however, there were unusual incidents which provided lighter moments.

One day we were returning from visiting one of our outposts and had driven miles across dry, low-lying country. The morning had been particularly hot and sticky so about mid-day we pulled up by a river bank with the intention of taking a dip to cool down and wash off some of the dust.

My driver and I stripped off and plunged into the cool water. We swam for a while then, considerably refreshed, we sat naked on a rock beside the water to dry off in the noon-day sun. Suddenly, a group of African girls appeared from the bush on the far bank to collect water. They soon spotted us and started to giggle, then pointing at me, they began to laugh almost hysterically.

"What's got into them?" I asked.

"It's you, Sir," my driver replied, reluctantly.

"What do you mean?" I asked. "They've seen a European before, haven't they?"

"Oh yes," he said. "But not naked. They're laughing because you're white all over - even your penis."

On another occasion, a white settler, looking very crest-fallen and sorry for himself, walked into my office and sat down. His crops had failed, he explained; debt had overtaken him and his marriage had failed. "I'm going to kill myself," he said.

"Not in my district, please. I'll have to investigate it." I replied, firmly believing that those who talk about it seldom do it.

"OK." he said, and left.

A week later I heard that he had driven over my boundary, some forty miles away and shot himself.

This incident reminded me of an Ismaili friend of mine who always stank of garlic. The smell was almost unbearable and I always felt uncomfortable close to him so, one day, I asked him why he consumed so much of the stuff. "Ah," he said. "It's a veritable life saver. My people firmly believe that eating plenty of garlic prevents cancer." A couple of weeks later, he committed suicide. Apparently, he had been involved with the manager of the local branch of Barclays Bank in some kind of fiddle. After my friend's death the manager was sacked but the bank never reported the matter to us.

One night, after dark, I returned to my headquarters to be met by my Sergeant who seemed very agitated. He saluted smartly and announced nervously, "Sir, There's been a problem."

It transpired that one of my plain-clothed Constables had brought in a man we had long wanted for stock theft and multiple murder. The Constable, an excellent officer and the backbone of my investigation team, was very tall and powerfully built while the accused was small and wiry.

During the initial interrogation, the accused had seen a chance to escape and lunged at the sergeant, throwing him off balance then rushed for the doorway. In a desperate attempt to halt him before he disappeared into the night, the Constable had swung his ham-sized fist and landed a powerful pile-driver blow straight down on top of the fugitive's head. Instantly, the accused dropped to the floor, stone dead with a broken neck.

I devoted considerable thought to the matter and eventually decided that I could attach no blame to either officer, after all, they were just trying to do their job to the best of their ability. The whole thing was an unfortunate accident and, albeit without due process of law, justice had been done . I searched for an easy way out and was just toying with the idea of recording it as a heart attack - let's face it, the blow must have jolted his heart somewhat and I felt qualified to diagnose since I had recently passed a First Aid examination - when, with the hint of a wink, my Sergeant said, "Sir, we'll send the body to the mortuary in the morning." I agreed because it would give me time to give the matter further consideration.

Next morning, the Sergeant, with a dead-pan expression on his face, marched into my office, saluted. "Sir," he said. "That prisoner must have recovered during the night because he's gone." I wrote him off in the records as an escaped prisoner.

Some weeks later, I discovered that my men had stripped the corpse, dumped it out in the bush and, during the night, Hyenas had conveniently disposed of the evidence. In any event, he had escaped certain hanging so my entry was half correct and a lot of hassle had been avoided.

One day I was called out to look at a lorry which had just run someone over. I inspected the vehicle for any obvious faults which may have caused the accident and then jumped into the cab to check the brakes. I hadn't driven many yards when I felt a sharp jolt. I stopped and quickly jumped out to discover that I had run over an African who turned out to be an employee of the Asian owner of the lorry. Seeing the lorry go past, he had rushed at it to climb aboard but had jumped short and fallen under the rear wheels. I was mortified and immediately drove into Eldoret to report the accident to my Superintendent.

"Sir," I said, quaking. "I think you'd better investigate this."

"Get on with it," he replied. "You killed him, you investigate."

Throughout this period, the liaison between Josie and myself flourished. We met frequently, either in Eldoret, or she would drive over in her Chevrolet to my house at Farm 35.

Though, by now, she was divorced, the question of marriage never arose. She was content to run her fashion shop in Eldoret and I was content, at least for the time being, with my post at the out-station. It seemed that the company we gave each other, the humour we shared and the sexual gratification that was paramount in our relationship, was sufficient for us both.

Josie was, sexually, quite adventurous and enjoyed experimenting with new positions and techniques. On occasions, it could even be said that she was a little kinky. Once, she asked me to take her out into the forest at night and make love to her so, wishing always to please her, I waited for a still, moonlit night and led her to a patch of woodland not far from the house.

We lay down in a cosy spot that I had taken the trouble to scout out the day before and we embraced. Gradually, we stripped each other and I applied myself to slowly arousing her to a pitch of delicious passion. Her response was immediate and it became obvious that the forest and the open air was having the desired effect on her. She became soft and malleable in my hands and squirmed and wriggled with ecstasy. As I slid between her parted thighs, I knew that we were on the brink of achieving the ultimate in sexual gratification.

Suddenly, the snort of a grazing buffalo somewhere not too distant from where we lay reminded me like a shot in the dark why I knew this patch of forest so well. It was the habitat of a considerable number of buffalo and I had frequently hunted them here. Josie stiffened and became immediately still.

"What was that?" she asked in sudden terror. I was lost for a reasonable answer. "Be quick!" she gasped, clutching my buttocks. "Be quick! I want to get out of here - now!" But to my eternal shame, the moment of glorious rapture had flown.

A few months later, we drove to another forested area and this time I was determined that we should see the thing through to a climax. As on the previous occasion, we embraced and passions were aroused but, just as we were about to become more intimate, my attention was diverted by the emergence from cover, about a hundred yards away, of a Bush Buck. At the time, my household was in need of meat so, before Josie realised what I was up to, I snatched my rifle, laid it across her naked stomach and shot it.

Josie was furious, jumped to her feet and gave me a damned good slapping with my cartridge belt. It hurt, but what followed was made the more enjoyable for it.

It was within the law for farmers to set trap-guns to protect crops from marauding animals and these would occasionally give us some headaches.

A rifle or shotgun would be attached to a couple of stakes and sighted about three feet off the ground. A trip wire would then be stretched from the trigger and fixed to another stake some few feet away in the line of fire. The idea was to discourage animals and, though warning notices had to be displayed in two languages, many human raiders of maize and other crops, as well as a few innocent ones, were hit and sometimes killed.

On frequent occasions, our local Veterinary Officer would be called up to the holding pens at Farm 35 to brand confiscated stock with our Police brand, 'DOP' in two inch high letters. The Vet would bring with him a couple of African assistants to tend the fire and the branding irons and we would detail our own men to hold the cattle down while he branded them.

On one such occasion, the Vet was busy about his task and, without looking, reached behind him and called for a freshly heated iron. The African assistant, his mind on other things, obeyed the command and slapped the iron into the Vet's hand - red-hot end first. The Vet screamed and cursed and immediately plunged the wounded limb into a bucket of cold water.

Some while later in the proceedings, after things had calmed down a bit, the Vet spotted the African bending over the fire and, without warning, rammed a red hot iron onto his left buttock. A puff of blue smoke shot up, the African leapt about eight feet in the air, screamed and took off quicker than a scalded cat. We never saw him again but if he's still alive he can be recognised by the 'DOP' brand on his arse.

In order to qualify for a salary increment, this same Vet had to pass an elementary oral examination in Kikuyu and an Administration Officer was assigned to the task of examiner.

"How do you say 'Come here' in Kikuyu?" the examiner asked.

The Vet knew this. "Ukahaha," he replied.

"Good," said the examiner. "Now," he continued, pointing at a storehouse across the yard. "How do you say 'Go there' ?" For a few seconds, the Vet thought hard then quickly walked across to the storehouse, turned and shouted, "Ukahaha!"

So as not to waste time, The Administrative Officer passed him as fluent.

I was with the same Vet on an occasion when he was addressing a large gathering of African stock owners on the proper care of their beasts and the necessity for dipping them against certain prevailing cattle diseases. He spoke in English through an interpreter who passed on his words to these tribesmen in their own language. I had learned a little of this particular language and so was able to understand both ends of the discourse.

My friend, the Vet, reached a stage in his address at which he felt it essential to stress the need for urgency in the treatment of the beasts. He raised his left arm and, in a dramatic gesture, jabbed the face of his watch with his right forefinger.

"The sands of time are running out!" he bellowed.

For a moment, there was a pause while the interpreter held a hurried consultation with one of the tribal elders. Then, seemingly happy with his translation, the interpreter rose to his feet and confidently announced to the assembled throng, "The Bwana says that his watch is busted."

Similar language problems often arose in court, particularly where it involved double interpretation; for example, English into Swahili, and then Swahili into any one of a vast number of tribal languages. A simple question like 'Where were you last night?' could lead to a major discussion between interpreters and witnesses which would eventually produce an answer such as, 'My Aunt's got toothache.'

Occasionally, a witness, or the accused himself, would play upon the Court's lack of understanding of one of the more obscure languages by replying with a string of nonsense so as to avoid giving a straight answer. Usually a whispered tutoring of the Judge would allow him to announce to the miscreant in his own language, 'Give me a proper answer or you'll land up in jail anyway, for contempt of Court.' More often than not, it did the trick.

Hunting was, as ever, my spare-time preoccupation and I would take to the bush or the forests in pursuit of game as often as time and other engagements would allow. As I have mentioned before, hunting was great sport as well as being the prime source of fresh meat, but it could also be dangerous.

One evening, in preparation for a bush pig shoot, I loaded the magazine of a rifle and had just leaned it against the wall in the sitting room, when a Brother Officer called to see me. I left him for a moment and went to my bedroom to change. Suddenly there was an almighty BANG! which almost made me leap out of my skin. I dashed back to the sitting room, trousers at half mast, and found the Officer standing by the window, white as a ghost and trembling uncontrollably. "I've just killed an African," he squealed in panic.

Eventually, when he had calmed down sufficiently to offer a stuttering explanation, he told me that he'd picked up the rifle to admire it, worked the bolt and aimed it at a figure in the far distance. Thinking that the gun was empty, he'd pressed the trigger and instantly, the figure had disappeared, apparently dropped to the ground, dead. When we dared to investigate we found to our relief, that despite being a good shot, the bullet must have missed its mark. I think the African was very lucky and, quite probably, he's still running.

I frequently hunted with a friend, Dr. Peak, a non-government Surgeon who practised in Eldoret. Although perhaps, he was not as expert as he might have been, Dr. Peak was an avid hunter and always keen to follow where I would lead. Like me, he was keen on hunting buffalo, an animal which I feared and which, for me, held a particular fascination.

One weekend, when neither of us had anything better to occupy us, we loaded the truck and, accompanied by a couple of bearers and a tracker, set off for the Kaptagat Forest to the north of Eldoret to hunt buffalo. The region was heavily forested and though it contained only a few buffalo, they were mostly lone bulls - large, angry and extremely dangerous. It promised to be an exciting weekend.

We started tracking at dawn but made sure we kept well behind our prey because, even though we were only twenty miles from the equator, at that altitude, 9000 feet above sea level, it was freezing and our fingers were too cold to operate a rifle bolt with any certainty.

We hadn't travelled far before the sun rose rapidly into a crystal-blue sky above the Cherangani peaks which formed the eastern flank of the forest and the ice which glazed the trees and scrub began to melt. Soon we were warm enough for the hunt.

With unerring skill, Juma, my Dorobo Tracker, picked up the tracks of a lone bull buffalo and beckoned us to follow him into a dense area of tall bamboo. We hadn't gone far when suddenly, from somewhere in the gloom ahead of us, came an enormous commotion. The large black shadow, enraged by our sudden appearance in his territory, lunged and crashed about snapping bamboo's as though they were grass stalks in his rush to escape.

Dr. Peak, who was some way ahead of me, raised his gun and fired blindly at the charging shadow - something which I had been trained never to do - but the frantic animal crashed on, stampeding down a steep slope snapping thick bamboo's with a sound like machine gun fire.

We tracked the animal for some hours but, to my great frustration, all we managed to find was blood-stained vegetation - the wounded bull had managed to evade us and got clear away.

A couple of weeks later, a brother officer, Tony Maxtone-Mailer, visited my area for some joint operations against cattle raiders and we took time off to hunt in the Kaptagat Forest.

Juma, as always, was soon on the track of a lone buffalo and we followed him into a dense thicket. For a moment he was out of sight then suddenly he came bouncing towards us, flew by and threw himself on the ground behind us. At that instant, an almighty crashing erupted from the vegetation about twenty yards ahead of us and out burst a bull buffalo, his head raised in full charge and his staring, blood red eyes intent upon our death.

The rifles we were carrying, mine a Mauser 10.75mm and Tony's a Mauser 9.3mm, were both a bit light for buffalo in these dense conditions but we had little choice and fired simultaneously. Although the beast's head dropped, his speed didn't and he passed straight between us, his right horn missing Tony by a whisker and his left side brushing against me as he charged on. We both swung round and fired again and he crashed into the undergrowth stone dead.

When we examined the animal, we discovered on his right side, which had just missed Tony, the horn was intact, but on the side that had brushed me, the horn had been sheered off close to the head. Had that horn been full length its point would have pierced my belly and the onrush would have certainly disembowelled me. I let out a howl of relief and shuddered for the rest of the day.

When he was certain that the danger had passed, Juma emerged from his hiding place and proceeded to slit open the buffalo's stomach. He thrust his arm in, rooted about and pulled out handfuls of steaming entrails and part-digested vegetation which dripped with a hot, green liquid. These he shovelled into his mouth with gusto, relishing a complete meal of meat and at least two veg. - while the poor animal quivered its last. We found Dr Peak's bullet - it had passed through the animals stomach and lodged against a bone on the far side.

We occasionally heard reports that, apart from the buffalo, this forest also contained a small isolated herd of elephant and close by them, two large bulls carrying very heavy ivory. On several occasions, Peak and I hunted them but in dense forest, thick with undergrowth, it can be very difficult even to catch sight of an elephant, let alone see both his tusks. Often, we came close but never succeeded in seeing what ivory the bulls carried before they caught our scent and were off at a fast walk which would last for four to six hours making tracking all but impossible.

My own hunting had always been conducted with a strong element of game conservation in mind but, many years after the above incident, a Government game warden went into the forest and indiscriminately killed the whole herd, nineteen elephants in all.

While controlled shooting meant that culling had to take place, at least it eliminated poaching in those areas where it was conducted. However, the policy in white farmed areas was to eliminate any game which threatened their crops on the basis that game and agriculture don't mix. At the same time we attempted to convince the Africans that, in their own farming areas, they did mix - after all, the game was there before they were - and we would do nothing to alleviate their problems with game unless human life was threatened.

Experience has taught me that colonial life, particularly in earlier times, tended to be lived to extremes - often primitive conditions, extremes of temperature, hard work and a rigorous life-style would lead to excessive indulgence during periods of leisure and I must confess that, at times, I was guilty of such excesses. I used to frequent one isolated club renowned for its prodigious drinking sessions which would sometimes last through the night and half the next day and on occasions, even longer.

The British couple who ran the club were pretty heavy drinkers but would usually retire from the scene at about 2 am, leaving the members to help themselves and sign chits for the drink they consumed.

One particular night, the wife had drunk more than her usual quota and just as she picked up her heavy, five-cell torch ready to light her way to their quarters out the back, she suddenly passed out behind the bar. The husband immediately called for help to carry her to bed and one of the members bent down and grasped her by the ankles. At his touch, the lady suddenly came to and sat bolt upright.

"You filthy bastard!" she screamed and promptly smacked him over the head with the torch. The unfortunate fellow reeled backwards streaming blood from a deep wound while she struggled to her feet and, supported by her husband, staggered off to bed, apparently unaware of the damage she had done.

Some days later when the poor chap returned to the bar, sporting a large bandage around his head into which many stitches had been inserted, our hostess turned to him with a pitying look and said, "My word, what have you done to yourself?" Apparently, she didn't remember, and nobody had thought to tell her that, just a few nights earlier, she had almost killed the fellow.

Needless to say, I was not immune from the consequences of these prolonged drinking bouts. One night, after an almighty session, I staggered to the car and set off in the direction of home but before I had gone far, I was suddenly blinded by the search light of the up-country express. The thought flashed into my mind that I must somehow have strayed onto the line or the train had left the rails. It was very close coming straight for me. I had to do something quick. I swerved, bounced off the track and ended up with the car balanced on top of an ant hill with all four wheels spinning clear of the ground. I watched in amazement as the train sped by. Apparently, I had encountered it at a point where the track came close to the road, then curved suddenly away from it. I spent a long, cold night perched on top of the ant hill.

On another occasion I attended a party at a house some way out of town. The party went on late into the night and, of course, I had far too much to drink. At 3.00am I was about to leave when I was asked by a charming, elderly Goanese couple, if I would give them a lift back into town.

"I'd be delighted to," I said, and off we went.

After only a couple of miles, I was obliged to stop to relief myself. "I won't be a minute," I said, hopping out of the car and heading for the bush beside the road. Suddenly, in the pitch dark, I took one step too many and plunged headlong down a steep embankment which ran close alongside the road. Due to the combination of drink and the fall, I passed out and when I awoke at dawn I found the old dears huddled together in the car, shivering with fear. They had no idea where I had gone to or what dreadful fate had befallen me and, later, on the frequent occasions that I met them at parties, they never again asked me for a lift.

It was around this time that I made two remarkable discoveries. Firstly; while driving home after a heavy drinking session, I found that I could more readily stabilise the road ahead if I closed one eye. Secondly; each time I went to bed after such a session, I found that everything kept moving sickeningly from left to right. However, if I crawled out of bed and spent the rest of the night on the floor, the problem was alleviated. These little tricks helped enormously to make my social life and its consequences more bearable and I must mention, that by the standards of the day in Kenya, I was considered to be a near teetotaller.

Eldoret is on the main Kenya/Uganda rail line along which the twice-weekly express travels between the capitals, Nairobi and Kampala. The engines had to be powerful due to the mountainous terrain through which they passed and the express was hauled by giant coal and wood burning monsters built by the English engineers Garrett. At 2.30 am the express, travelling at full speed, would thunder through one small up-country Government centre waking the half dozen English families who were the sole inhabitants and whose houses were situated close to the track. On one of my visits to the Police out-station there, I heard a rumour that this little community had the highest *per capita* birth rate of any white settlement in East Africa.

The Police out-station and its adjacent buildings in which my men were housed were of brick construction with corrugated iron roofs. One day, after a bout of particularly heavy weather, I was asked by the Sergeant in charge to visit the station because he had a tragic accident to report. Apparently, during a severe thunderstorm, one of Constable ran to the shelter of his quarters and stood at the window waiting for the storm to abate. Suddenly, the building was struck by a bolt of lightening which came through the roof and drilled a neat hole about one inch in diameter through the top of his head and penetrated several inches deep. He was killed instantly.

One day, a rather odd character arrived in my district as a settler from the UK.

He bought a farm and immediately announced that he would build himself a house on it. We all thought little of this since he was reputed to have been a builder in London before his emigration.

The construction which began to appear was, to say the least, a ramshackled affair - part wood, part stone, part mud and part corrugated iron. Many began to question the truth behind his reputation.

Our builder friend thought about his plans for a few days then decided that the house needed more storage space in the form of a cellar. He excavated furiously for a few days until he had a fine capacious cavity below the ground-floor level then, as he stood back to admire his handy-work, the whole building collapsed into the hole.

Undaunted, and despite the disapproval of his neighbours, he set about rebuilding. This time he constructed, as the centre-piece, a large fireplace and chimney mostly of hard-baked mud over a timber frame. After the house was finished he moved in and for a time enjoyed the comfort of large log fires - until the mud baked dry and the timber frame of the chimney burst into flames and burned the whole house down.

During the house building operations, he set on a team of labourers to build a dam across a nearby stream. His knowledge of dam construction was about as complete as that of house building and he neglected to include an adequate spill-way in his plans. Soon after it was completed, there were considerable rains which filled the dam to a level where it burst and was completely swept away causing considerable damage to the neighbouring property.

Whenever my duties allowed it, I would take time off for a spot of hunting and over a period I established a number of bases around my district from which I could venturing forth into favoured hunting grounds. One such place was at Timboroa, a small railway halt south of Eldoret on the main line to Nairobi.

At an elevation of around 9,000 feet, Timboroa was reputed to be the highest rail point in the British empire and boasted a 'dak' bungalow, a kind of cafe-cum-bar at which trains without restaurant facilities would halt to allow passengers to obtain food and drink.

On my first visit, I met a elderly English couple who, together with their daughter, owned and operated the Timboroa Saw Mill situated in an isolated spot a few miles back into the forest. Their nearest neighbours, apart from the little railway halt and the dak bungalow, were about fifteen miles away. They kindly invited me to stay the night and I readily accepted since it was an ideal location from which to hunt in the surrounding forest. On my arrival there I discovered an additional benefit - their daughter, who was small, slim and very attractive.

The couple were regular drinkers in the dak bungalow where all was quiet until the old lady, who was normally a kind and considerate soul, got drunk. Then she would become angry and violent and there was hardly a window in the place through which, at one time or another, she hadn't thrown her poor husband. Not long after my first visit, the daughter married and moved away and then the old man died leaving his wife to live alone in the forest.

As night fell, the old girl would dismiss her staff, lock and barricade herself in the house, go to bed and drink herself into stupor before passing out for the night only to emerge the following morning as if nothing had happened.

On one visit to the area, at about midnight, I received information that she had not been seen for over twenty-four hours so immediately, I set off for the house to investigate. I arrived at 1.30 am in the middle of a heavy rain and thunder storm to find her servants huddled in an out-house uncertain what to do. I knew she kept a loaded shotgun and a handful of spare shells on her bed and that, at the slightest noise, she would fire through the bedroom walls, so nobody had the courage to approach too close.

The only access to the old lady's bedroom was through a small window which was secured by shutters both inside and out. Knowing of her shooting habits, I didn't relish the thought of breaking in and I could hardly order any of my men to do so. I was in a quandary and I was terrified.

There are people who will tell you they are afraid of nothing, they are either idiots or liars. Fear is human nature's armour. I know - I have spent most of my life in fear. If danger threatens, you immediately become alert and your reactions sharpen. But in the prevailing circumstances perhaps my greatest fear was of displaying fear itself before subordinates.

Finally, I decided that the only course open to me was to break in and risk the consequences. I found a hefty iron bar, ordered my men to keep their heads down and smashed through the shutters and the window. After a moment's pause, I scrambled through, expecting a blast from the shotgun at any second, but there was silence. I shone my torch towards the huge bed which appeared to be unoccupied apart from the shotgun and an empty whisky bottle and after a quick glance about the room, I threw back the bed covers. There was the poor old girl - dead - but with something of a happy smile on her lips. Her heart had eventually given out.

In Eldoret, fire was a not infrequent hazard among the tinder-dry buildings and, driving home late one night with my orderly, I spotted flames leaping from the roof of a hardware store in the main street.

There was no one else about, so we sped off towards the little improvised fire-station which we found was also deserted. If we didn't do something quickly, half the town would be ablaze so we leaped into the fire engine (the old, red-painted Ford Model 'A' two-seater), and roared off.

Before stopping at the fire, I drove furiously up one street and down another with the Orderly frantically clanging the bell to alert the sleeping town. No-one appeared, not even the night patrol constables who, I knew, should have been about somewhere.

Eventually, we screeched to a halt in front of the store, smashed our way in through a side door and, using a couple of hand-held extinguishers, which were the only means at our disposal, we managed to bring the fire under control.

Just too late, someone arrived on the scene and pointed out to us a fire hydrant close by in the street. We connected our hose and I went back into the store to finish off the damping-down. In fact, the fire seemed to have caused little damage - not as much as I caused with the powerful jet from the hose which, in my anger at the non-appearance of any help but myself and my orderly, I took great satisfaction in aiming in all direction around the store.

At the scene of another fire which raged amongst a group of tinder-dry African dwellings, I spotted an African vandal slashing the fire-fighters hoses. Before I could do anything to stop him, a native fireman dashed up behind the vandal and, in his eagerness to minimise the damage, cleaved his scull in two with his axe. The dwellings were home to a number of women and children and in my opinion, vandals such as that one, who could have killed the lot, are best put permanently out of the way. I fully supported the fireman in his, perhaps hasty, action and had the death recorded as resulting from 'Injury from a falling beam.'

Towards the end of my period of command at Farm 35, I became due for three weeks leave but, just before it, I was asked to take temporary command of another out-station as well, while my opposite number there took his own three weeks leave. On arrival, I discovered that the Inspector had been making overtures to an English girl who had come out to stay with relatives on a neighbouring farm. Since I was deputising for him, I considered it an essential part of my duty to carry on with her where he left off and we soon became friends. She was a little older than I although, it transpired, quite innocent of some of those matters which I considered were the most important in life.

She had been planning to spend a few weeks in Nairobi and since it was my intention to travel that way to spend some of my leave on the coast, I offered her a lift which she readily accepted and, in the event, she decided to travel down to the coast with me. As soon as my colleague returned, I dodged rapidly through the handover formalities, dashed out to the farm and, together with my new-found companion, I was on my way before he could discover what had gone on during his absence.

At the time, I still had my old Vauxhall 26 h.p. tourer which was never built to withstand the rigours of East African roads - unlike the American cars which I owned later. In those days, American roads were largely rough and unmetalled, just like those of East Africa. I was expecting a few problems but, as it turned out, we had a trouble free run over five hundred miles of rough, earth roads all the way to the coast.

We booked into a partly constructed beach hotel to the north of Mombasa - it was then the only hotel between Mombasa Island and Kikambala thirty miles to the north where stood the first hotel ever constructed on the coast. Our accommodation consisted of two adjacent 'rondavels', (circular mud huts with thatched roofs), connected by a partly screened pathway and it was fairly primitive.

My companion selected one of the rooms and started to unpack, shyly indicating that I should go to the other and do the same. Naturally, I was a little disappointed but instantly obeyed, determined to pursue my seduction of her in a slow and gentle fashion.

The following afternoon, I visited her in her room and, responding to signs of willingness on her part, I kissed her and an interlude of mild petting took place. Two days later, after a token reluctance, she allowed me to get into bed with her and there the trouble started.

The bed was a narrow wooden frame spanned by sagging canvas webbing upon which was laid a thin kapok-filled object calling itself a mattress. She climbed in first and when I followed, the whole lot sagged so far that it was impossible to lie beside her. That, in itself was not the problem - I had no intention of lying beside her anyway, at least not for long - it was simply that we were trapped in what resembled a narrow trench which rendered love-making all but impossible.

We hadn't progressed very far when I was forced to give the job up and sheepishly apologise for the failure. She smiled weakly and I returned to my room. It wasn't until a week later, and after she had shyly indicated her desire to do so, that we managed to overcome the problem, to our mutual satisfaction.

We spent our time pleasantly enough, swimming, fishing and walking the beaches until, suddenly, I started to run an intermittent, high fever. For a couple of hours at a stretch, I would feel like death before suddenly returning to normal. This wretched condition persisted until we left the coast and then for the whole of the journey back to Eldoret.

Early in our stay on the coast, I warned her of some of the hazards of Kenya that lie in wait for the unwary, but her reaction lead me to believe that she didn't fully understood my motive for telling her. It was merely my concern for her health and comfort but she was convinced that these hazards were all my fault,

There were Mango flies, I told her. These would lay their eggs in clothing or the like, while they hung out to dry. The grubs would hatch and burrow into the flesh of the wearer and the first sign of the invasion would be a swelling which soon reached the size of a boil, having a white head just like one. When it was judged to be fully developed, you squeezed it and out popped a maggot.

Then there were 'jiggers' which could be a real pest. These are a species of flea which burrow into the toes, feet and ankles and lay their eggs under the skin. At worst, all that the victim feels at the time is a tiny pin prick and a mild irritation which soon wears off. As days pass, a small white sack forms under the skin and grows rapidly to the size of a pea. At this stage, the best solution was to get an African servant to perform a minor operation to extract it - they were, by and large, experts at it. They would use a blunt safety pin to break the skin and remove the sack intact, the danger being that if the sack were left in too long, or was broken, the baby 'jiggers' would themselves burrow in and increase the problem twenty-fold. Many Africans lost toes or chunks of flesh from their feet through neglect or mishandling of the problem.

On the return journey, instead of the direct route to Nairobi, we decided to take a diversion through Tsavo and into Tanganyika, camping by night and taking a total of three days for the journey.

The heart of the Tsavo region, though now-a-days home of the much famed game reserve, was then almost totally unoccupied and undeveloped and, for the four hundred miles from Mombassa to Nairobi, except at remote trading centres, we never saw another vehicle.

Nights were spent on a ground sheet beside the car and we were bitten constantly by mosquitoes and kept awake by the howling of Jackal and Hyena and by the distant grunting of hunting lions. Though I had by me, my Mauser .404 heavy magazine rifle, the poor girl shook with fear all night and by morning was showing distinct signs of distress.

About half way, the steering on the old Vauxhall suddenly became extremely heavy and I knew that the rough terrain was beginning to take its toll. We struggled on to reach a small trading centre where I jacked up the front end of the vehicle and discovered that the near-side king pin had fractured and all but a couple of inches of it had vanished. There was no hope of finding a spare in this remote region so I searched round for anything that might serve as a substitute. Eventually I located a thick heavy bolt which I forced into place and off we went again.

My lady-friend, already stressed by the rigours of the journey and the fear-filled, sleepless nights, was not too impressed by my engineering efforts, particularly when she was forced to suffer the horrendous vibration and the front wheel wander which ensued. Still, I suffered intermittent bouts of fever and our relationship was, to say the least, becoming strained.

At daylight the following morning, after another awful night, we set off again but hadn't gone far when the engine petered out. A quick inspection revealed that the fuel pump diaphragm had split and, of course,

I didn't carry a spare. I was carrying, however, enough reserve petrol for the journey, stored metal containers.

I took one empty can, punched a hole in the bottom, jammed open the bonnet and secured the can above the engine. Next, I disconnected the fuel pipe from the pump and wedged it into the hole, sealing it as best I could with strands of cotton and toilet soap; (soap is insoluble in petrol). I filled the can and, again, we were mobile. The only problems were, the imperfect joint constantly leaked petrol onto the engine, trailing a cloud of stinking fumes back into our faces, and the necessity of stopping every fifteen or sixteen miles to refill the can.

It was not a pleasant journey and, when I look back, I shudder - a constant dripping of petrol onto the hot cylinder block and just behind the front seats, twenty gallons of spare fuel in thin four gallon containers belching petrol fumes through their ill-fitting caps at every bump in the road. Had it ignited, the fire-ball would have been spectacular and visible for miles.

Another night spent in the bush did nothing to improve our rapidly deteriorating relationship. Somewhere out there in the dark, a herd of wildebeest lowed and shuffled nervously. Lions were on the hunt. The pandemonium grew and grew until, just before dawn - panic, as the lions moved in for a kill and the whole herd stampeded. They passed so close that we felt the ground tremble and we were choked with the dust from their flying hooves. My companion was near to breaking point. The discomfort and danger was not what she had expected from a romantic trip into wild game country.

At sun-up, we continued our journey in silence and eventually arrived at a fast-flowing river crossing. There was no bridge, just a hand winch concreted into the far bank above flood level. The object being that one of the party would wade across, retrieve the wire rope, bring it back and fix it to the front axle, then return to the far bank to crank the vehicle across if it showed signs of digging in or stalling. I set about the task of adjusting the make-shift petrol feed so that it survived the crossing and, judging there to be no crocodiles at this particular place, I said to her, "Wade over and get the rope."

"No! No!" she yelled, and burst into tears.

"Stupid girl," I said, amazed. "What's got into you now?" From that moment, the fate of our relationship was sealed and we spoke no more.

Eventually, we reached Nairobi where I managed to obtain a new king pin and pump diaphragm before continuing our journey up country which proved uneventful but was pervaded by the uneasy silence.

I dropped her off with her family and feeling near to death, crawled into town to see the Government doctor. He took one quick look and said, "You've got mumps. Go home, go to bed, drink lots of fluids and I'll see you the day after tomorrow. By the way," he added, as I stumbled out of his office. "Be very careful not to catch a chill."

Desperate for anything that would give me relief, I obeyed his instructions to the letter. I went straight home, ordered all doors and windows to be closed and dived into bed under a mountain of blankets.

The heat was almost unbearable but, between bouts of delirium, while servants bathed my steaming brow, I drank copious quantities of liquids 'til it made me sick. I didn't want to catch the chill the doctor had warned me about. Never before or since, even in a bout of severe malaria, have I ever felt so hot and so sick.

True to his word, the doctor arrived thirty-six hours later. He took one look at me and his jaw dropped. "Blimey," he said. "You don't look too good."

"No," I whimpered. "It's the temperature."

"I'm not surprised," he said, eyes wide with disbelief. Then, waving an arm in the direction of the servants, he ordered, "Open all the doors and windows." Then, pointing at me, "And you, strip off and have a cold bath. We must get that temperature down immediately."

"But what about the chill?" I pleaded.

"Don't be a fool, you can't catch a chill with a temperature as high as that."

I took three weeks sick leave and happily, I had no swelling of my private parts and only a little around my neck.

She, the English girl, was so distressed by the return trip that, soon after our arrival back in Eldoret, she administered a severe flea in the ear to the Station Inspector whom I had relieved, and promptly returned to England. I never saw her or heard of her again. I think she'd had enough of Kenya Police Officers to last her a lifetime.

I saw no good reason to tell Josephine of the events of the trip since I would soon be departing for the coast and a new posting. Of course, she knew that I'd been on holiday, but I told her nothing of the girl I'd taken with me... not until many years later.

Coastal Light Entertainment

few weeks after my return from holiday, I received a notice of
posting. I was to travel from Eldoret to the coast where I would
be stationed at Police Headquarters in Mombasa - but in what
role, I was not informed.

My recent experiences along the route to Mombasa in the old Vauxhall
made me doubt its capacity to endure another such trip so I searched
around for a tougher and more reliable alternative. Eventually I came
across a 1932 Chrysler Coupe which, in contrast to the town-bred gentility
of the Vauxhall, displayed all the course characteristics of a car born to
travel the dusty, unmetalled roads of the American mid-west.

I thought the Chrysler was a grand old car even though it did have a
few faults when I took possession, for example, the massive straight-eight
engine had a tendency to twist viciously then thump down in an alarming
manner each time I accelerated hard. This was due to the fact that two of
the engine mounts had sheared leaving the engine free on one side to pivot
about the axis of the prop shaft; the starter motor bushes were worn,
forcing me to start it by hand cranking. The petrol feed to the engine was
a leaky 'autovat' system which appeared to be designed only for level
motoring so that on long hills, the engine would eventually stall through
fuel starvation. Each time this happened I had to get out and refill the
'autovat' by hand before it would start again. Changing a tyre could also
be a problem since they were mounted on split-rims which had to be
withdrawn using a three-clawed crank in the centre of the wheel.

All things considered, she was a bit of a wreck but, since my meagre salary didn't extend to repairing these 'minor' faults, I had to put up with them. When tyres became worn, even right through the canvas, I had to make do and mend by employing a commonly used trick of binding rope around the rim and the tyre to protect the exposed inner tube and prevent it from bulging out. This, of course, gave a rather bumpy ride. Otherwise, the old girl went like a bomb and she was my pride and joy.

When the time arrived to depart, I crammed as many of my possessions as would fit, into the car and, leaving just enough room for my servant, Ajuro, I tied the rest to the outside and we set off for the coast.

We had to travel some considerable distance before I became accustomed to the eccentricities of the new car but eventually I began to relax as we sped along at a good pace leaving in our wake a cloud of dust from the rough earth road.

Part way down one long, straight stretch, we found ourselves keeping pace, at about sixty miles an hour, with a down-country train where the line ran parallel to the road. We waved to the passengers who cheered and waved back from the carriage windows. Suddenly, to my horror, I saw that the road ahead turned sharp right across the rail track and in those times, the crossings were all open ones with neither warning signs nor barriers.

One thing I had learned on the journey so far was that my brakes were all but ineffective because the brake shoes were worn away leaving just the rivets screaming against the brake drums when I applied them.

My heart pounded. We had no chance of stopping and, at this pace we would either be crushed by the train or dive off the road into the dense bush ahead with heaven knows what consequences. I plumped for the only alternative - to race the train to the crossing.

I accelerated, cramming my foot hard to the floorboards and causing the half secured engine almost to leap out of the bonnet. Ajuro squealed and covered his eyes as we swerved across the track, barely twenty feet ahead of the speeding train. Since then, I am forced to stop and look both ways before venturing across the track at any of our UK crossings.

Next morning, we arrived in Mombasa and I went immediately to Police HQ and reported to the Provincial Commander.

"Take over traffic," he said, barely acknowledging my arrival. "Oh, and if at any time you find you're not too busy, help out anywhere else you can."

The length of Kenya's Indian Ocean coastline and for a distance of about ten miles inland was not strictly a part of Kenya Colony although, in practice, it was governed and policed as if it were. In fact, it belonged to the Sultan of Zanzibar and was designated The Coast Protectorate with its police headquarters in Mombasa under the control of the Provincial Commander.

The Sultan exercised powers in the Protectorate and enacted certain laws which were intended to ease the daily burden of its people. One such law stated that traders were allowed to alter the fashion in women's clothing only once every ten years so that the spending of fashion conscious women would be curtailed and would not bring destitution on their families and thus deprive children of essential food. I think that many present-day husbands in the UK would welcome the introduction of such legislation here.

There were three British Inspectors at headquarters, one in charge of prosecutions, one in charge of C.I.D. and now myself in charge of the traffic division. We were all quartered together in the European section of town in an ancient colonial-style house which was built to withstand the rigours of an English winter but, unfortunately, not the overhead equatorial sun and for most of the time was unbearably hot. The house was, however, quite a grand residence and added a certain edge to our main preoccupation when off duty - the pursuit of the local European ladies.

A short time after my arrival, one of my companion officers fell for an attractive girl who came from a good, but quite old fashioned, family. He was smitten with her and, for a while, seemed to be progressing favourably in his suit. In those days, respectable daughters were always chaperoned, particularly in the company of young Police Officers, and knowing this girl's family, it was certain that any time he arranged to meet her, they would not be alone. One morning he appeared for breakfast in a state of considerable excitement and said to the two of us, "Chaps, make sure you're here for tea. I've got her mother coming."

It was a hot, sticky, uncomfortable day most of which I spent in the office filling in routine accident reports. When I arrived home at the appointed hour, I found that our friend had made the best arrangements he could for the comfort of his guests; table laid on the verandah with a newly laundered white linen cloth, cucumber sandwiches, finest quality tea and small, delicate cakes served on the best china, and all with the obvious aim of making a good impression on his darling's dour parent.

In due course, we three officers, the girl and her mother sat down for afternoon tea, amid polite conversation which flowed smoothly around recent social events and police matters. Suddenly, regarding a recent crime which had taken place in the locality, the girl's mother commented, "I thought it was dreadful." To which, my companion officer, who was too busy drooling over the girl to really concentrate on what her mother was saying, replied,

"Yes, fucking awful."

The old dame glared at him in disbelief. then, without a word, seized her daughter by the arm and dragged her unprotesting from the house. We, his fellow officers, were astounded because we had never heard him swear before, even when we were alone, he was always the perfect gentleman but the romance was at an end and my friend never saw the girl again.

Some years later, he married a delightful lady who worked as a Government Veterinary Officer and whom he adored. I'm almost certain that she never heard him say that word throughout the whole of their happy married life.

A few weeks after my arrival in Mombasa, while I was still settling in to the routine of the Traffic Division, I received a message that there had been a serious accident a few miles away on the mainland. Accompanied by a couple of my men, I hurried to the scene and discovered a British Naval lorry leaning at a crazy angle at the side of the road with a crowd of Naval personnel sat around looking bruised and sick .

Some roads in these areas consisted simply of two, two-foot wide parallel tarmac strips on which vehicles ran to prevent them sinking in soft sand or puncturing their tyres on the sharp coral rocks. This form of road construction presented two major problems; when two vehicles approached each other from opposite directions, one was forced to give way and risk the consequences; any vehicle travelling at speed was in danger of leaping the tracks with the obvious results. Something of the latter had befallen this vehicle.

Apparently, the lorry, driven by a British rating, was taking a party of Naval personnel to a distant beach for a picnic. For some reason, the lorry had to swerve and the front wheels left the tarmac. As the vehicle bounced along out of control, the passengers on the back were thrown violently from side to side and one unfortunate nineteen year old Wren struck her head on one of the coconut palms which fringed the road.

The blow broke her neck in several places and stretched it out to double its original length. She was, of course, killed instantly. I never was particularly squeamish, but the sight of this poor girl with her head almost disconnected from her body, shook me rigid.

119

I immediately arrested the driver and charged him with manslaughter but, within days, the Navy exercised their rights and took him out of my custody to deal with him themselves. I was furious at their high handed attitude and, later, on two separate occasions, when the Military tried to do the same, I stood firm and prosecuted the offenders in civil courts.

A few weeks after this incident another fatality occurred outside a bar on Kilindini Road which lead down to Mombasa's docks. A Chinaman hailed a passing taxi which swerved across the road to pick him up but, unfortunately, it was travelling too fast and pinned the poor man against a tree. On investigation, I found him to be pretty well flattened and missing one ear which had been ripped off and crushed into the trunk of the tree. I charged the taxi driver with manslaughter and left the ear where it was as evidence.

At the trial I mentioned the ear and its condition, as an indication of the speed of the taxi at impact, so the Judge, Mr Justice Thacker decided to view the evidence personally. When we arrived at the scene, I searched in vain for the ear but it had vanished.

"Well, Officer," the Judge said, impatiently. "Where is it?"

"Er... I don't know, sir," I replied. "I left it here on the tree."

"Disgraceful," he barked. "Missing evidence, eh! Consider yourself admonished."

Three months later, I was standing beside a roundabout in the centre of town when an old American Coupe came sweeping round it with tyres screeching and obviously, barely under control. It hit the curb, then straightened up and slowed to near walking pace so I stepped into the road and flagged it down. To my surprise, the driver was none other than Mr Justice Thacker.

"Awfully sorry, Officer," he said. "It's my son's car and I've never driven it before."

"Disgraceful, your Lordship," I barked. "Consider yourself admonished." He stared at me for a second, then recognition spread across his face.

"Good God!" he squeaked. "You're *that* Police Officer."

After that, when I was of much more senior rank and he was a circuit judge, we would always meet in his chambers when he visited my Province, for a glass or two of sherry and laugh about the old days.

Late one night, I was on duty at Police Headquarters when information came in that a killer, whom we had been seeking for some time, was in town. This character, a Sikh, was dangerous, having knifed one man to death and seriously sliced up another and all for no apparent motive. So, detailing a Sergeant and two Constables to accompany us, I hurried off with the informant who led us to the Asian area of town.

"He's in there," he whispered, pointing at a particular bungalow, then scurrying of into the night before he got drawn in any further. The Sergeant and I crept close to the bungalow and peered through a gap in the curtains of the only room that showed a light. What we witnessed nearly gave us hysterics.

There, naked except for his turban and a leather belt holding his ceremonial knife, was our man. He was busy preparing a young Asian girl for his pleasure by lying her on the bed and spreading her legs as wide as they would go. Satisfied with the arrangements, he backed away across the room then with a flying leap, displaying extraordinary accuracy, indicative of much practice, he penetrated her at the first go.

"Let's get him," my Sergeant growled, springing to his feet ready for action. I seized his arm.

"Wait," I said. "Let him finish. Then he'll be worn out and give us no trouble. Besides which, it'll be the last time the poor devil will get it - in this life anyway."

When the Sikh had finished, we broke in and he gave himself up without resistance. The poor girl lay on the bed, wide-eyed and naked, holding her breasts and quaking with fear.

Sundowner parties were a regular feature of the social calendar which I would attend whenever duties allowed me to. At one of these Sundowners, I met a couple who lived nearby. He was a mild mannered fellow, tubby and balding, probably aged forty or more and she, Margaret, was a small, rather mousy woman aged thirty-six and my impression was that she was shy and reserved.

We chatted for a while then, just as the party broke up he said to me, "We're having a beach picnic tomorrow, since you're on your own, would you like to accompany us?" I was not very keen but the next day was Sunday and I had little else to do, so I accepted.

At 10am the next morning, I drove to their house and found them on the verandah. Margaret was dressed for the beach and beside her was a large picnic hamper and a pile of towels. I couldn't help noticing that, in her present, scanty attire, she had a rather splendid figure and was altogether more desirable than I had first imagined.

"Do you mind if we use your car?" she asked.

"No problem," I said. "It'll easily take three in the front."

"Ah," said the husband. "I'm afraid I can't come. Urgent business, you know. Got to drive into town immediately." I expressed my regrets that he couldn't come and Margaret and I loaded the hamper into the car, waved goodbye and set off for the coast together.

We followed the coast road for several miles to a beach fringing one of the many lagoons which lay between the reef and the shore. The beach was deserted so we spread the towels in the shade of the coconut palms and made ourselves comfortable.

For a while, we chatted about this and that, and the more we talked, the more I realised that my first impression of her - that she was shy and reserved - was wrong. It was more a case that she was dissatisfied with her humdrum existence and though, in a way, she was fond of him, she said very little in the presence of her dull and unattractive husband.

The tide was in so we slid into the cool water of the lagoon and, for half an hour or so, we swam and splashed and played and chased a small turtle which had come into the lagoon with the tide. By the time we returned to our picnic spot, our relationship had grown closer and less inhibited.

"We'd better get out of these wet things," Margaret said and, as she slipped one strap from her shoulder, I made a move towards the privacy of the palm trees. "No, no," she protested. "We're all right here, under the towels."

I obeyed. Soon we lay naked side by side and I had the chance to view the whole body which, until recently, I had paid little heed. She had a nice flat stomach with a small pout of muscle just below her trim waist, slim, but well shaped hips and thighs. Her breasts, though a mite pendulous, were shapely enough and fascinated me. For a moment, there was silence. Suddenly, she heaved herself up onto one elbow and, fingering the hairs on my chest, she said, "Do you believe in platonic friendship between a man and a woman?" I was completely taken aback by this pointed question and stammered something like,

"Er... I suppose there could be circumstances....but no, not really."

That was enough for her and she writhed and pressed her naked body against mine. We kissed and, before long, we were making love. "We're not in a hurry," she whispered and then commenced to display a prolonged and persistent vigour which I found quite surprising from one of such small stature. Meanwhile, the sun had moved, diminishing the shade under which we had originally settled and leaving me with a sunburned bum.

Later, she revealed to me that she hadn't had sex for four years because, by nightfall, her husband was too tired and she never fancied it in the morning. I, it seemed, filled a gap in her life and, for as long as our relationship lasted, she seized every opportunity she could to visit my quarters for an hour or so of energetic passion. I don't know about the early morning or night-time, but she certainly fancied it during the day.

A few days after the picnic I was called to the scene of an accident and found a most distressing situation. A group of African children had been playing on a railway bridge leaning over the parapet to watch the trains below. At one stage, a train thundered under the bridge and they immediately dashed for the other parapet to see it emerge. Unfortunately they ran straight under the wheels of a passing lorry.

Four of them suffered ghastly mutilation and where killed instantly while a fifth was dreadfully injured and barely alive. Immediately, I had the injured child rushed to the hospital and the bodies transported to the mortuary. I considered myself by this time to be inured to blood and guts but the horrible sight of these mangled little children made even me shed a tear.

To my surprise, the driver of the lorry had not absconded, as was usually the case in this type of accident, the fear of a charge of manslaughter being normally sufficient to make them scarper before the authorities arrived on the scene. Just as rare, there were three witnesses, one Asian and two Arabs, who claimed to have seen the accident and all swore that it wasn't the African driver's fault.

I checked the vehicle over and found that the brakes and the steering where functioning correctly, certainly better than my own car, then we drew a plan of the scene and took measurements. Meanwhile, the driver sat huddled in a corner of the bridge talking to my Constables and shaking with fear at the prospect of five years in jail for manslaughter.

Most Africans love children who, in their eyes can do no wrong, so the driver was convinced that, no matter what the facts of the case were, he would be blamed. He was amazed when I told him that I considered him not to be at fault and he was free to go. I left my men to take statements and clear up while I, thoroughly depressed by the incident, took myself off for a beer.

Normally, we, the Police decided whether or not an inquest was necessary or whether to prosecute or not but, in unusual cases like this one, we submitted a report, endorsed with our opinion, to a Magistrate, if there was one within reach. He would study the report, initial it and pass it back. Seldom did a Magistrate ever disagree with us or order a hearing unless we asked for one. In this case I had the file returned to me marked 'Closed. No Further Action', within forty-eight hours of the accident and I wonder just how long it would have been dragged out in this country, regardless of the agony suffered by the driver and others concerned.

Apart from occasional incidents, such as the one described above, which were very distressing to me, life in Mombasa's traffic department was pretty routine; driving offences, vehicle inspections, licensing etc. But occasionally, when duties allowed, I was called in to assist other divisions on assignments which proved to be a little more exciting. One night, myself and my two companion Inspectors were asked to take a party of Police to raid a shanty town on the outskirts of Mombasa. Here, it was suspected, a much wanted gang of murderers was holed up and we were determined that their freedom was about to end.

We set off in two Police, fifteen hundred-weight pick-up trucks and, as we approached the township, we parked one of the vehicles, manned by a Corporal and two Constables, by the roadside to ambush any of the gang who tried to escape. We moved the second vehicle closer to the hideout and parked it on a ledge overlooking the road. Quite incidentally this second vehicle had on board a device called a 'Tanganyika Jack' which was a species of winch used for rescuing heavy vehicles from mud or soft sand. It took the form of a heavy, metal banded, wooden case about 15" x 4" and 3'-6" long, containing a steel shaft and a crank handle. It weighed about half a hundred-weight.

We left the pick-up and crept towards the hide-out but, as we got close, we must have been spotted by a look-out because all hell broke loose as the gang burst out of the hut, waving machetes and screaming blue murder. One of them was shot and killed by one of the other Inspectors and I put two soft lead bullets from my Smith & Wesson .45 revolver into another.

Unknown to us, the ringleader had parked an old banger of a car round the back of the hut and seconds after the gang broke out, it roared out from the hiding place and tore off down the road. We yelled to the ambush party to warn them of his approach then finished our business with the rest of the gang.

When, eventually, we hauled our captives back to the first ambush point, we found the ring-leader's vehicle crashed into the earth bank with the driver dead at the wheel. Apparently, the Corporal had heard our yells and, as the vehicle approached, he stood up in the rear of the pick-up, grabbed the first thing which came to hand, the 'Tanganyika Jack', and hurled it like a javelin at the vehicle as it passed below. The jack went straight through the windscreen cleanly breaking the ring-leader's neck and killing him stone dead.

Our operation was deemed a great success and the manner of its outcome saved much time in Court proceedings than it would otherwise have done.

This type of operation was always hazardous and, considering some of the desperate characters we had to deal with, we were often lucky to come out of it alive. Another incident which took place at about the same time illustrates just how hazardous it could be. A brother officer who was stationed up-country, conducted a raid on a Mkamba African village about forty miles from Nairobi. As they approached the village, an arrow was fired from the doorway of a hut and struck him in the centre of the forehead. Although the arrow penetrated some way into his head, he didn't lose consciousness, in fact he didn't even fall down. He thought about pulling the arrow out and chasing down the villain who'd fired it but was immediately faced with a dilemma - was it a smooth bladed game arrow or a barbed war arrow covered with poison. He concluded that caution was the best policy and decided to seek medical help, however, there was no telephone (that came years later) and he had no driver in his party. With no second thoughts, he snapped the arrow off a few inches from his forehead, clambered in to his vehicle and drove the forty miles over rough earth road to Nairobi.

Arriving just before dawn, he staggered, covered in blood, into the European Hospital and confronted the night duty Sister. She took one look at the wound with the arrow sticking out of it and promptly fainted. Next he stumbled over to the Sister's quarters block, (we police always knew where that was), and, by now almost unconscious, knocked one of them up pleading for help. She also fainted. Finally, the Matron, who was made of sterner stuff, was called and she quickly organised treatment. Fortunately for our compatriot, the arrow was smooth bladed and not poisoned and, almost miraculously, he made a full recovery.

Later, he was furious with himself for discarding that part of the arrow shaft which would have borne the bowman's "signature", the mark which would have identified the owner, who could then have been picked up and prosecuted.

For some months before my arrival in Mombasa, Headquarters had been planning more modern accommodation for its Inspectors and soon, the three of us were moved from our old colonial house into flats which occupied the upper three floors of what, then, was the tallest building in Mombasa. The lowest of our floors, some eighty feet above ground level, contained a huge lounge with bedrooms off each end, a kitchen, a bathroom and a shower room and here, my two companion Inspectors set up home. Stairs led to a second floor containing a large bedroom, a bathroom and shower and a spare bedroom, and this floor I occupied in regal isolation. Yet more stairs led up to the third floor under the dome which crowned the whole building.

In contrast to the old house which was uncomfortably hot and sticky, our new accommodation, due to its height and the fact that instead of windows it had open stone trellis-work, promised us more daytime comfort and less sleepless nights. One minor snag presented itself, however, there were no lifts, so we got plenty of exercise.

In the first few month after I moved in, my most frequent visitor was Margaret. Whenever her husband was tied up on urgent business in the town or away up country on a conference or the like, she would climb the stairs to my flat and we would indulge in hours of very pleasant love-making. Time and time again she proved to me that, at least in private, she was not the shy timid little creature I had first taken her to be and she never hesitated in whatever daring sexual adventure took her fancy.

One evening I was taking a shower prior to attending a Sundowner when she arrived. "Won't be a minute," I called, and she went into the bedroom to wait. A few minutes later, with only a towel round my waist, I walked into the bedroom to find her standing by the bed in just her underwear.

"Come here," she said, giggling in a most tantalising way. "Now, turn round and close your eyes. I've got something for you." I was a bit wary but she was so excited I obeyed. "Now, put your hands behind you for your present." I did so and in a flash she had handcuffed me.

It appears that, while I was still in the shower, she had found a pair in an open drawer and it had inspired her. The knowledge that she had me under her power heightened her excitement so she soon had the towel off me and began to live out every fantasy that this new situation engendered.

For a while, I played along with her games, let's face it, they were very pleasurable, but then she found one of my ties, formed a slip-knot and attached it to my most delicate part. Now I must confess that being towed around the room trussed up in this manner is not the most enjoyable experience I've ever had but - worse was to follow. She found my whippy,

126

leather-covered swagger cane and laid it on my bare buttocks with a will. Though the activity raised Margaret to a fever pitch of excitement, it really did hurt me and, for the next week or so, I found that sitting down was very uncomfortable.

After this session, and possibly because of it, the relationship between Margaret and I began to cool. Our meetings became less frequent and our lovemaking more orthodox. I had also started to develop a twinge of conscience about her husband whom, although I seldom met him, I began to realise was a nice fellow and was sadly mistreated by his cheating wife. But, as one door closes, another, it seems, inevitably opens.

About this time, I was in the habit of having a noon-day drink on the patio of the Dolphin Hotel, either alone, or in the company various acquaintances including one who was a war correspondent.

I soon observed that each weekday a car would draw up to the hotel entrance and out would step a beautiful woman, probably, I guessed, in her late thirties. She was tall and slender with lovely auburn hair and I found her altogether most attractive.

The Navy driver would open the door for her, and first, out would come one slender leg followed slowly by the other allowing me a tantalising view of her thighs. Then she would lean forwards to emerge from the car permitting me further excitement by a glimpse of her superb cleavage. I was transfixed, but as she swept past into reception she looked neither to the left or right.

Too shy to approach her, I stationed myself on the Dolphin patio every day for over a fortnight, longing for just a glance of recognition from her, but to no avail. I was racking my brains for a means by which I might get to know her when fate stepped in.

Headquarters had offered to provide temporary accommodation for the Captain in charge of the local Military Police and lodged him in one of our spare bedrooms. He was a affable fellow who's arrival introduced my companion Inspectors and myself to a whole new social round and one evening we were invited to a 'do' at the Military Police Mess. Several ladies had also been invited and, as I scanned the room for likely female companionship, who should I spot but my auburn haired lady from the Dolphin Hotel.

"Oh, Arlene," our host said. "She's a Royal Navy Confidential Secretary. Come on, I'll introduce you." This time, much to my surprise, she smiled in recognition and we chatted and danced as if we had been friends for years. I was delighted

Later she told me that each time she had arrived at the Dolphin, she had noticed me on the patio and, on occasions when I was alone, she had deliberately hitched up her skirt and parted her legs as she got out of the car, just to tease me.

The evening was hot and unbearably humid and the room was filled with smoke so, as the party drew to a close, Arlene said, "Shall we take a walk along the beach. It's a full moon."

We drove to an isolated stretch of beach and strolled hand in hand along the edge of the lagoon and, though the night air was cool, hot passion was rising. Eventually, we reached the end of the beach and as we turned, she put her hand on my cheek, kissed me and with the moonlight glinting in her auburn hair, she said, "Will you share my bed with me."

I was almost speechless. Only yesterday, I had been ogling her from the Patio of the Dolphin apparently with no hope of ever speaking to her, and now, here I was, less than twenty four hours later, being propositioned by this peerless object of my desire. I couldn't believe my luck.

"Oh, yes!" I whispered, and held her close.

She kissed me again. "Here on the beach, or back in my room?" I'd had some experience of love-making on the coral sand of a tropical beach, and it's terrible stuff. It gets everywhere and, for the next few days, you keep finding sand in places you didn't even know you had places.

"At your place," I replied.

Arlene occupied a penthouse on top of the Dolphin Hotel which I had so often seen her enter, and though she was married, her husband lived elsewhere on the continent and she never mentioned him.

From the start, she displayed a total lack of inhibition and seconds after we entered her room, she shed her clothes and proudly displayed to me her beautiful body. Immediately, I was made aware that her lovely auburn hair was perhaps not entirely natural.

Experience had already taught me that, when with an older woman, I need do little to arouse her, and Arlene, who was some fifteen years my senior, was no exception to that general rule. Her imagination was vivid and her knowledge of the art of love-making was complete and, for the few months in which our relationship flourished, she exercised all that imagination and all that knowledge to, I believe, our total, mutual gratification.

The tropical full moon seemed to inspire her and, on those glorious nights when the moon was high and the sky cloudless, we would head for the open air and an hour or so of unrestrained passion. One spot she favoured on these occasions was atop a large water storage tank which stood three feet high and was surrounded by a four foot high screen wall on the hotel roof beside her penthouse. There, when the moon was bright, we would spread a mattress and lie together naked beneath the sky until either passion was spent or the moon went down.

One night, minutes after we had settled ourselves down on the tank, two middle-aged lady residents wandered onto the roof in search of cool night air and strolled past within a few feet of us. Fortunately we went unnoticed but, seconds later, they both came over and leaned against the tank wall and, for fully fifteen minutes, reviewed all the latest hotel scandal.

We were stark naked and I, for one, was fully aroused for the ensuing passion. Had they turned there heads for just a second, they would have had enough scandal to keep them going for years.

Sometimes, especially after a gin or two, Arlene's usual ice-cool behaviour in public would slip and I remember on more than one occasion, in one of the bars we frequented, she jumped up onto a table and danced to the music, but only when it was the Glenn Miller band.

After a lot of gin, (and occasionally, I would buy her doubles instead of her usual singles), she got a considerable kick out of inflicting pain and I was quite surprised to learn how pain can intensify the pleasures of sex.

With no husband around to bother us, Arlene and I made the most of our time together. Although just a little bit possessive, she was a beautiful woman, a thrilling lover and a most cherished companion and, if she were still alive today, she would be aged about ninety-five. For years after we parted, I regretted ever having treated her unkindly.

A few days after my first meeting with Arlene, I bumped into an old acquaintance from the UK who was, indirectly, to do me a big favour. I had just left my office at the traffic division and was heading for home when a voice hailed me.

"Peter! Is that you?"

I turned round and there, dressed in whites and carrying a tennis racket, was Walter Carman, a long-standing friend of my older brother.

"Walter," I replied. "What on earth are you doing here?" He explained that he had joined up at the outbreak of war and that his regiment was stationed here in Mombasa.

"Fortunately for me," he said. "My CO's a generous soul and I get plenty of time off to play tennis.

Walter was the son of a wealthy Norfolk family and had never wanted for money but, unlike his father who was the driving force behind the large family business, Walter was a mild mannered chap, in fact, the perfect gentleman, with little personal ambition. He was, however, a tennis fanatic who had once played at Wimbledon and having achieved the rank of Corporal and been selected to drive for his Commanding Officer, was given plenty of spare time to indulge his passion.

We arranged to meet again later in the week for a set or two and, for several weeks, until his regiment departed for other shores, we had regular encounters on the court. Of course I was usually no match for him but on one occasion, with enormous effort on my part, I did manage to beat him.

I showed Walter around the town and, on occasions, he would accompany me as my guest to one of the many Sundowners and evening parties, and it was at one of these that I introduced him to Margaret.

By this time, our relationship had grown stale and she and I rarely met. I sensed that she entertained a certain bitterness towards me for my lack attention to her needs and since I was just embarking on my affair with Arlene, I would have preferred her to be 'off the scene'. Walter proved to be the ideal substitute.

They took to each other instantly and I suspect that Margaret took some pleasure in pushing me aside for her new love. I didn't see Walter for many years after that, not until we came across each other at a shoot in Norfolk when he said to me,

"My god! That woman you introduced me to. She was something, wasn't she." It seems that they had kept each other very contented for some considerable time. Just before I left Kenya for the last time, I bumped into Margaret on the street but, before I had chance to ask her about the years since our last encounter, she blushed and said, "I'm late for an appointment," and rushed off in the direction from which she had just come.

The usual routine of Police work continued with no shortage of violence and harrowing scenes and our social life carried on through an endless round of mess parties, Sundowners and the like. Each unit of the British forces stationed in Mombasa would periodically hold a mess party to which we, the Police, were always invited and at which we had the opportunity to meet new faces including ladies, both attached and unattached. The forces always stuck to tradition and each party was for either officers, NCO's or other ranks, but never for a mixture of ranks.

Every few weeks, we would reciprocate and throw a mess party of our own to which we would invite members of all the forces, regardless of rank, just as long as they were considered to be decent folk. Our do's, at which the lowest ranks were at liberty to converse with the highest, and vice versa, proved to be extremely popular and never was there any unpleasantness or any disrespect between the guests.

It was at one forces mess party, not many months after I had first met Arlene, that I was introduced to Sandra, a pretty, young Naval Rating fresh out from England. I was immediately enchanted by her youth and freshness; she was then only twenty and, for a change, a woman younger than myself. I was still young, unmarried and saw no reason for exclusivity in my relationships, so I asked her for a date. Arlene, then aged thirty-nine, was, however, of a different opinion and, when she found out about what she considered was my infidelity, she went crazy.

They say that the two most beautiful things in life are a woman in love and a ship in sail, but their master you must be. Be you not, then to hell they will take you, and if to hell I must go, then give me a ship.

At our next (and last) meeting, Arlene flew into an uncontrollable rage and, at one point, I seriously believed that she might attempt to kill me. In the end, she spat viciously at me, swore vengeance and vowed never to see me again.

For the next few weeks, I kept a low profile, staying well away from parties and anywhere else I thought I might run into Arlene. Instead, I kept to my work and spent all my leisure time in the company of the delightful Sandra.

Sandra was like a breath of fresh air; lively, pretty, with a perfect figure and, as far as I could tell, with very little experience of the male of the species. We drove together to various beaches, swam and laughed and kissed and gradually, we grew closer and closer.

One day, she came to my flat in preparation for a drive up the coast to a beach we had found, however the weather was none too good.

"Let's stay in today," she said. I was about to protest that there was nothing to do in the flat when I spotted the twinkle in her eye and the penny dropped. The time had come, she decided, to consummate our relationship and my protest evaporated.

After six joyous weeks of our, more intimate, relationship, I began to notice remarks that, I suspected, hinted at an even closer bond - marriage. I never actually countered these remarks fearing, I suppose, that by doing so, I might disturb the present idyll, but my silence must have been read by Sandra as tacit encouragement.

At about this time, I heard persistent rumours amongst my acquaintances that Margaret's husband was on the war-path having been told, possibly by Arlene, that his wife was being unfaithful. She, Arlene, had been heard muttering foul threats that I 'was in for it' and obviously had neglected to inform the poor chap that I was no longer his wife's lover but had been replaced by my friend Walter Carman. These rumours bothered me only slightly. However, another matter arose which scared me rigid.

One bright afternoon, Sandra breezed in, grinning from ear to ear and bubbling over with excitement. "Look!" she squealed. "I've picked up a sample for our bridesmaids dresses." In her outstretched hand was a piece of heavy silk material of a ghastly electric blue colour. Instantly, my stomach turned to jelly and I was too shocked to speak, even to utter a faintest bleat of protest.

It seems that in the face of my silence, she and her cronies had got it all worked out and, that night, she went home as happy as she had come. With my whole being in turmoil, I retired to bed, but, for the first time in my life, I couldn't sleep. I was not ready for marriage and the idea that I was trapped filled me with shear panic. Some time around dawn, I came to a decision.

At 9 am the following morning, I requested an interview with my Provincial Superintendent and a few minutes later, I entered his office.

"Sit down, Mills," he said. "You look like you've got a problem."

"More than that, Sir," I replied. "I've got three problems. First, I've got a young girl pressurising me into marriage; second, I've got a married man gunning for me for seducing his wife, and third, my relationship with a thirty-nine year old lady has developed into a 'hell-hath-no-fury-like-a-woman-scorned' situation. For an instant he stare at me wide eyed.

"By god, you never do things by half, do you? What do you want me to do?"

"Sir, please...an immediate posting." He pondered for a while then, with a sigh, he said,

"I think you're right. I'll see what I can do. Report here, same time tomorrow morning."

It was the first and only time I have ever asked a favour of a senior officer and all day and night I was on tenter hooks praying that he could find me somewhere far enough away for safety.

At nine the next morning, he called me in. "Got any Court commitments or other outstanding work?" he asked. Since I hated hanging around at Courts, I always took subordinates with me to act as witnesses, so Court appearances never presented a problem.

"None, Sir," I replied.

"Well, you're in luck," he said, smiling. "I've spoken to Leslie, the staff Officer at head-quarters. It so happens that an emergency has developed in the Marsabit area and we reckon you'll do for the job. When can you be ready?"

Marsabit, I knew was in the Northern Frontier District and I had heard mess talk about the wild, almost uninhabited, desert terrain around it. To me it was a dream fulfilled and I was overjoyed with the posting. "Immediately, sir," I replied and breathed a gigantic sigh of relief.

I dreaded breaking the news to Sandra whom, I suddenly began to suspect, may be pregnant, but knew that I couldn't just leave without, at least, attempting to explain myself. In the event, she took it very calmly. She was not pregnant she said and seemed to resign herself to my sudden departure with no ill feeling.

Some weeks previously, I had made the decision to part with my old Chevrolet. The faults which were present when I left Eldoret had grown worse and I began to fear that the engine on its dodgy mountings would soon part company with the vehicle altogether. Besides, it didn't seem quite proper that such a dangerous and illegal vehicle should be driven by the head of the Traffic Department. Although I considered it, the expense of repairing the old bus would have been excessive so, reluctantly, I let it go and bought instead, a 1934 American open-topped Ford V8 Coupe.

All the following day, I spent packing and stowing my belongings into the Ford. including several things which I considered might be necessary in the country to which I was heading. Some items, I had to obtain in a rush from various parts of town owing to the urgent nature of my departure but, by evening, I had the car loaded high with all the essentials. I had enough clothing, my shotgun, light and heavy rifles, two revolvers, hundreds of rounds of ammunition, two hunting knives, a torch, some spare batteries, and, because rumour had it that the desert produced a glare akin to the snows of the Arctic, I took two pairs of sunglasses. I took toiletries and the minimum of bedding. For medical supplies, a few bandages, some quinine, aspirin and a little pure carbolic acid in case of wounds. I had been told that if the acid were poured directly into the wound, it would penetrate deeply enough to kill any germs and so prevent blood poisoning. My kitchen-ware consisted of a few chop boxes with crockery, cutlery and cooking pots sufficient for just myself. For the car, I took spare fuel, water, oil and inner-tubes and this time, I included a few non-repairable spares – fuel pump diaphragm, fan belt, distributor cap and two road spring main leaves. I also took my small Kodak vest pocket camera, several spools of film and a marching compass, leaving just about enough room for Ajuro and his little bundle. The rest of my few possessions, I left in storage, to be collected – heaven knows when.

By the time I was done, I felt supremely confident that I was equipped for any emergency that this new adventure could throw at me.

Late that evening, I handed over the Traffic Department to my Asian deputy and very early the next morning, Ajuro and I left the coast for Nairobi, Marsabit and the Northern Frontier District.

The Magical Northern Frontier

I was travelling into a different world and I knew it. The little I had learned from chatter in the mess, told me that the Northern Frontier was a vast, arid, empty region; no roads, no towns, no comforts, no parties, no women; in fact a place where a white man had to call upon all his resources of self-reliance and self-preservation just to survive. For me, this was a dream come true, the kind of adventure for which I had yearned since boyhood and, at last, I was on my way.

Ajuro, I'm certain, was not filled with the same enthusiasm. His preference was for a town, a comfortable room, running water and the society of like-minded souls but he remained silent and, at least for the time being, he was content to follow me where ever I went.

We drove the dusty and, by now, familiar road inland from the coast and, way after dark, reached a point some sixty miles short of Nairobi in the heart of game country. I pulled off the road and, as we made our beds on the ground beside the car, the air was filled with the fantastic sounds of the animals as they went about their nightly business. Dawn revealed that, not only were there large herds of plains game grazing within a hundred yards of our position and, in the distance, vultures were dropping down on what would certainly have been the remains of a lion kill but also, nearby, a couple of Rhino browsed the bush unaware of our presence. I was tempted to shoot one since, at that time, I had not yet shot a Rhino, but duty prevailed, much to Ajuro's relief, and we pressed on towards Nairobi.

Completing the three hundred and thirty miles journey to Nairobi from the coast, I went straight to Police Headquarters and reported my arrival to the Staff Officer.

"Ah, Mills," he said, raising his eyebrows. "You made good time."

"Yes, sir," I replied, seeing an opportunity to score a few points. "I was told it was urgent." For the next hour or two he briefed me on my posting and the area in which I would serve.

I would be attached to the North West District of Marsabit which was experiencing increasing problems with raiders from Ethiopia and Sudan who would cross the border and commit terrible slaughter and mutilation among our own tribal groups. Not that the raids were entirely one-sided, warriors from our side would, in turn, cross the border to carry out equally horrific vengeance attacks.

Inter-tribal rivalry of some sort or another had been going on in the area for hundreds - even thousands of years but, in the face of a sudden increase in this murderous activity, the authorities had decided that the time had come to make a determined effort to stamp it out. It had been decided that this "battle area", consisting of some thirty-five thousand square miles of mostly trackless desert and scrub, was to be called 'The North Horr Detachment' and would be under the overall command of the Marsabit District Headquarters.

Marsabit was controlled by a District Administrative Officer with a handful of tribal police, called Dubas, and a Superintendent who commanded some three hundred and fifty African Kenya Police. These latter were split up into 14 platoons each consisting of a Sergeant, a Corporal and twenty-three Constables and it was a number of these platoons that I was to command.

Each platoon went out on patrol duty for three months at time and were transported by lorry, together with sufficient rations and supplies, to one of several border strong-points from where they became mobile by camel. Each platoon had a riding camel section consisting of a Corporal and five Constables mounted on camels which were owned and trained by the Police. To these were added sufficient baggage camels to carry enough food, water and weapons for the platoon's anticipated activities. The baggage camels were recruited, together with their owners from local nomadic tribes, each owner providing and leading, by a rope attached to the lower jaw of the first one, a string of four camels. At times, a platoon would take on as many as forty or fifty baggage camels.

Border strong points were situated at, or near to, water holes which were scattered at rare intervals in the region of the border. A platoon would dig in behind rock defences and despatch scouting parties to seek information about raiding parties and to locate their tracks if possible. For about half the time, the whole platoon would leave the strong point on long-range patrol with the objective of intercepting raiding parties who would sometimes penetrate as far as one hundred and fifty miles south of the border, or to chase and engage those who had already slipped through the net and massacred some of our tribesmen. It all sounded like 'Cowboy and Indian' stuff and I was eager to get on with it.

At this point, the Staff Officer smiled and beathed a sigh indicating his satisfaction that he had told me sufficient for the time being, the rest, I would have to find out for myself. No doubt too, he had been assessing my fitness for the job and my ability to withstand the hardships that he knew lay ahead of me.

"Well Mills," he said, standing. "You'd better be on your way." And he dismissed me with a wave of the hand.

As I left Police Headquarters, I considered reporting to Government House and signing the visitors' book as was the tradition, but decided to postpone it until the next time I visited Nairobi and had actually achieved something worthwhile.

I promptly left Nairobi and heading North, drove through Thika and Marang'a and, as we approached Nyeri I could see, rising to the west, the forested heights of the Aberdares where I had stayed with the Blain family and had my first taste of this magnificent country. Yet further north, to the East of the road approaching Nanyuki, the massive, snow capped bulk of Mount Kenya towered impressively above us.

Late that same evening we drove into Isiolo, the Administrative Headquarters of the Northern Frontier District where I reported to the Superintendent of Police who put me up for the night and who hastened me on my way early the following morning.

Isiolo was the headquarters of the Provincial Commissioner in charge of the Northern Frontier District. Also stationed there were a Superintendent of Police and his assistant, a District Commissioner, a game warden (George Adamson of 'Born Free' fame) and was, at the time, the only centre which permitted the wives of British officials to reside with them. North of Isiolo, for a distance of 400 miles to the Ethiopian border, lay a vast empty area containing every kind of desert and scrubland which was administered from district headquarters located at Garissa, Wajir, Mandera, Marsabit, Moyale and Lodwar. The mere sprinkling of forces they commanded had to cover the entire area from the Indian Ocean to the Uganda border, a border of over a thousand miles.

137

After a good nights rest and a decent breakfast, and as I prepared to take the road again and head north on the last leg of my journey to Marsabit, the Superintendent confided in me that Marsabit had been plaguing him for ages for an extra officer. "Perhaps now, they'll get off my back," he chuckled. "By the way," he continued, "I'd leave your car and take the police lorry from here on if I were you." I thanked him, but declined the offer, preferring to rely on my old Ford since it had brought me so far without problems.

I soon regretted my decision. The appalling road conditions forced me to drive slowly preventing adequate cooling and that, coupled with the heat of the afternoon sun, caused the radiator to boil constantly. I also ran the engine short of oil and, still forty miles short of Marsabit, in the heart of the Kaisut Desert the inevitable happened, a piston smashed through the side of the cylinder block.

By pure good fortune, a Government Stock Control Officer was travelling this normally deserted road some way behind me and, only a couple of hours after I had broken down, his lorry came rumbling into view. We transferred my possessions and, abandoning the Ford at the roadside, continued the journey, arriving in Marsabit just as darkness fell.

Marsabit is situated on top of a five and half thousand foot high mountain which sticks up like a gigantic mole hill from the centre of flaming desert country. The upper levels are clothed in lush forest and, much to my delight, abundant big game inhabits the mountain, especially in the dry season. Compared with the desert below, the climate is heavenly; pleasantly warm by day and cold at night calling for fires to be lit.

"About time," was the unceremonious greeting I received from the Divisional Police Superintendent when I reported to him the next morning. "I want you to get up to North Horr immediately. We've had information that a band of armed Habbash horsemen are raising hell in the area." Apparently, I was to be given no time at all to settle in or to receive a briefing on the conditions in the region. "I have a lorry and men standing by," he snapped. "Get up there quickly and try to locate and engage them." He gave me no more information, just handed me a slim file containing a brief history of the Marsabit district and added, "Up there, any black we spot armed with a rifle, we shoot on sight." With this, I saluted, turned on my heel and left. In due course, I would add a bit more history to that slim file.

In the courtyard below, the lorry waited filled with my small party of Police and festooned with dripping canvas water carriers. I climbed aboard and, with the party belting out their fighting songs to impress the women-folk they were leaving behind, we set off into the darkness.

For just a moment, I felt a twinge of apprehension; I knew virtually nothing of the terrain, the local customs, the practices to be followed or, for that matter, anything else about the area and I had been thrown in at the deep end. Ajuro too, was worried. He sat beside me nervously clutching his bundle, eyes wide and, no doubt, wondering what horrors were about to leap at him out of the night. But then, I told myself, I was in charge of this little 'army' and whatever we were about to encounter, we could handle, and I thought no more about it.

This little I had learned, from studying maps while stationed in Mombasa; North Horr stood at the north-western edge of the Chalbi Desert, at the centre of which lay a dried-up lake bed. The route from Marsabit to North Horr crossed the desert and the lake bed, passing a couple of open water holes at Karawe and Warump on the way. To the east lay the Huri Hills and the Dida Galgalu Desert, to the south, the Koroli Desert and the looming bulk of Mount Kulal and to the west, the shores of Lake Rudolf.

Lake Rudolf had been the objective of an expedition which left the coast in 1886 and travelled to the southern tip of the lake (then known to the Turkana people as 'Embasso Narok', the Black Lake). The expedition, some 700 strong, travelled up country via Nairobi and, on the way, attempted to scale, the hitherto unclimbed, Mount Kenya. Although they came within 3000 metres, they were forced back by freezing weather and the lack of proper equipment for such a difficult task and failed to reach the summit.

The expedition's leader, a wealthy Austro-Hungarian named Count Samuel Teleki von Szek, named the lake 'Rudolf' after the murdered son of his Emperor, Leopold II and then continued up the eastern shore past Mount Kulal which, the expedition's reporter said, was 'sanded smooth two or three times a day by 80 mph winds'.

Eventually, the expedition reached the northern end of the lake and encountered the Gelubba people who lived around the delta region where the River Omo feeds into the lake. Here, the expedition's reporter describes a meeting with one of the local Gelubba tribal chiefs and it was this very chief who I was to meet some years later, being the first white man he had encountered since meeting Count Teleki von Szek in 1887.

Stretching away to the north of the base at North Horr, right to the border with Ethiopia and beyond, lay empty, sandy, semi desert and it was here, it seems, that the worst of the inter-tribal warfare had suddenly escalated.

We made our way slowly down the steep, rough tracks which descended Marsabit's four thousand foot escarpment to the desert below and drove off into the night across the desert and the dried-up lake bed which formed the terrain between Marsabit and our destination at North Horr. For the most part, we navigated by the stars because no previous vehicle tracks were evident in the darkness that surrounded us.

A few of hours before dawn we drew to a halt and the Corporal in charge came to me and saluted. "All right to camp here, sir?"

"I suppose so," I said, slightly puzzled. "But surely, we must be quite close to North Horr."

"Yes, sir," he replied, looking at me as if I were out of my senses. "But it's still dark." Here, I learned my first and perhaps, most valuable lesson of the Northern Frontier District - never, never enter a base camp, frontier strong point or for that matter, any camp site, whether travelling by vehicle, on foot or by camel - after sunset. To do so would instantly bring down upon you a hail of withering fire from vigilant and nervous sentries. We posted sentries and camped on the lake bed around the lorry.

Just before dawn, we de-camped and drove the last ten miles, arriving at North Horr as the sun began to rise above the desert to the east of us.

I wasn't expecting North Horr to be much of a place, but as we approached, I saw that it was even less of a establishment than I had imagined; just an open water hole beside a low sandy bluff on top of which stood the fort - a sand-bag construction surrounded by barbed wire. A hundred yards or so to the west, stood a small collection of Doum Palm Bandas, (wooden huts), surrounded by a ring of white-washed stones and this I took to be the Police barracks. From the highest part of the fort jutted a rickety pole on top of which a Police flag fluttered proudly in the morning breeze.

As we approached, the blare of a bugle drifted across the intervening desert sounding the alarm and calling all the fort's personnel to action stations. There followed a great hullabaloo as the full compliment of the base, in khaki and tepees, raced to man the defences, snapping bayonets onto their rifles as they ran.

My driver halted the lorry just short of the perimeter defences and waited. After a short pause, the base's Senior Sergeant emerged from the fort's entrance and, with a ring of steel blades glinting in the rising sun behind him, marched stiffly towards us. He was tall with impressive shoulders and eyes like black diamonds. He approached, halted and having identified us, snapped me a smart salute.

"Tamaam sir," he barked, and standing rigidly to attention, he proceeded, rapid fire, to give me a list of all the base's current assets. "Three Sergeants, eight Corporals, fifty-two Constables, sixty-three rifles, eighteen thousand and ten rounds of ammunition, twelve riding camels, forty baggage camels, eight copper water barrimels (carried by camels), two tribal elders present in camp." He paused only for breath, and then, "Three platoons, each of two NCO's and twenty three Constables, patrolling the border a hundred and fifty miles to the north. Others at Marsabit, resting, sir!" This was "Tamaam", a complete status report which inevitably followed first contact with any active unit on the frontier. The Sergeant ended by saying that there was no bad news and only two men to face disciplinary action. He had done his bit and now I was in charge. From now on, if anything went amiss, it would be my responsibility. He snapped me a final salute and remained rigidly at attention awaiting my orders.

It was a moment when I began to realise the enormous weight of my new responsibilities. Here I was, not yet twenty-four, having just travelled seven hundred and fifty miles in the last eighty hours across all manner of wild terrain from the relative comfort of the civilised east coast, to find myself suddenly in operational command of some two hundred and forty armed men campaigning in hostile desert in this, the most isolated and far-flung outpost of the Empire. I was, to say the least of it, a little nervous. But, of course, I couldn't show it. Instructing the Senior Sergeant to stand down the defences, I ordered him to report to me again in two hours time.

In anticipation of the imminent arrival of a new officer, the Senior Sergeant had ordered his men to build a Banda close to the barbed wire defences surrounding the fort for my sleeping quarters. This was a small circular hut constructed of local Doum Palm trunks with fronds forming the thatched roof and with a few planks placed on the earth floor. In the event, I discovered that poisonous sand snakes had a habit of making their home under the plank floor so I decided the safest policy was to sleep out in the open. I had my possessions unloaded from the lorry and carried into the Banda.

Two hours later, to the minute, the Senior Sergeant reported to me as ordered and I asked him first to take me on a tour of the base, after which we sat down for a discussion on the region and its troubles. He proved to be a frontier tribesman with good local knowledge and a great deal of valuable experience in the region so, despite the fact that as a white officer, I was supposed to be super-human, I decided to 'come clean' with him concerning my own inexperience.

I had, I told him, no knowledge of the area, of its people or their customs, I didn't even have an accurate map of the District; I was entirely ignorant of local Police methods and tactics and requested him to give me guidance and back-up for a few days at least. He was very patient and understanding and suggested that, in a couple of days time, we should make a foot safari to a frontier base called Dukana. This, he said, would serve as a good introduction to the command. I readily agreed to the idea and thanked him for his tolerance. Next, I mentioned the Marsabit Superintendent's orders concerning the Habbash raiders and asked him if he'd heard anything of their whereabouts.

"Not a word, Effendi," he replied.

'Good,' I thought. 'Then, sod 'em. If the Superintendent wants to come and chase 'em, he can. I'm sure as hell not going to.'

At dawn, three days later, the Senior Sergeant reported to me at my Banda "Safari tyari, Effendi," he barked. (Safari ready, sir). This was a moment I had been keenly awaiting, my first venture on patrol. I had only one slight worry - I had never ridden, or even mounted a camel before and it was essential, in my position as commander that I maintain some vestige of dignity.

Lined up ready, under the command of another Sergeant, was a platoon of twenty-five men with the riding camel section already mounted and, behind them, loaded with all our necessary provisions and equipment, was a bunch of stinking baggage camels who's leaders were in a quarrelsome mood and seemed, at any moment, ready to knife each other. At the front stood a Corporal holding the rein of a very pale and ill-tempered looking camel. I glanced first at the Corporal and then at the camel. This, I thought, must be for me and my apprehension grew.

Guessing that I hadn't the slightest idea how to mount a camel, the Corporal discreetly twisted its lower jaw until it howled, then yelled 'Ho, ho!' whereupon, it sank meekly to the ground. He then stood on its folded foreleg and said, "Tyari, Effendi." and I stepped forward to mount. "Stand on his left knee," he whispered. "And keep your weight on until your well over the saddle." I soon learned that the second you relieved your weight from his leg, the beast would shoot up like a jack-in-a-box and if you weren't in the saddle before then, you'd be flat on your back in the sand.

Once mounted, with a rifle tucked into the rifle bucket slung beneath the saddle and my trusty .45 revolver, I was ready to go, so, raising my arm cavalry-like, I shouted 'Forward!' and we were off.

After a few hundred yards, I felt confident enough with the camel's swinging paces to turn my head and scrutinise the unit on the move and all seemed well. As I turned, I caught sight of my servant Ajuro who, unfortunately for him, had to walk with the foot men. He stumbled uncomfortably along beside the baggage camel on which our chop boxes were slung, looking very dejected. Now, forced to live in this desolate region so far from the civilised life he loved, I think he had given up all hope of a prolonged life and had resigned himself to an early and miserable fate.

In addition to chop boxes, and weapons, I took with me only a camp bed, a ground sheet and a folding table and chair. In fact, during the whole of my time in the Northern Frontier District, I never did carry a tent, considering it to be an unnecessary burden. Instead, I slept in the open and if it rained, which it very occasionally did, Ajuro would rise and flick the ground sheet over the camp bed allowing me to remain reasonably dry.

This first Safari was to last for twelve days giving me a great opportunity to learn something of the terrain in which we operated and to experience at first hand the rigours of the survival in the desert which, by day, baked under a remorseless sun and, by night, chilled you to the marrow.

The Senior Sergeant taught me, very discreetly and diplomatically, some of the ways of the desert patrol; how best to select a safe camp site, how to mount effective sentries, how to use the contours of the land to travel unnoticed, how to move unheard through the thorn bush, oh, and a host of other vital instruction, including the routine of 'The Dawn Stand-to' and what action to take if the enemy were sighted or mounted a sudden attack.

By the time we returned to North Horr, I felt confident enough to take proper control of my command and even to start throwing my weight around a bit.

Close by the North Horr base there were two large, yellow sand hill, each about a thousand yards long at the base and three hundred feet high. The ground on which they stood was course, black shale and, I was told, the hills slowly shifted in the persistent strong winds which blew sand up the windward side and down the other, although this phenomenon was seldom seen to happen.

The idea that two such large features of the landscape could possibly move intrigued me, so, not long after I arrived at the base, I had a large wooden stake driven into the ground at the base of one of them and occasionally checked to see if any movement had taken place. By the time my tour of duty in Northern Frontier District was over, the hills had moved nine feet.

A few weeks after the first Safari, an incident was to occur which was to convince the men under my command that I was in touch with the supernatural and thus, endow me with considerable prestige.

The Senior Sergeant came to me one morning with the suggestion that a company parade should take place for my inspection and said it should be organised for the following afternoon. I just happened to know that a total eclipse of the sun was due to take place at the very time the parade was to take place.

"No, Sergeant," I said. "Arrange it for the morning after. You see, my God is going to take away the sun and the afternoon will be dark."

He retreated to the barrack lines and I could see huddles of men in excited conversation who cast many secret glances in my direction. 'Another mad white man,' they were thinking.

Dead on cue, at 2.30 the following afternoon, the moon commenced its slow passage across the face of the sun and in due course the shining glare of the desert turned pitch dark. In an instant, the Sergeant raced across from the barracks, saluted and in a state of high excitement, stammered, "Sir, the sun has gone, it's gone dark. What do we do?"

"Don't worry, Sergeant," I replied in a slow, priest-like voice. "I've asked my God to give the sun back to us and I'm sure he will." Slowly, the moon slid by and day-light returned leaving the company open-mouthed with wonder. In those days, such phenomena had an electric effect on primitive peoples and much camp-fire talk ensued - and probably lives on in legend to this day. My reputation was established.

For the next few months, I remained at North Horr, sending out patrols into the more troubled areas way to the north and occasionally venturing forth with them myself. Always, whenever we selected camp sites in the forward, danger areas, we would carefully prepare the site before bedding down for the night. Unseen, we would scrape holes in the sand behind rocks and any convenient cover we could find. Then, about an hour before

144

dawn, we would 'Stand to' and secrete ourselves in the holes with arms ready to hand, bayonets fixed and one up the spout.

The favourite tactic of raiders such as the Shangilla was always the sudden dawn attack and we had no intention of being taken by surprise. Strangely, during the whole of the three years I spent in the Northern Frontier District, we were never attacked in camp. Partially, I believe, due to the fact that we mounted efficient sentries and our ability to choose good, defendable camp sites.

Primitive tribesmen of the region such as the Gelubba were extremely dangerous in combat owing to the belief, promulgated by their witch doctors, that, if they were fired upon, the bullets would turn to water and leave them unharmed. Thus, a charging warrior may see his companions fall on either side, but he, being still alive would persist in the belief and press on with his attack.

Although the area for a distance of about a hundred and twenty miles south of the border was an exclusion zone into which local, friendly tribes (tame tribes, as we called them), were forbidden to enter, they were mostly nomadic and inevitably did. On one long patrol, we encountered the tracks of a Shangilla scouting party in the vicinity of a nomad encampment and decided to try to engage them. For two or three days and nights, we stayed close by, encircling the camp with a ring of defensive positions in the hope that the Shangilla would attack but, for two days and nights, all was quiet. At dawn on the third morning, we lay vigilant in our 'scrapes' and all around I heard the faint click of rifle bolts as the men readied their weapons for the onslaught. I had loosened my .45 in its holster and my finger was on the trigger of a sub-machine gun. Beside me lay a ten shot .303 with one extra round up the spout. We were ready.

"Sir," the voice of my Sergeant, lying alongside me. "To the North. Enemy!" Suddenly, screams and shouts broke out and I could see in the dim early light a large group of figures running and leaping in the air as they rapidly approached the camp. 'Come on you bastards,' I thought. 'We'll do for the lot of you.'

"No one fire until I do!" I yelled and levelled my sights on the nearest of the bunch as they bounded towards us. By the time the range had closed to a hundred yards, I was ready to fire and began to squeeze the trigger when suddenly, the Sergeant raised his arm.

"Sir, stop!" he bellowed. "They're ours." My heart was racing but, heeding his warning, I held off and watched as the warriors got nearer, still yelling and dancing. The Sergeant sat up and, with a great sigh of relief, said,

"They're 'tame', returning from a raid of their own over the border. They're "Kula Amoring"." (throwing screaming fits to demonstrate their success). Thank god I didn't open fire. Had I done so, and my men had followed suit as ordered, I reckon we'd have killed at least thirty-five of them and that wouldn't have gone down too well with the rest of the 'tame' tribes-people we were supposed to protect.

In this remote region we were very isolated, having no means of communication between ourselves and headquarters in Marsabit and, as Police Commander I was left very much to my own devices, reporting to them whatever I considered important and only when I considered it necessary. During the first three year spell I spent in the Northern Frontier District, having no official books in which to make entries, I kept no records other than a diary of events and reported, only at rare intervals, those things which I considered would prove useful later. Generally, I would submit a report about six months after the event it referred to, and then, I wrote it in a manner which would lead to consideration for commendations or awards for members of my force.

Some two years after I first arrived in the Northern Frontier District, headquarters decided that it was time to experiment with some sort of radio communication and each force was issued with an old military Type 'twenty two' Morse transmitter. At times, it could be quite useful but more often than not, it allowed HQ to interfere with my procedures so, if they got difficult, I would simply go off the air.

So complete was our isolation that, for one period of seven months, I saw no other European and spoke no English and once went nine weeks eating only game meat and maize, having no tea, coffee, wheat flour, milk or any fats or oils.

The first three months after my arrival at North Horr, I spent touring the area of the frontier which lay under my command, visiting all my platoons and the border strong points and assessing our problems and our strengths. Where the terrain allowed it, I travel by vehicle, failing that, by camel and even on foot.

My vehicle was a short wheel based, hard sprung, two-ton Ford V8 lorry with no doors on the cab so that we could de-bus rapidly if ambushed and with back wheels much larger than the front to allow an easier passage over hot, loose sand and the like. I also had a rifle bucket installed to the right of the steering wheel to keep the weapon close to hand in case of sudden, unexpected attack.

Having on several occasions in the past, and in less hostile territory than this, been troubled by vehicle breakdown, I determined to take precautions and loaded all the gear I could find against the day when it happened again. I carried drums of water and petrol, spare springs, cylinder heads, rear axle half-shafts, tyres, tubes, distributor cap, rotor arm, fan belts, spare battery, charger cut-out, plugs, radiator hoses, universal joints and many other non-repairable parts, not to mention a mass of odd nuts and bolts, bits of wire and tools. To break down on the frontier could prove lethal, and perhaps, only for the lack of some small tool or item of repair. Despite its registered capacity, the addition of all this 'essential' equipment meant that the lorry seldom travelled with less than a three and a half ton load.

I took to travelling, whether by vehicle or by camel, with a personal escort consisting of a Sergeant, a Corporal and thirteen Constables. This was ten men short of that which headquarters considered a minimum force for safety in the forward areas, but I considered that the greater mobility afforded by my slimmed-down force was well worth the risk. When on camel safari, myself and six of the men were camel mounted while the rest went on foot.

Travelling by lorry could prove difficult. Though we navigated the desert by compass trying to follow contours and catchment areas, it was often necessary to detour miles and miles off course to find safe routes up or down escarpments and across dry river beds or other natural barriers and though, over time, we striped the desert with vehicle tracks, it was never hard to get lost.

Throughout the District we were seldom more than forty-five miles from a water hole, however, this didn't necessarily mean that you were certain of obtaining water. First you had to find the well and even when you did, it might be dry.

First excavated, possibly in biblical times or even earlier by long forgotten ancestors of the local nomads, the water holes were generally small and often very deep and since most of them had little or no vegetation around them, you could pass close by and not spot them.

Occasionally, there would be a member of my party, and sometimes a local tribes-man brought along as a scout, who claimed to know the way to a particular water hole but all too often they would prove useless and get us hopelessly lost.

147

Sand Grouse, which were abundant in the desert areas, often proved useful in guiding you to open water pools some of which were more or less permanent, while others, merely temporary, caused by isolated local showers; or to 'sand rivers' which flowed for just a few hours following storms at their source, possibly hundreds of miles away. Just after dawn, flocks containing up to several hundred grouse would flight into these pools to fill their bellies and, if they had chicks, their breast feathers, with water to fortify themselves and their young against the searing heat of the day. Follow their flight lines and you would be certain to find water but it could be as much as fifty miles or more away.

Although, as I have already mentioned, a strip of land stretching 120 miles south from the border, was declared a prohibited area which our tribes-people were forbidden to enter, they were nomadic and inevitably did, especially if they had heard that rain had fallen in the area. Almost as inevitably, they were attacked by Gelubba raiders and others who crossed the border. These attacks would lead to counter raids and to a continuation of a chain of events which had persisted for hundreds, even thousands, of years.

The motives for the constant raiding were neither religious nor territorial, nor was it principally slavery, even though young girls and boys were sometimes taken for the purpose. These were warrior people intent on an enjoyable outing while proving their manhood and impressing their women-folk with their bravery in battle.

Further North

Having spent my first few months touring the territory and gradually getting to know its terrain and its problems, I came to the conclusion that, despite the increased mobility afforded by my slimmed-down patrol, we were still too slow arriving at a trouble spot. Often, I would hear rumours that a band of Gelubba or Shangilla raiders had crossed the border and were on the prowl, but by the time we had travelled north, they had struck their target and, triumphant, had fled back to the safety of their own land. North Horr was too far south of the main problem areas so, ignoring the possible risks and my orders from Headquarters, I decided to get nearer to the action.

I ordered two platoons to make ready complete with sufficient supplies and equipment for a prolonged absence. Next, I detailed the Senior Sergeant to recruit a party of local tribesmen to act as labourers to clear rocks and bush to create a track for the vehicle. Then we set off north to establish a forward base somewhere between North Horr and the border.

The journey was arduous and not without danger since the terrain was unknown. Occasionally, we were forced to cross a dry river bed and, where they were steep and not too high, we dug away the banks to make a slope shallow enough for the lorry to negotiate. Some fissures we encountered were narrow enough for a make-shift bridge which we constructed either from Doum Palm trunks or simply by heaping rocks into the crevasse until it came level with the banks.

Progress was slow but eventually the whole entourage arrived at Lug Banya, a dry river course at the northern tip of Lake Rudolf, (now Lake

Turkana). At this point the Omo River, who's source is in the mountains of central Ethiopia just west of Adis Ababa, flowed into the Lake through a long, densely forested delta most of which lies north of the border in Ethiopia. Not far to the west of the Omo lies the border with southern Sudan.

The area either side of the Omo River was the home-land of the Gelubba people, a loose collection of six groups who had no paramount chief and who had never been dominated or administered by any outside power, colonial or otherwise. With no knowledge of white supremacy in Africa and totally untouched by civilisation they existed in much the same way as they had since the dawn of time. They fell into two main divisions, each with its own chief and elders but with a common language; those to the west of the Omo were called Merille and those to the east, Gelubba.

These people had some peculiar customs including the drowning in the Omo of any twins that were born. Their principal occupation was stock herding which was carried out mainly by the young men of warrior age who would sleep at night on the ground amongst their animals to deter thieves.

The Gelubba, at least half of whom had fire arms, though mostly ancient French Fusil Gras purchased from Ethiopian Habbash traders for a few head of stock, were constantly raiding and were considered to be a damn nuisance to all their neighbours. Occasionally, for larger raids, warriors from several sections of the tribe would come together, but we had information that if all sections were to combine, they could field a formidable force some two-thousand strong. Even when retreating during an engagement they presented considerable danger to their pursuers by holding their guns over their shoulders pointing backwards and, while still running, press the trigger.

Although further north than I had first intended, it was here at Banya, one mile south of the tip of Lake Rudolf and close to its eastern shore, that I decided to establish a fort. The few maps of the area that existed showed considerable variation as to the exact position of the Kenya/Ethiopia border but one thing was certain, Banya was just about on that border.

I set all hands to cutting down the squat thorn bushes which grew in profusion on the area I had chosen. This opened up a clear field of fire all round and the thorns we used as a perimeter defensive barrier in lieu of barbed wire. At the centre of the cleared area, we dug holes in the sand to use both as defensive positions and to sleep in and, finally, we set up bent old thorn tree trunks from which we flew the Police flag and the Union Jack.

Once we were settled and in a satisfactory defensive position, I took stock of our situation. The site I had chosen for the fort was just six miles south of the nearest Gelubba village, a good deal nearer than we had been at North Horr and when trouble broke out here, we would on the spot to put a stop to it; a far more satisfactory state of affairs, I thought.

Less than 2000 feet above sea level and so far inland that it received hardly any rain at all, the terrain around Banya was just about the hottest, most inhospitable place I had ever visited.

On pretty well every day of the year, it was plagued by hot, gale-force winds which developed about midday and lasted till dusk. Frequently, these winds would stir up 'dust devils', mini tornadoes with core wind speeds of over a hundred miles an hour which often did considerable damage within encampments. Dust devils would suddenly form and then meander on an unpredictable course sometimes rapidly and sometimes just creeping along. At times they would become stationary and would excavate a hole in the ground of considerable proportions, occasionally uprooting a thorn tree so that, after it subsided, the air would be filled with falling sand and debris.

At times, the nights could be cold but, for an hour and a half after dawn, the temperature and the quality of the atmosphere were a heavenly respite, then the daily inferno would start. An hour or so later you were dehydrated and could sweat no more and could brush the white residue of salt from your arms and legs. We had never heard of the need to replace salt lost through sweating and salt tablets were just not available.

Prevailing winds came from the west across the surface of Lake Rudolf and would force water ahead of them causing a rise in level along the eastern shore. Since most of the land to the east had, in prehistoric times, been a part of the lake, the land was little higher than the lake itself so each afternoon, large areas of land were quickly flooded to a depth of several feet. With the water came some of the lake's inhabitants intent on sunning themselves in the newly formed shallows. Crocodile, Nile Perch, some over a hundred pound in weight, Barbel and Tilapia were often to be found and frequently, we would wade about in the water and shoot them to provide a welcome addition to our diet.

Among the many annoying pests that either flew or crawled upon the earth, there was one which I found particularly aggravating, due partly to its painful bite and partly to its unnerving persistence - the Camel Fly. A sandy coloured insect similar to a large wasp, you were seldom aware of its approach until suddenly you felt its vicious bite. Continually on the prowl for blood, they were a constant nuisance and no matter how hard I swatted them, I never seemed to kill them or even cause them much injury and back they would come for more blood. Finally, in desperation, I would catch them, pull their wings of and throw them away. As often as not, finding that they could no longer fly, they would crawl across the ground and up your leg to draw more blood.

The Gelubba knew nothing of national boundaries. As far as they were concerned, we were hostile enemy invaders who had come to occupy their homeland and, at any moment, I feared a sudden attack by large numbers of them. My party, being only fifty strong, could easily have been overwhelmed and the immediate objective, of curtailing their murderous raiding activities would be lost. I needed a stratagem, a way of impressing upon them that we were invincible and by that, establish our superiority over them. As ever, God answered my prayers.

It was necessary for us to draw water daily from the lake and one morning, I accompanied the water detail, leading a group of camels down to the shore. Suddenly, we sighted a small Gelubba warrior party, some armed with rifles, creeping through the thick bush quite close to us. It soon became obvious that their intentions were less than friendly, in fact they were about to attack us and, within seconds, came screaming out of the bush towards us. We immediately opened fire and there was dust, confusion and bodies flying in every direction. One warrior, armed with a rifle and brandishing unsheathed wrist knives, lunged at me but a fraction of a second before he could slash my stomach open, I downed him with a shot from my .45. The skirmish was over almost as quickly as it had started with the surviving Gelubba fleeing and disappearing into the bush like rabbits with their tails on fire. Anticipating reprisal attacks, we strengthened our defences and in future, instead of camels, we used the lorry to draw water.

It transpired that the attacker I had killed was the cousin of a local Gelubba chief and it seemed that, since he was both well related and a renowned warrior amongst his clan, his death at our hands had made a deep impression on his people. A few days later a group of unarmed Gelubba elders approached the fort and as we sat down to talk, with the aid of some of our 'tame' tribesmen who had some language similarities, I determined to drive home the message that we were in charge and we would stand no nonsense; in essence, I told them to behave and obey orders or we'd massacre them.

I made one particular point which was aimed at preserving the day-to-day well-being of myself, my men and our animals, that was, to stop watering their stock within sight of where we drew our water because their cattle churned up mud and fouled our water. If they continued, I told them, I would set fire to the lake.

They didn't stop so, after a few days, I took a party to the lake at watering time and waited until we saw the Gelubba with their stock approaching through the distant haze whereupon, we emptied a forty gallon drum of petrol onto the water. We retreated into the bush then, when the Gelubba were only a few hundred yards away, I fired a couple of tracer rounds into the lake.

The result surprised even me - a few flashes and then, Whoosh! a massive sheet of flame spread over a vast area, topped my an enormous cloud of black smoke. The Gelubba herdsmen screamed, jumped in the air and took off like the devil was after them. The fire burned for a long time ending as a vast sheet of flame burning a few feet above the lake's surface; rising petrol fumes, I suppose.

Later, we learned that this little exercise had been a resounding success and had gained me the reputation amongst the tribe of being a powerful medicine man who was capable of dangerous magic.

I could gather very little intelligence concerning the activities and the intentions of the Gelubba and despite the awe in which they evidently held me, I didn't trust them to behave as I had ordered them. After all, their habit of raiding and killing their neighbours was centuries old and wasn't going to be stopped in five minutes. So, in order to strengthen our position against their treachery, I withdrew two additional platoons from less troubled areas some distance away and ordered them up to Banya. Now, I was in a position to send out regular patrols without leaving Banya under strength.

Occasionally, our patrols would encounter raiding parties and immediately engage them killing a few and, from the blood stains we found, wounding more. But then, we would withdraw and allow them to collect their dead.

Although the Gelubba were the source of most of my present problems, the region around Banya was by no means the only trouble spot in my command area. It was vital therefore, that I keep in close touch with the rest of my force but without wireless communication, that was difficult.

I gave the matter some thought and lit upon the idea of using two-man, camel mounted parties as runners between my various forward platoons and strong points. They could move fast, carry their own supplies and were less vulnerable to attack than any other size party. As it turned out, they could cover around eighty miles over most terrain in twenty-four hours - not ideal, but the best that could be achieved given the circumstances.

News filtered through to me that a friend from my time in Eldoret had recently died from blood poisoning. Apparently, he had been trying to 'drill' a hole in a metal sheet by firing at it with his .303 rifle. A fragment of bullet had rebounded and penetrated his elbow and, within forty-eight hours, he was dead.

News of this incident gave me cause to think about my own medical situation. Extraordinary as it may seem now, we were not issued with any proper medical kit - not even a first-aid book and, being hundreds of miles from the nearest medical aid and in disease-ridden, dangerous locations, we were, to put it mildly, vulnerable. My father would have been appalled.

The medical supplies, which I had collected myself, consisted of Quinine, Castor Oil, Aspirin, a few bandages and that was about it. I did have some Aquaflavin for wounds and a little pure Carbolic acid as a last resort against blood poisoning but the possibility of serious wounds, Appendicitis and the like, didn't bear thinking about, but then, we were all young.

I had not been inoculated against typhoid, I carried nothing with which to treat dysentery nor did I have filters or purification tablets so a constant hazard to health was drinking water of which, conditions demanded, we needed a great deal. Open water holes and excavated wells were never clean, being contaminated with baboon droppings, snake droppings, mud and other unidentifiable detritus so I employed a method I had been taught using 'Andrews Little Liver Salts'. Stir a packet of the salts into a few gallons of contaminated water and the filth precipitates quicker than boiling and filtering. It may seem unscientific, but it worked - I'm still alive.

On long 'foot' patrols I usually walked in the morning, lay up for four or five hours during the worst heat of the day then rode my camel in the afternoon, so care of one's feet was important. Protecting the feet in socks and tough boots would seem to be wise but this could lead to all sorts of problems so I normally went barefoot in open sandals. If I hadn't walked far for some time, I would pre-harden my feet by soaking them in methylated spirits and the application of talcum powder at night helped to keep them in good condition.

The Gelubba had been considered by high command to be a threat to the western flank of our military forces moving against the Italians occupying Abyssinia, (Ethiopia), and it filtered through to me that a combined Police/Military punitive expedition was to be mounted against them. As a result, the Northern Frontier District (NFD) Police were, for a time, placed under military overall strategic command but, in the event, the advance of our forces into Abyssinia was so rapid that the manoeuvre was never implemented.

This temporary change in the structure of higher authority had very little effect on my own command other than, for several months, at regular monthly intervals, a military convoy would emerge out of the dust of the desert to deliver rations to my forward base at Banya for our own use and for distribution to my other forward bases. Mostly wooden boxes, each contained twenty-four tins of good old bully beef which we didn't need and didn't want. Most of my men were NFD Mohammedans and wouldn't eat beef that hadn't had its throat cut and been bled and besides, we had ample fresh meat from our own flocks of sheep and goats - but the wheels of the mighty military machine were turning and we couldn't stop them.

I concentrated all my bully beef supply at Banya and used the unopened boxes as bricks to reinforce the fort walls and build pill boxes. A couple of thicknesses stopped rifle bullets and I'm sure that when, in the distant future, archaeologists excavate the ancient site, it'll give 'em cause to ponder.

When out on patrol, we would drive sheep and goats ahead of us to kill as we needed meat, and these, we bought from 'tame' tribesmen further south and paid usually in trade goods which were far more attractive to the vendors in remote areas than money - the going rate for sheep and goats was about fifteen pence per beast. For this purpose we mostly carried bolts of plain white cloth which was much in demand in the area and suited our purposes very well.

Funny thing was, while driving the flock ahead of you, one animal, either sheep or goat, would always seem to take the lead and remained always out in front. When the furthest point of the journey was reached and you turned to head back for base, probably by quite a different route, this particular beast always seemed to know exactly which way to go. I think they possessed some sort of instinct rather like a homing pigeon.

At times, when on patrol, we would find signs of raiding parties at border water holes but no immediate signs of the raiders themselves. This set me to thinking that I ought to devise some kind of trap for them when next they returned. On patrols I had acquired some ammunition of the bores most used by the raiders and some of these I would doctor. I removed the bullet from the case, trebled the powder load using stick cordite from my heavy rifle ammunition then replaced the bullet. I would leave the doctored ammunition lying around the water hole for the raiders to find. The greatly increased muzzle pressure developed when these rounds were fired was more than sufficient to burst the breach of any rifle. Although I heard rumours of injuries, I was disappointed never to actually come across a raider with one hand or half his face missing.

Each morning I used to conduct sick parade but, whatever the alleged ailment, I was only able to offer one of the three medicines I had available; Quinine, Castor Oil or Aspirin.

One morning, all six reporting sick requested Quinine. My Orderly, however, being a resourceful chap, had seen two half bottles and poured one into the other. It seems that Quinine and Castor Oil are not a compatible mixture because, by the time I reached the third man with his dose, the first to have taken it collapsed in apparent agony. By the time I reached the fourth, the second went down, writhing. The remaining two declined my medicine so I gave them each an hour's pack drill.

In the early days of the occupation of Kenya, the Turkana tribe, who were cousins of the Gelubba and who's homeland was the west of Lake Rudolf, exercised a particular form of greeting to strangers arriving in their land. The young warriors would charge the strangers, yelling, leaping in the air and brandishing their spears. To them, this custom was a display of friendly greeting but to the newcomers it appeared to be a threat which unfortunately resulted in many Turkana being shot and killed. There were highly strained relations for years until their customs became better understood.

The main problem in dealing with Gelubba elders was that ultimately, they exercised little control over those of their tribe of the warrior age group. Friendly contact or agreement with elders was by no means a guarantee of peace. None of the countries on who's territories they lived, Ethiopia, Sudan or Kenya, had ever held dominion over them. They existed as they had always done since the dawn of time and I, I decided, would be hard-pressed, as an agent of civilisation, to have any lasting effect on their less desirable activities.

A year or so before my arrival in Banya, there had been a massacre by Gelubba of Gabbra and Rendille people, our main local 'tame' tribes who were the subject of cross-border raids by the Gelubba. Elders of the Gabbra and Rendille had agreed to meet the Gelubba elders near the border under a flag of truce to discuss ways of ending the bloodshed between them. Our administration was very suspicious of the intentions of the Gelubba and advised strongly against the meeting, but the Gabbra and Rendille elders went anyway.

The *baraza* (conference), convened as agreed, and for two days, there were heated discussions but no serious incidents. On the third day however, the Gelubba elders lost control over their warriors who proceeded to massacre all the Gabbra and Rendille elders. The scene of this horrific incident was close by my fort where the ground was littered with bleached skulls and thigh bones.

Some years later, before I finished this tour in the NFD, word passed to us that the Kenya Police had at last acquired its first aircraft, an Auster. Request was made that, at every Police base, a strip of ground, three-hundred yards long by fifty wide, should be cleared of trees, rocks and pig holes and be demarcated at each corner by a pile of white-washed rocks or similar for use as an airstrip.

I soon had an area cleared alongside the fort and for the white corner demarcations, we collected the bleached skulls and bones from the site of the massacre. In the event, I never did see an aircraft land there but, in any case, an Auster didn't have the range to reach Banya. Had it done so, I wonder whether His Majesty King George 6th would have approved of reports that his Empire's most far-flung outpost sported a bully beef fort and a human skull demarcated airstrip.

I established communications of a sort with a section of the Gelubba tribe who were encamped only six miles away from the fort by first, planting a pole from which flew a white flag, in a clearing two miles from them and placing under it a bolt of the white cloth we used as trade goods. Then, we erected another pole and white flag in a position five-hundred yards from our outer defences. The bolt of cloth disappeared and three days later, four unarmed Gelubba elders, driving a sheep before them, appeared and halted beneath the second pole. Accompanied by my Orderly, both of us visibly unarmed, I walked out to greet them.

157

I soon discovered that their form of greeting was to say 'Na Faya', to which one replied, 'Na Faya' and this was repeated three times. Then, hands were held and rubbed together before any meaningful discussion could start.

Conversation was impossible but by the use of improvised sign language we seemed able to express our thoughts adequately enough and after brief declarations of friendship and co-operation, the meeting was over and we went our separate ways, the elders to their encampment and us, my orderly driving the sheep they had given us, back to the fort.

After that first meeting, whenever we wanted to contact them, we simply hoisted a white flag on the two poles and, a couple of hours later unarmed elders would appear and await escort through our defences.

Wide spread and frequent patrolling of the area seemed to be the best method of controlling the activities of raiders but I was careful to avoid a predictable routine and always ordered personnel remaining at the fort to keep active to avoid encouraging an attack on a weakened garrison.

If I suspected that raiders were active in an area, we would lay up in ambush, sometimes for as long as a week behind some elevated ridge which overlooked flat country. In the clear air, we could see for many miles and would look out for dust, the flash of sunlight on a spear blade, smoke or, at night, the glow of fires. If something suspicious was sighted, a prolonged discussion would take place - what was it? Dust from stampeding game, or what? Where had it come from? Where was it heading? Then if I thought we were on to something, I would despatch a small party to investigate or, if it looked worthwhile, I'd take the whole patrol to intercept.

More often than not, these ambushes would end in a wild goose chase and, at best we would catch sight of Gelubba fleeing in the far distance. On the rare occasions that we got close enough and were able to exchange fire, the Gelubba would split up into small groups and take off in all directions. When they did, it was fatal to dissipate one's own force to follow each of the separate groups because the Gelubba would waste no time in re-forming and launching an attack if they thought they had the advantage over a small party.

On average, my men were good rifle shots though, strangely enough, most were more accurate at night than they were in daylight. This was because they tended to look straight at the target rather than through the sights on the same principle as bow and arrow shooting.

One day while out on patrol with a full platoon I was searching for a water hole which none of us had ever visited before, when we sighted what we thought was our objective way down on the plain, some one thousand five-hundred feet below us. It was late afternoon and I was tired and in great need of water so the prospect of travelling many more miles to find a gentle way down to the plain didn't appeal to me.

"We'll go down the slope," I said to my Sergeant. He peered over the edge in amazement and slowly shook his head.

"It's very steep and rocky sir. Too steep, I think for camels, especially loaded ones." I ran out of patience.

"Sergeant!" I yelled. "We're going down." And I rode my camel over the edge.

The next hour was for me was one of sheer terror. On a camel, the rider's head is some twelve to fifteen feet above the ground and when travelling down a slope, a camel doesn't squat like a horse but keeps its back legs straight, so when I looked down, while fighting not to be bounced over the animal's head, I could see the rough, stony ground where I would land if I fell, some forty feet below me. The poor beast slipped and skidded on the loose scree and instead of extending its front legs forwards to slow its progress, it stuck all four out sideways in desperate attempts to stabilise itself. It was obviously scared stiff - and, I can tell you, so was its rider.

My panicky attempts to slow the camel by pulling on one rein or the other, or both at once were useless. Half the time its head would twist right round to face me snapping and snarling and with its feet flying in all directions.

We travelled in this perilous fashion for the whole of the fifteen hundred feet, the camel almost rigid with fear and me frightened out of my wits lest I should be thrown and bounce, broken and bleeding all the way to the bottom. It was more than a sigh of relief that I breathed when, eventually, we made it to the plain below and it took all of the hour and a half, until the rest of the party had descended, for me to recover what little composure the embarrassment of the event would allow me.

When we reached it, the water hole which had been the objective of my perilous descent, turned out to contain bitter water which was quite undrinkable. The following morning, as we moved off, the Sergeant turned to me and, with a dead-pan expression, asked, "Do we go back up the slope, sir?" I didn't offer him a reply.

Camels were a wonderful beast of burden but sometimes they could cause problems. Occasionally, one of a string of four baggage camels would suddenly take it into his head to refuse to cross say, a dry river bed or to climb a steep hill, and would start bucking and kicking in an effort to throw its load. This would start the other three bucking as well and the cry would always go up, "What's it carrying!" If the load contained items essential to our survival and they were breakable, the animal was immediately shot, otherwise men's lives could be in danger.

The cause of death was recorded as 'Duccan' and the owner paid twenty shillings compensation. As long as the camel, or for that matter any other animal, had died of a disease rather than any other cause, we were allowed to pay compensation, twenty shillings (£1) for a camel, two shillings (10p) for a sheep or goat. And the only disease that Nairobi seemed to have heard of was 'Duccan', so, in my reports, everything that died, died of 'Duccan'.

Back at Banya, we continued to strengthen the fort and make a show of our presence to the nearby Gelubba in order to dissuade them from making any more attacks on our 'tame' tribesmen. Things seemed quiet for a while, until, one morning, a small party returning from night patrol reported to me that they had found tracks which led them to a flimsy palm frond shelter just fifteen hundred yards to the north of the fort. The Gelubba had constructed the shelter under cover of darkness and, observation showed, were using it nightly, but for what purpose we couldn't be certain.

Maybe some of the warriors were bringing women there for illicit sex, maybe they just wanted to be closer to us or maybe they had a more sinister intention - we never discovered.

In any case, I had to assume the worst and decided to make a real show of its destruction so as to further establish my superiority over them. I conveyed a message to them via the elders that if they didn't stop using the shelter, I would ask my god to destroy it by fire. My scouts kept watch and reported that, each night, the Gelubba were still using the shelter, so I finalised my plans for a spectacular show of my god's awesome power.

Over the proceeding few months, we had taken possession of a variety of weapons mostly from raiders coming over the northern border with Abyssinia and among these were a dozen or so Italian Breda light machine guns and a quantity of ammunition. I had assigned a two man team to each gun and put them through a course of tuition so that we now had a proficient machine gun section.

Crop raider and .577 double barrelled heavy rifle

Another crop raider downed

Buffalo hunting, Kaptagat Forest

*Above: Tony Maxtone-Mailer with buffalo which, if it had two horns,
would have disembowelled Peter*

Below: Some good ivory

*On the move.
Camels in the
Kubi Furr Pass
between Banya
and Buluk*

*Mounted Section,
North Horr*

*Baggage Camels,
Banya*

Police District Headquarters, Wajir

Wajir

Emergency Defences, Dukana

Frontier Fort, El Roba. The 'Keep'

Frontier Fort, El Roba. The 'Keep' after further building

Frontier Fort El Roba. Men at action stations inside the fort.

Frontier Fort. Todenyang

I had the distance to the palm frond shelter carefully paced out and the machine guns set up on their tripods all in one straight line and sighted accurately on the target. Each gun team was issued with three magazines containing twenty-eight rounds per magazine and every third one a tracer round.

That night, a few hours after sundown, I ordered the teams to man their guns, hold them steady and then rapid fire until all three magazines were empty. It was a spectacular sight - in one thunderous cacophony, twelve bright lines of tracers, about a thousand rounds in all, rent the blackness, all converging on the one distant spot. As the firing ceased, we saw flames leap from the target. Next morning I sent a scouting party to assess the damage and on their return, they reported that the shelter had burned to the ground and that there were many blood stains and tracks indicating a sudden panic withdrawal.

For a few weeks following this incident, we had no trouble from the Gelubba so I felt confident enough to absent myself from Banya for a while to undertake a safari I had been contemplating for some time. I needed to make my presence felt and acquaint myself with the territory to the south, on the eastern shore of Lake Rudolf, and planned to travel down the full length of the lake, some one hundred and seventy-five miles I planned then, to turn east and travel the eighty odd miles to North Horr before turning north to Banya again.

We set off and headed towards the Omo Delta which formed the northern shore of the lake. This was Gelubba territory and I knew that we were being watched but was fairly certain that the recent demonstration of power by my god and his machine guns would be sufficient to deter any attacks for a while at least.

At the lake, we turned south to traverse the area now covered by the Sibiloi National Park and Crocodile Sanctuary which then, was low lying land subject to flooding from the lake. Although we encountered a few nomadic tribal groups we heard of little trouble and no raiding in the region so we progressed southwards at a steady rate, camping by night close to the lake shore and posting sentries just in case of sudden attack.

About half way down the length of Lake Rudolf, we came to a swampy inlet which seemed to extend about seven miles inland and yet was only a couple of hundred yards across. It looked very shallow and was covered with green vegetation, to all outward appearances just a waterlogged grass field and I saw no reason why we shouldn't just wade across but, for some reason, the rest of the party hung back and seemed reluctant to approach it. I called up my Sergeant, (not the same one who had advised me against descending the escarpment), and said,

"What's the problem, Sergeant?"

"It's the men and the camel leaders, sir. They say they can't cross and we should go inland and round it."

Feeling bloody minded, I said we'd cross, but the camel leaders insisted that they couldn't (wouldn't), so I said to the Sergeant, "Right, you take the patrol round the swamp and my Orderly and myself will cross here and wait for you further south." He looked a bit doubtful but couldn't refuse an order so off they went, taking our riding camels with them while I splashed in to make what I thought would be a short crossing. As ordered, my Orderly followed and, as he did so, I heard him work the bolt of his rifle. At that time, Lake Rudolf teemed with crocodiles but, of course, not in such shallow water.

We had waded for some distance before I noticed that the water was up to my knees so I stopped and looked carefully around for tell-tale signs of nostrils poking above the water before venturing on. The further we went, the deeper it got and we soon began to encounter a softer and softer bottom. Again, I scanned the surface of the water nervously and myself, worked a round into the breach of my rifle.

It was too late to turn back now, imagine the loss of face if the rest of the party had to return to the north bank to collect us. Discipline would be shattered to say nothing of my own embarrassment.

Still further and even deeper, and the further away the southern bank appeared to be. Eventually, After struggling manfully through chest deep water with our feet sticking in the glutinous bottom and in fear of suddenly losing a leg, or worse, we began to feel harder ground beneath our feet and finally made it to the southern shore.

To say that I was scared would be an understatement and I discovered then that fear comes in phases; first fright, then terror, then a distinct drop in temperature, then the 'So what the hell if I get killed, I ain't scared' phase, then the cycle repeats itself over again, or so it always was with me. Had we retreated, the incident would have been campfire talk for ever, and ever; we would have lost face, and my biggest fear of all was that of showing fear.

We pressed on south to Loiangalani, then a small settlement on the eastern shore of Lake Rudolf, where I camped down for a week.

Loiangalani is now a tourist camp mainly used by fishing parties out to catch Nile Perch and Tiger Fish. Though peaceful now, when the tourist camp was first established, a canoe-born party of Gelubba warriors came down from the north and raided it, killing most of the staff.

When we arrived, it was a lake-side village which was the home of the entire Elmolo tribe, then numbering exactly eighty-nine persons, men, women and children who were the last remnants of a dying tribe.

They lived in a collection of skin covered huts by the lake and since there was little or no grazing for endless miles in every direction, just lava rock and sand desert, they could keep no stock for milk or meat. They survived largely by spearing Nile Perch and giant Tilapia in the lake and, very occasionally, a hippopotamus or crocodile.

All of them had horribly thin legs and arms and were badly afflicted by ulcers caused by the, almost exclusive, diet of fish. Despite their miserable plight, the Elmolo were keenly hospitable people and immediately offered guests a portion of the very little they had.

From my first encounter with them, I felt desperately sorry for the Elmolo and determined that I would do whatever my own limited resources and time would allow to help relieve their pitiable condition. From then on, for the duration of my service in the Northern Frontier District, I made a point of visiting them twice a year and would camp down for a week or two close by their village.

The Elmolo's method of fishing was harpooning from rafts which they built by lashing together four or five Doum Palm trunks. From scrap iron they made barbed harpoon heads which were attached to shafts with home made cord and another cord was attached to the shaft so that it could be retrieved after throwing. Drifting around the lake, they would harpoon the larger fish, Nile Perch up to two hundred pounds and Tilapia up to twenty pounds.

Hunting hippo was an altogether more dangerous proposition and required, not only a co-operative effort, but also considerable courage on the part of the Elmolo fishermen. Hippo can be extremely aggressive and tend to attack anything which approaches too close. The flimsy rafts of the Elmolo could easily be upended by an angry hippo and their crews slaughtered in seconds.

Three or four rafts would set out, each with two crew and loaded with chunks of lava rock. They would approach a group of hippo, who would submerge for up to two minutes at a time feeding on bottom vegetation. Each time they surfaced the crew would lie flat on the raft so as to remain inconspicuous then, as the animals submerged they would paddle closer until a hippo surfaced within harpooning range. Immediately, the crew would hurl their harpoons and hang onto the rope attached to the harpoon head. The other rafts would paddle furiously alongside and, as the stricken animal surfaced ready for battle, they would also hurl as many harpoons as they could and hang on to the ropes as the hippo thrashed and fought for freedom. The rafts would be quickly lashed together and then they would all stone the animal with the lava rocks until the hippo either died or, more often, managed to escape.

A hippo, though hard won, was much prized by the Elmolo because its yield of meat and fat to eat, hide and bones to make housing and artefacts would give them a short but welcome period of relative plenty and nothing of the animal was ever wasted.

On my visits, I would accompany them on a hunting foray onto the lake and using their method of approach until we came near enough to a hippo, I would shoot it. The sound of the bullet hitting the massive bone of the animal's skull made a crack like a sledge hammer hitting a lump of rock and on each visit I would shoot two or three hippo which would keep them supplied for some time. When they were brought ashore for butchering, I found that each of the animals I shot for them had, at some time in its life been a target for the Elmolo hunters, and most of them more than once because they were covered in old wound scars and bristled like hedgehogs with harpoon heads from previous engagements.

On one of my visits to the Elmolo, I was suffering from veldt sores - like large, very painful boils which appears on the ankles and which disable one completely for a couple of days. The cure, I had been told, was to immerse the affected area in the lake, which I did. Almost instantly, a vast shoal of tiny Tiger Fish fry appeared and started nibbling at the white head of the boil. All I felt was a slight tingling sensation and it wasn't long before they had cleaned out all the puss and rotten matter, leaving the sore to heal from the bottom upwards. On each subsequent appearance of veldt sores, apparently caused by certain minerals present in the soil, I would take off for a couple of days camping by the shore of the lake to take the cure.

After our stay with the Elmolo, we headed north past Mount Kulal which rises to seven thousand five-hundred feet and stands about fifteen miles to the east of Loiangalani and the shore of Lake Rudolf. Beyond Mount Kulal lies the Chalbi Desert which I had crossed before when I first travelled from Marsabit and we now turned north east and headed again towards North Horr, the original base of my Detachment command.

The Chalbi Desert is an area some one hundred and thirty miles by forty and is formed from part of the dried up bed of the original, much larger Lake Rudolf which shrunk to its present size in prehistoric times. Occasionally, large parts of the desert would be flooded when heavy storms in the hills hundreds of miles to the north in Ethiopia filled the normally dry courses of the rivers Balal, Ririba and Kore and for a few weeks, these areas would be impassable. Very quickly, all the water would be gone and the whole desert surface would again become crazed, dried up mud with the exception of the northern fringe which was covered by a layer of fine crystallised soda giving the appearance of a vast, glaring, white snowfield.

The upper slopes of Mount Kulal and, further south, the Ng'iro Range and the Ndoto Mountains were covered in lush vegetation and were heavily forested but, despite their good grazing and relatively gentle climate, none were inhabited by the Rendille tribe, in whose country they were. Instead, the Rendille remained a desert wandering, nomadic people and would only enter the mountain forests when particularly good hunting attracted them. During periods of prolonged drought in the lower regions, large quantities of game, particularly elephant and buffalo, would climb higher and gather in the lush mountain tops.

The northern slopes of the Ndoto, though extremely precipitous, had a special attraction for elephant - wild plums, which grew there in profusion. In the season, Elephant would smell the fallen fruit and slowly climb the slopes to gorge themselves and, since the plums rapidly fermented once they were on the ground, the elephants would soon become drunk. This was a signal for the Rendille hunters to climb up above the herd and suddenly create the maximum disturbance by rushing about yelling and banging tins or anything that would make a racket. The elephants would charge off in panic and, if the hunters were successful, one would lose its footing, fall over the edge and plunge, helpless, to its death.

To the north of the Chalbi Desert, towards the border with Ethiopia, stood the Huri Hills with Huri, the highest peak reaching an altitude of 4000 feet. Despite their bulk and a length of some thirty miles, no water was to be found on them; no rivers or streams, no pools or wells and even though there was a complete absence of trees, they were covered in an abundance of grass.

Throughout the year, the Huri's experienced heavy, damp mists accompanied by strong winds and it was very cold - such an enormous contrast to the burning desert below. At times, when the mists were particularly dense, nomadic tribesmen would venture up from the desert and, by skimming the top of the grass with a vessel would collect sufficient water for their immediate needs from the dew that had settled there.

On our return from one safari to the border, we were travelling down the length of the Huri's when we were witness to and extraordinary display of weather. About mid day, we were at a high point with good views over a large part of the Chalbi when, without warning, a patchwork of every kind of climatic condition suddenly began to develop over the desert. Every ten miles or so, in all directions, nature produced something different; violent thunder storms - the worst I've ever seen, tornadoes, dust devils, areas of brilliant sunshine, channels of hurricane force winds which raised the dust and blackened the sky, torrential rain and hail storms and patches of what appeared to be stationary mist. If Dante's inferno ever existed on earth, this was it. My men and I halted and mesmerised, watched it for over an hour when, just as quickly as it had started, the phenomenon suddenly subsided.

Some time later, as we camped down at a water hole a party of Ethiopian refugees who had fled across the border to escape a flare up of violence in their own land began to arrive. Smallpox had broken out amongst them so I pulled my camp back half a mile from the water hole to avoid contact but, through necessity, continued to draw water from it. After a few days, I found to my horror, that some of my followers were removing clothes from those who had died, for their own use in the future and were washing them in the water hole. Immediately, I had all the clothes burned, stopped drawing water and de-camped with due haste.

At North Horr, we stayed for a few days while I reviewed the situation with the rest of my command who were stationed there, then decamped again and travelled the hundred or so miles north back to the border fort at Banya.

Considering the conditions under which we had to operate in these northern regions, we were, in truth, very vulnerable. The terrain and the weather were some of the harshest in the world requiring the utmost care and skill in the exploitation of our meagre resources just to survive, let alone the fact that we often surrounded by large parties of armed, hostile primitives and sometimes with as few as fifteen men.

I never overlooked the fact that young warriors could not marry nor could they gain any standing amongst their fellows until they had killed another human being. To survive at all, we had to impress them and customs had to be observed.

Each night, at base camp, the whole compliment were ordered to fall in and, to the sound of the bugler playing 'The Last Post', the flag was lowered with due ceremony. At dawn, the sentries would call out the quarter guard and, as the flag was raised, the bugler would sound 'Reveille'. All very important 'dasturi' (customs) which told observers that we were here, we were strong and we meant business.

I have to admit that, at times, you began to wonder why on earth you were sweating away your life in some god-awful, far flung land just to protect a handful of heathen savages. But the truth was, there existed an under-lying strategic reason.

Kenya's northern desert belt provided a four hundred mile natural defensive barrier against the possibility of invasion from the north and east, of settled Kenya. So it had to be policed and intelligence gathered, not only on native incursion but also on that of foreign powers.

One of the greatest causes of discomfort and hazards to health at Banya were the mosquitoes. As darkness fell, they would rise in untold millions and their humming sounded like a distant jet plane. At night, the Gelubba kept constant fires of cow dung, the smoke from which drifted across their settlements in an attempt to keep the mosquitoes at a distance. Any camp followers who accompanied my personnel would build 'nests' at the top of any suitable thorn tree and there, they would spend the night at a height above the flight level of the mosquitoes.

I introduced a device to minimise the nuisance to night sentries by constructing wooden frames which rested on the men's shoulders and were draped with mosquito netting, thus holding it away from their bodies. As they moved silently around the perimeter, this contrivance gave them the fearsome aspect of churchyard ghosts. For myself, I constructed a large 'dining' mosquito net under which I had considerable freedom of movement after dusk. Nevertheless, I reckoned on about thirty bites every night.

Most of my men suffered chronic malaria from mosquito bites, as did the Gelubba. But I was extremely fortunate, I never got it once during the whole of my service on the frontier.

The traditional native treatment for a malaria attack was to wrap themselves in a blanket and lie in the sun so as to develop a very high temperature. This resulted in profuse sweating which, in less than forty-eight hours, alleviated the attack.

When, eventually, Mepacrine and Palludin became available, we, in our wisdom, forced the men to take them at daily parades. This, we learned later, was a grave error since, when, after years of service the men returned to their homelands, they succumbed to severe malaria because the drugs had destroyed their natural resistance. As soon as this fact was recognised, the practice was stopped.

The Gelubba homeland lay in the territory either side of the Omo river delta where it drains into the northern tip of Lake Rudolf and it stretched northward for a hundred miles or so on either bank, roughly on the border between Southern Sudan and Ethiopia. Though it was north of the Kenya border, I twice made expeditions into the area and found that, for miles back from the river, the country was covered in dense thorn bush, so dense that, even on foot, passage through it was extremely difficult. Game tracks and stock trails through the bush eased progress somewhat but seldom seemed to lead in the direction one wanted to go.

On each expedition, we came across Gelubba encampments hidden deep within the bush but, each time, we found in them only old men, women and children never men of warrior age. They, it seemed always retreated into dense cover at our approach but remained close, ready to attack if they thought their families or stock were threatened.

The truth is that, under such conditions, a co-ordinated defence was almost impossible and in the poor visibility afforded by the dense bush, spears and knives would probably have been far more effective than guns. I quickly realised that I should never have endangered the lives of my men just to satisfy my own curiosity and appreciating that the tribe considered the territory to be theirs to defend against all intruders, I made no further incursions after the second. However, we had made a show of strength and I felt convinced that we had demonstrated to the Gelubba that retribution could swiftly follow any major atrocities on their part.

Life in the Northern Frontier District was always lived on the edge. Whether on the move or encamped or behind the defences of one or other of the border forts, we were continually under threat of attack by hostiles and it was essential to keep constant vigil. Neither were there many comforts to ease the rigours of the daily routine; the burning heat by day, the cold at night, the constant thirst, the bouts of harsh weather, the miles of difficult terrain, all multiplied the discomfort and stress suffered by the men. Inevitably, the strain would tell and someone would begin to 'lose it'.

Most of my men were down-country tribesmen serving a three year tour on the Frontier and occasionally one from a higher cooler region would crack and say that the heat was killing him and he could go no further. Initially, I was in a dilemma; I could hardly give him a travel warrant and tell him to catch the first train home for a rest - there were no trains., nor for that matter, any roads. We certainly couldn't halt the patrol until he felt better, nor could I turn him loose in the desert, he wouldn't have survived for two days on his own. I had no choice, so in these circumstances, I always followed the same procedure; I instructed my NCO's to disarm him except for his bayonet, fill his water bottle and leave him saying, 'You can always follow our tracks if you feel like it.' They always did, the fear of lion or raiding hostiles soon cured them.

When on patrol in these dangerous areas, I fielded scouts to both flanks, to the rear and in advance of the main party, their job being, not to fight heroic battles on their own but to give instant information of any possible threat or impending attack straight back to the main group. Spotting a potential enemy in dense thorn bush country could pose particular problems and they could be on you before you even knew they were near. One ploy was for a scout to lie down on the ground from where he could see for a considerable distance in every direction below the lowest branches of the thorn trees.

At night, when camping down in the danger zones, especially when we had seen evidence of a raiding party in the area and we considered that an attack was likely, we would make a lot of noise pitching camp, even firing a shot or two, to make sure the hostiles knew where we were. Then, an hour or two after dark, in complete silence, we would relocate to a new, pre-selected site, one or two miles away. The raiders, having pinpointed us at the first campsite, would withdraw and only approach again just before daylight, by which time we would be close up behind them and take them by surprise.

At night, I would post double sentries around the camp, the first would be mobile and visible and the second guarding his companion from some hidden vantage point.

Africans love to chatter and, if left to it, my men would do so all day long in a high-pitched voice audible for miles. When on the move, the best policy was, always, to maintain complete silence so as to avoid attracting the attentions of would be attackers and, if we arrived at the scene of any trouble, we could do so unannounced and catch the culprits red-handed. I ordered complete silence with the threat of severe disciplinary action for any breaches of the order.

I found that, marching in desert conditions during daylight hours caused me a considerable thirst problem. If we were on the move soon after dawn, I would have sweated myself dry by 9.00am and could brush the salt deposit off my skin. If then, I drank to quench my thirst, I would soon develop a raging thirst that nothing would quench and further drinking would only make me feel sick. I fell into a routine of drinking nothing between dawn and dusk but quaffing copious quantities throughout the hours of darkness.

Our camels, which were bought from indigenous tribes-people, we had to break and train for their allotted tasks ourselves and this activity, conducted somewhat like a rough version of a wild west rodeo, provided enormous amusement for all concerned.

After a wrestling match, a rope would be tied to the lower jaw of the candidate and another to its tail. The man at the front would drag the camel along by its tether, screaming and yelling to persuade it to follow him, while a second hung onto the tail rope, leaping and bellowing similar words of encouragement while belabouring the wretched beast with a long stick. Either side of the camel, more men walked along shouting and banging empty tin cans to keep it going straight. The animal itself would be snarling and roaring and kicking out at anyone who got too near. When angered, camels have a nasty habit of kneeing anybody who gets too close to their front end and when they do it, they mean it, so the tail rope man had to act as break if the beast suddenly got too near to the lead rope man. This hullabaloo continued twice a day for several days and our usual practice was to break three or four camels at a time so you can imagine the uproar this procedure created.

For the next stage, heavy sacks filled with sand would be lashed to each side of the camel and after a few days of this, a brave Constable would be goaded into mounting and riding the beast. Real rodeo stuff with every man at the post yelling encouragement and rolling about with laughter.

Eventually, the animal would be accepted as broken and we would pay the owner the going rate for it - £1.00. Unlike horses, camels forget and, if they aren't ridden for some time, they have to be re-broken and the whole chaotic procedure gone through again.

When local family groups of nomadic tribesmen moved to new camping grounds, they often did so by moon light and as they travelled, particularly over sand or soft ground, they made no sound save for the camels wooden neck bells, a different tone for male and female. All you heard was the musical note of the bells as the shadowy train drifted slowly across the moon-lit sand.

In the heat of the day, in open sandy terrain, mirages are common and it's strange to see a large camel train, clear in every detail, walking along thirty feet above the ground - upside down.

It's very easy to get lost in flat, featureless bush country. With vegetation above head height, visibility is restricted to the nearest bush and there are no reference points. It's dangerous for even an experienced person to lose sight of his starting point unless, of course, he's on a long-distance journey and can follow a compass bearing.

In low country on the equator, you die very quickly from thirst and quite a number of people lost their lives by leaving their vehicles and venturing into the bush to shoot a buck, a guinea fowl or some other game they'd spotted, then becoming totally lost in even a short distance.

In one instance, we found tracks which indicated that the poor unfortunate, in his last desperate effort had even crossed his own vehicle tracks without realising it, because they continued into the bush on the far side and eventually led us to his body.

Two Englishmen, travelling through desert country by car, came to a sand river which was normally dry, but which happened at the time, to be flooded from a rain shower in nearby hills. Often, these flash floods would flow for only a few hours, then would cease and the river bed dry up in no time at all. Instead of waiting, this intrepid pair foolishly decided to attempt a crossing and committed the cardinal sin of not removing the fan belt first. The water was deeper than they thought and as they reached the deepest part, the fan blades became immersed and the shaft sheared driving the blades through the radiator and immobilising the vehicle.

Error followed error and, instead of staying with their vehicle, where eventually, they would have been found, they decided to walk the considerable distance to their destination. Then, apparently seeking a short cut to avoid a long diversion that the track made, they got lost and both perished of thirst.

Many normally dry sand river beds flowed with water only once in ten years or more, usually caused by heavy rain storms in hills or higher ground which could be a hundred miles away. An innocent traveller could be crossing a dry sand river on a scorching hot day with not a cloud in sight while, unknown to him, a massive torrent of water could be rushing at breakneck speed down the water course ready to swamp him.

Over years, thorn trees and other vegetation would grow up along the margins and often large quantities of debris would have collected in the river bed. Flood waters would pick up the debris forming a barrier ahead of the water. Acting like a dam wall, the barrier would cause a huge build-up of water which would batter down and sweep away anything which lay in its path. The first warning of the flood water's approach was a trembling of the earth followed by air bubbling up through the sandy bed of the river and an ominous, ever increasing rumble like distant thunder. And you'd better be out of the way when it arrived or you and your vehicle would be swept away and lost.

During one patrol to the northern border, we made for an isolated water hole to camp for the night and replenish our stocks but, as we approached, we found it was already occupied by a band of Abyssinian Habbash irregulars - villainous ruffians, festooned with rifles and bandoleers. There were about a dozen of them and, after the usual greetings, an argument broke out about which side of the border we were on and who had a right to be there and who hadn't. To avoid an immediate violent confrontation (though we outnumbered them four to one), I pulled back a few yards and ordered my Sergeant to deliver to them a notice which I wrote on a Police letterhead. In my best, but almost illegible handwriting, it read:

'In the name of My Majesty King George the 6th
and that of the Kenya Government
I hereby am required to both request and order you to withdraw, failing
which any force necessary to evict you may be used without warning.
I remain My Majesty's Humble Servant,'

...and I signed it with a flourish.

This was I thought, reasonable diplomatic jargon and all very serious stuff and my Sergeant marched stiffly towards them and handed it in a ceremonious manner to the who appeared to be the leader of the band. Of course, they couldn't read and, in any case, they knew no English. Instead, they thought I had made them a gift and were suddenly all bows and smiles and friendly chatter.

Soon, they were sharing their few supplies with us and us likewise with them as if we were the best of friends. We shared the water hole for the next few days swapping stories of our adventures in the most cordial of relationships and when they left, the leader begged me to visit what he called their 'headquarters' some forty miles north of the disputed border.

A week later, on a whim, I did so and they brought out the red carpet, all fell in, lined up smartly and I was invited to inspect the 'parade' and the encampment. After the inspection, they invited me to sit in the place reserved for honoured guests and brought out the 'tegge', a powerful, pungent beer brewed from the honey of wild bees.

The following morning, feeling a little worse from the copious quantities of 'tegge', we left, and parted the best of friends.

Eight months later, I received a message via HQ that the Foreign Office had ordered me instantly to submit a report (twelve copies), explaining why I had illegally entered Abyssinia with armed Police and terrorised innocent civilians. Diplomatic channels don't always get the facts right.

We encamped one night in densely bushed country part way between Banya and another forward patrol base at Buluk which stood some thirty-five miles to the south east. All was quiet until, in that darkest hour before dawn, we were awakened by a sudden outburst of yelling and shots and agonised screaming. The fracas seemed to come from a position about a mile away but, owing to the darkness and the dense bush, I could do nothing until daylight except for the usual 'Dawn Stand-to' defensive procedure.

At first light, we advanced on the position we had pin-pointed and found a most pitiful sight. There were six or seven badly mutilated corpses and another six or seven poor unfortunates sprawled in the sand but still alive, their penises and testicles cut off, most speared through the thighs and desperately trying to hold onto their entrails which spilled out through gaping wounds in their stomachs. The whole scene was a blood-bath and covered in a mass of flies.

I photographed these poor individuals and quickly called a council of war. There was no possible medical aid we could render; we had no first aid book, no needle or thread, no radio, no vehicle and it was three hundred and fifty miles across waterless desert to the nearest medical aid. There was nothing we could do for them and they were all doomed to suffer a prolonged and dreadfully painful death in the next few hours. We were left with no alternative so I ordered my men to shoot them. I withdrew and, as I counted the appropriate number of shots, the thought went through my mind that this was technically murder, barbarous murder, but what else could I have done for these poor unfortunate people?

Before they died, we managed to elicit from them that they were some of our 'tame' Gabbra tribesmen who were on a scouting mission to locate a 'soft' Gelubba target for a reprisal raid but they had been caught unaware by a party of Gelubba warriors and a case of 'those who live by the sword shall die by the sword' quickly followed.

Later, so I was told, my photographs of the incident were laid before the British Parliament as an example of the problems that existed, when Kenya was trying to elicit more funds to provide better policing of the Frontier.

Prior to British occupation of the area, the tribes from both sides of the border were armed, more or less, equally. But, in our 'wisdom' we disarmed the tribesmen on our side of the border, leaving them only spears and bows and arrows with which to defend themselves against raiders, many of whom carried rifles.

To enforce our rule, we shot on sight, without prior warning, any African found carrying a rifle within a belt stretching 130 miles south of the border. This put our 'tame' tribesmen at a great disadvantage and, since our own forces in the area were numerically so few for such a huge tract of land, we simply could not provide the protection they needed and they suffered heavy casualties.

Despite my inability on the occasion mentioned above, I did have a couple of medical successes. The first concerned one of my African Constables who reported to me one morning that he couldn't pass water and had a terrible pain in his penis.

As always, we were totally isolated, cut off from any medical aid and neither I, nor any of my men had the faintest idea what to do but the poor man was so distressed, I had to make a rapid decision as to treatment.

I figured out that there was some sort of obstruction and that this must, somehow, be dislodged but with what, I hadn't a clue. Suddenly, a resourceful Corporal produced a thin porcupine quill and rounded off the sharp point. I soaked this in boiling water laced with Aquaflavin, greased it and pushed it up his penis. I was surprised how easily it slid in and, on a second and deeper penetration - Hey Presto! The problem was solved. This rapidly became evident when I withdrew the quill since myself and all those present were liberally sprayed and the only one of us left smiling was the Constable himself.

My second medical triumph, (not all that surprising since both my father and my uncle were doctors), came some years later when I was visiting a remote airfield. A gang of African workers under the control of an English engineer, whose name, I remember was Adams, were employed to lengthen the runway. In conversation, poor Adams confided in me that he was in terrible pain from a slipped disc. As we camped down for the night, Adams told me that, after dark, Hyenas were stalking the camp and proving to be a bloody nuisance and was there anything I could do about it.

"I'll take my truck after dark," I said. "I'll drive round a bit and see if I can spot any in the headlights."

"Good," he said. "I'll come with you."

The truck had no door on the cab and I had a rifle tucked into the rifle bucket to the right of the steering wheel so, if we spotted one, I'd be ready to dispose of it.

We did a circuit of the airfield and, just as we turned onto the runway, the headlights picked out a single Hyena loping along ahead of us. I accelerated to come up behind it and, at about forty miles and hour, I steadied the truck, pulled out the rifle and leaned out of the cab to shoot it. Suddenly, the front wheels dropped into a drainage ditch which had been cut straight across the newly cleared strip. The front of the vehicle dived into the ditch, hit the far side and leaped out again followed by the rear end doing the same resulting in the front axle being torn away from the chassis. Adams and I had our heads smashed against the cab roof then our backsides slammed down hard onto the almost solid seat, then up again, then we were both hurled out of the sides of the truck and, for a minute of so lay, dazed on the strip.

As I staggered to my feet, feeling for broken bones and lurching towards where Adams lay to see if he was still alive, he suddenly leapt to his feet and cried, "I can walk, I can walk. My back's cured." The severe jolting had evidently reset his slipped disc and he was like a man reborn. He had neglected to inform me that, that very morning, he had instructed his men to dig a three foot deep drainage ditch across the lower end of the runway.

Many years later, I pulled in one night at a newly established bush motel and as I walked in, I received an ecstatic greeting from the proprietor who had instantly recognised me - it was Adams.

"Doctor," he cried. "For you, everything's on the house." And he lead me over to the bar and bought me a drink. "You know," he said. "All those years of pain, but since that night, I've never had the slightest twinge."

At intervals of many months - and once, eight months - during my tour of duty on the Northern Frontier, I would retreat from the desert and take a well-earned rest of two to three weeks at the Administrative Centre on the cool heights of Marsabit. Here was a little civilised society amongst such company as the District Officer and the Superintendent. These gentlemen did, albeit infrequently, travel their jurisdiction and on the whole led a fairly active existence but it was mostly on my visits to Marsabit that I met them and it seemed all too soon that my rest was over and I would return refreshed to the desert forward areas.

Each twenty-five man frontier platoon was relieved by freshly rested ones from base at Marsabit, supposedly once every three months. However, for one reason or another, these tours always seemed to get extended so the men's delight at their return there was all the more cause for celebration.

Ten miles or so from Marsabit, as the lorries started to grind up the escarpment leading to the summit, the men would start to bang on the sides of the vehicles and sing of their warlike achievements. The nearer we got to the town, the louder it got and if they had killed, the excitement was feverish.

To the women-folk, these were their returning warriors and once they heard the clamour, they would instantly drop everything and tear off down the track to greet them, screaming about what they hoped their man had done and dancing as they went. No need to go into detail about what happened that first night but in the morning, some of the women could be seen sleeping outside in the sun to indicate to everyone the virility and staying power of their man.

Light Relief

I enjoyed living 'rough' in a hot, isolated environment such as the deserts of the Northern Frontier District and, as far as I could tell, I even thrived on it. The years I spent separated from the company of white men, without shelter, medical aid, shops, wireless and, refreshingly, without the interference of higher authority, proved blissful and they passed all too quickly.

The conditions under which my men and I were forced to live were, to say the least of it, unhealthy and positively unhygienic. For the most part, we obtained our water from stinking wells liberally dosed with baboon and other animal excrement, snakes and other miscellaneous drowned fauna. We never boiled it, we just baled out the well a few times, left it to stand for a while until the muck had settled then drank it. Often, as I have mentioned before, I would stir in a little Epsom Salts which seemed effectively to clear the top half of the water and make it reasonably palatable.

In the desert, meat would go 'off' in a couple of hours or so and very shortly afterwards would turn green, therefore I took a little care to inspect any game we shot prior to it being cooked.

Most desert antelope suffered from measles and, of course, tape worms, which, if ingested could be a considerable hazard to health. My servants were instructed to show me any meat before it was cooked and if it had started to smell I told them to curry it. If measles cysts were present, they showed up like pieces of tapioca when the flesh was cut, then I would instruct them to roast it for an extra half hour which, hopefully, would kill any infection and when it came to eating the meat, I would cut round and flip away the cysts. We were not inoculated against typhoid, para-typhoid, hepatitis nor even small pox despite the fact that so many of our men were carriers of the disease as well as dysentery and malaria.

It seemed to me that the simple precautions I took were effective enough coupled with the fact that, without medicines, antibiotics and the like, I must have developed a degree of natural resistance. But it may have been just good fortune that I managed to survive against the biting insects, the internal parasites and the sundry diseases in this 'white-man's grave'.

As I have said, rest periods, during my tour of duty in the Northern Frontier District, I spent in Marsabit. Considering its isolated location amid trackless desert and dense bush country, Marsabit was, even then, a quite substantial settlement - cool, moist and green atop its high mountain.

Maize, bananas and sundry other crops were cultivated by the locals and about a third of the area was designated as a game reserve. Here I was able to follow my passion for hunting, both for food and for sport, where the mountain, it's southern and eastern foothills were heavily forested and teeming with game.

At the southern end of the mountain lay Lake Paradise of Martin Johnson fame. The Johnson's, on an earlier photographic expedition, had landed a small amphibious plane on the lake only to discover, when they came to leave, that the lake was too small for take-off and its shores were bounded by tall trees. They were forced to make camp for several days while they felled an enormous number of trees before they had a sufficiently clear route to get airborne.

Around Marsabit, conflict inevitably arose between farmers and the wildlife. Elephant and buffalo in particular would raid the crops, mostly at night and what they didn't manage to eat, they would trample.

Some animals, especially elephant, would become very bold and refuse to flee even when crowds turned out to beat cans and hurl rocks and fire-brands at them. They would stand their ground, become very aggressive and threaten to charge anyone who dared to approach too close. Not only were the growing crops at risk from the invaders, even the little thatched stores built by the farmers were torn down and crops already harvested were stolen.

A stalemate had been reached, demanding a drastic solution, and I arranged with the local farmers that, if elephant invaded, they were to tell my Orderly who would pass the word on to me wherever I happened to be. Beside me, for such occasions, I kept my 0.577 rifle to which, for night shooting, I attached a three cell torch using two of a vehicle's shortest rear leaf springs and a bolt, clamping it to the barrels. I had pre-aimed the sights and the torch beam at a spot twenty yards away so that I didn't have to aim, merely shine the torch on the target and squeeze the trigger.

One evening, a game of Bridge had been arranged between myself, the District Officer, the Superintendent and an Army Veterinary Officer who was camping down at Marsabit for a few days. He, together with a Farrier Sergeant Major, was in charge of a party driving a herd of Abyssinian ponies down into Kenya for army use and had stopped off for a rest and supplies. As we sat down to play, I had my rifle beside me, just in case. The District Officer took one look at the rifle, then at me.

"I say, Mills," he said. "If you're really so keen to win, we'll give in right now." I assured him it wasn't a threat and we dealt the first hand.

About ten thirty, I had just laid out my hand as dummy when my Orderly rushed in.

"Pardon me sir," he said, excitedly. "The elephant have arrived."

I excused myself, grabbed the rifle and we set off into the night. I followed him for about two-hundred yards until we came upon a bunch of locals all pointing to a spot somewhere in the darkness. Slowly, I advanced towards where they had pointed and, at first, began to smell the beast then I saw a shadowy mass some way ahead of me. I switched on the torch and, for a few seconds could only see the light reflected from the maize stalks, then, two white spots of light - reflections in the animal's eyes. The elephant had swung defiantly to face me.

Quickly taking stock of the situation, I decided on the gentler method of dissuasion and yelled, "Bugger off!" whereupon, it slowly turned to display its side. I shone the torch on the heart shot, one third of the way up the body and angled in behind its near shoulder blade. This would direct the bullet through the top half of the Elephant's heart. I fired both barrels almost simultaneously, the beast staggered about ten yards and toppled over dead while the rest of the herd made a rapid retreat. I hurried back to the Bridge party to find my partner, the Army Veterinary Officer, just playing his last card of the hand to win the game.

When shot through the heart, animals can behave unpredictably, particularly elephants, since they have a very large heart. If the heart is at the contracted phase of the beat when the bullet hits, the damage will be massively increased as the heart expands, and death is very quick. However, if the heart is expanded when the bullet strikes, upon the immediate contraction, the damage is apparently lessened and the beast can do a good deal of damage before it eventually succumbs.

At night, on occasions when I found myself without a torch, I would fasten a lighted cigarette end over the foresight with a rubber band then, lining up the foresight and the glowing cigarette against a paler patch of sky, I could bring the gun down, aim and know exactly where the bullet would strike.

Large game was so abundant in the Marsabit area that my services were called upon on numerous occasions in attempts to control them. I was in thick bush one night searching for the culprits of a rather devastating crop raid when I spotted a large elephant standing within range. It stood side on to me but all I could see was its head. Though I favoured a heart shot to be certain of a kill, I had no choice but to go for a brain shot. I fired and the animal dropped only to reappear a split second later exactly where it had just been. Amazed, I fired a second time and again it disappeared, this time for good.

We waited until the rest of the herd moved off and then approached the spot where the elephant had fallen and to my surprise, there was not one, but two elephants lying side by side, stone dead. The second one had been standing exactly behind the first. A similar situation often arises when shooting buck and gazelle in thick bush you shoot one and end up killing two.

For my accommodation while staying in Marsabit, I had a small wattle and mud 'rondavel' built just in the forest edge above the main settlement. Often at night, elephant would use it as a scratching post and I would lie inside, gun at the ready to fire through the walls if it looked like collapsing. It never did, and soon, having satisfied its itch, the animal would move off.

Some nights, often for a good few hours, there would be as many as forty or fifty elephant feeding noisily round about but somehow, my flimsy home remained largely intact and I remained unharmed.

Not so Michael (Mickey) Walker, the Superintendent. He had, at great expense and not a little trouble to himself and others, designed and constructed a beautiful ornamental pond in the garden of his residence and filled it with plants and small, pretty fish imported from the settled area of the country.

On the day the pond was finished, filled with fresh water and the fish introduced into their new, exotic home, he had a succession of visitors to whom he displayed this new and, for the area, unique, garden embellishment, with evident pride. But that same night he had intruders. A herd of elephant raided his garden and drank the entire contents of the pond - fish, plants and all.

Although he was superior to me in rank, Mickey was not my boss because the North Horr Detachment, which I commanded, was under the direct authority of NFD headquarters at Isiolo. Nevertheless, he and I became great friends and, during my visits to Marsabit, we hunted together quite a lot. His house, a wood and iron structure with slight pretensions to colonial grandeur, was small but comfortable and, on odd occasions I would stay there instead of in my rondavel.

One evening, Mickey had a lucky escape. He was dozing in front of his fire when, out of the corner of his eye, he suddenly spotted a snake's tail protruding from a hole in the wooden wall above the stone fireplace. He grabbed a heavy stick, seized the snake's tail and started pulling, ready to club its head as soon as it appeared. He pulled and pulled but the creature managed to wedge itself securely inside the wall so Mickey moved closer to see if there was a way to dislodge it. Suddenly the snake's head appeared from another hole about a foot away from the first and launched itself, fangs bared, to strike its attacker. Thanks be to heaven, it missed as Mickey leaped backwards and went sprawling head over heels over the chair he had just been sitting in.

In order that certain food stuffs would stay fresh longer, Mickey had a cupboard built on his verandah, but this had the unfortunate effect of attracting hyena at night. About midnight one night, he heard a noise and crept outside with a hurricane lantern and a shotgun with the object of clobbering a couple of the beasts. He searched the verandah, then the garden but could find no sign of them so, frustrated, he returned, only to find a large hyena standing on the verandah, snarling and blocking his way into the relative safety of the house. Quick as a flash Mickey fired both barrels at the beast which bounded straight at him. Luckily for him it missed and, with a yelp, disappeared into the night.

Hyena were troublesome especially during the wet season when the game dispersed into the plains areas surrounding Marsabit. They were faced with a choice of either following the game to hunt or, the easier option, staying put and scavenging from humans.

Nightly, they would prowl the settlement on the scrounge for anything faintly edible and they were dangerous so, along side my 'rondavel', I had a trap constructed to discourage them. This consisted of a small wire net enclosure five feet long, fifteen inches wide and about four feet high, open at one end and closed at the other. A foot or so in from the open end, I fixed a rifle so that it pointed down at anything which entered. I attached a length of picture wire to the trigger, passed it over a pulley and hung a piece of rotten meat from it at the closed end of the trap.

It was simple but effective. Hyena, jackal and occasionally leopard would be attracted to the meat, circle the enclosure for ages, clawing at the sides of the trap but eventually, being unable to resist, would enter the open end, grab the meat and pull it out. This fired the gun and the bullet, striking either the neck or the head, invariably killed.

Out in the bush, hyena could not only be a damned nuisance, but could be a serious threat to life and limb. They were generally very numerous and extremely persistent, and if nothing was done to discourage them they would become very bold and a positive hazard to humans.

Constantly prowling the fringes of the camp, they would seize the opportunity to dash in and snatch anything smelling of meat or skin, and cases were reported of half a face or a chunk of thigh being torn off people sleeping in the open. If we were camped for any length of time and they became troublesome, I devised a couple of methods to frustrate them.

I would get my men to dig a hole about four feet diameter and about seven feet deep. A pole was driven into the ground either side of the hole and a line strung between them from which a large chunk of rotten meat was suspended about four feet above the centre of the pit. A hyena would be drawn to the meat and circle the hole, leaning over as it did trying to reach the meat. Eventually, it would lean too far and tumble down the pit to be shot or speared next morning.

Another method I invented which entailed little effort utilised empty paraffin cans. The four gallon cans were rectangular in shape and I would have the tops sliced diagonally and the four pointed flaps pushed down inside the cans. A chunk of meat would be placed in the bottom of each can and they would be placed upright, just outside the camp-site. Hyena would smell the meat and shove their heads into the cans, trapping themselves by the pointed flaps. Although they were plenty powerful enough to break free, they would bang the tin around a few times, howling horribly, then just lie down quietly and wait for the men to shoot them.

The Masai used a method when their cattle were being harassed and killed by hyena. They would boil up large quantities of game and cattle meat and then mix with it quantities of 'cotton soil' to create a heavy, sticky porridge. They would leave this out in large open pots and the hyena would gorge themselves until their stomachs swelled and they became virtually immobile. By dawn, the hyena would be lying about close by, trying to sleep off the impossibly heavy meal and could easily be speared.

I was called out on one occasion to tackle a large bull elephant who was raiding a banana plantation and menacing the settlement who farmed it. I approached the plantation and suddenly came upon the bull facing me head on with his trunk raised stripping bananas from a tree. I fired and the bullet hit him in the Adam's apple, passing just above his heart and pulverising the arteries. The Bull took a step backwards and fell on its side, dead. As it lay there, its penis swelled to a full erection, some thirty inches long and five inches thick. The women from the settlement quickly gathered to butcher the animal and seeing the erection fell about laughing and giggling and making smutty remarks to each other. I never saw this happen again and assume that the cause arose from the damage the bullet had caused to the blood flow. I am told that hanging can have the same effect on humans.

In butchering an elephant for meat, the Africans first gutted it, taking all the delicacies of offal, trunk and fore-feet. Then they one or two would disappear inside the carcass and cut off chunks of the heart and the like and hand them out to friends and family. Nothing was wasted.

Rhino are funny animals, aggressive and intensely stupid and, if startled, will charge at almost anything. Found mostly in bush or wooded country, they always seem to turn up at the most inopportune moments. During all my time in Kenya, I had many confrontations with them but only ever shot two.

Ploughing through the sand of a dry river bed one day in a lorry driven by an African, I was anxious that he should keep going hard to avoid becoming stuck. About half way across, I spotted a Rhino about forty yards away to one side. He was just standing there watching us with no evident malice in his tiny mind, so I took no more notice. Suddenly, the lorry lurched.

"Go faster," I yelled to the driver. "Put your foot down!" But, not hearing me over the roar of the engine, he turned to me to find out what I wanted and immediately, the lorry became bogged down in the soft sand.

At that moment, an idea must have flashed through the Rhino's mind 'cos his ears pricked and he pawed the ground - a sure sign of trouble. 'Here's a great opportunity,' he thought and lowering his mighty head, came straight for us. I had heard tales that locomotives passing through bush country where Rhino were plentiful had often been charged by them so I had to do something fast.

I had with me only my light Mannlicher .316 rifle and that was loaded with soft nosed bullets for shooting meat for the pot so I knew I couldn't kill him before he killed us. Quick as a flash, I raised the rifle and aimed at the base of his front horn. The impact, though it caused the Rhino little harm, made it swerve and, thank heaven, it charged by just missing the rear of the truck. The last I saw of it, it was still going.

Rhino horn has always commanded a very high price. Arabs want it for making the best dagger handles and the Chinese for grinding into powder as a medicine. It appears that, when taken by a male, it causes intense irritation in the penis, resulting in greatly enhanced sexual desire. I'll have to take their word for it since I've never taken it myself - or ever felt the need to.

Before the Army Vet and the Farrier Sergeant Major left Marsabit with their ponies, they and two other itinerants, (One of which, if memory serves, was George Adamson of 'Born Free' fame), gathered at my rondavel one evening for a drink. Talk flowed, time passed and gradually the event turned into an epic boozing session. After several hours, the Army vet suddenly staggered to his feet, grabbed the Farrier by his hair forced open his mouth and wrenched out a set of false teeth.

"I alwaysh have to do thish, hic," he said. "Or, when he gets pished, hic, he'll shwallow 'em and choke."

These sessions became a feature of our social life at Marsabit and on one such occasion, a new game was invented. A mark was made high up on the wall of the rondavel and contestants had to stand, (if they were capable), and with one hand, aim a weapon, usually my .577 heavy rifle, and hit the mark. This rifle was a formidable weapon weighing 15 lbs, firing a 750 grain bullet propelled by 100 grains of Cordite. The muzzle emitted a white flame four feet long, the recoil nearly broke ones shoulder and the resulting smoke nearly choked you. The concussion inside the rondavel was extreme and would blow out the oil lamp. Once, it even exploded all the valves in my old Zenith battery radio.

We were sitting round the table one night getting happily drunk when one guest, who was well beyond his limit, thought of a new game. He pulled out his .45 revolver, put the barrel to his head and, as he pulled the trigger, flipped the barrel up towards the ceiling as he fired. He managed to do this rapidly three times in succession, luckily, successfully missing his head, before we got the gun away from him.

Early in the morning after these sessions, the Police Quarter Guard N.C.O., having heard shots and revelry throughout the night and knowing the usual form it took, sent up a party to patch up the walls of the hut.

Inevitably, after such jollification's and 'rest' at Marsabit, I would return to the Northern Frontier to continue the job of patrolling and policing and, when time allowed, a little hunting.

When camped on the shores of Lake Rudolf, I would occasionally hunt crocodile often to provide meat and skins for native fishermen. This could be an exciting and often quite dangerous occupation.

Crocodile, which infested the lake and could grow to man eating size, would crawl up sand or mud banks to sun themselves, often in groups of a dozen or more. Having good eyesight, they would shuffle off into the lake if you approached within a hundred yards or so, so arriving at the spot they had just left, I would lie down in the depression on the land-ward side of the bank, keep my head down and wait.

After half an hour or so, the crocodile would think it was safe to return and draw themselves back up onto the bank again and suddenly, a head or back would appear on the bank above me. Inevitably, this meant that several more would be out of the water or in the shallows at the edge of the lake. Of course, you had to be careful not to place yourself too near or get yourself in a position where you were between them and the water or you could be in serious trouble. As soon as the first animal became visible, I would stand up, pick my targets and fire. Mad panic would ensue; snapping of jaws, thrashing of tails and the whole lot would charge back into the safety of deep water.

Like hyena, crocodile can be trapped and, if encamped by a croc infested river, my men would sometimes employ this method. They would dig a trench from the water's edge, about two feet wide stretching inland about fifteen feet. At the land-ward end, they would hammer in a stake and attach to it a chunk of rotten meat. During the night, a croc would smell the meat and crawl up the trench to get it. Apparently, they cannot reverse or climb out of the trench, so the poor beast would still be there in the morning. Such a prize would be the subject of many a camp fire story-telling, an entertainment loved by Africans.

My men loved fish, an excellent source of food which, when we could get them, would be gutted and roasted on sticks over the camp fire. Lake Rudolf contained a plentiful supply with Nile Perch up to 200 lbs, and large shoals of Barbel and Tilapia. When encamped on the shore, we would wait until, in the heat of the afternoon sun, large Nile Perch would drift into the shallows and cruise around with their fins and an inch or two of back cleaving the surface. Standing up to our knees in the water, we would wait motionless like herons until one cruised past, then we would shoot it.

Large shoals of barbel would sometimes congregate, shoulder to shoulder, in the breakers along the shore line. All we needed to do was to shoot one of them and six or seven more would be knocked unconscious by the concussion of the bullet hitting the water. It amazed and distressed me to see that, though they had been knocked out a few hours before, gutted and were roasting over the fire, they would still be flipping their tails this way and that, apparently still trying to escape.

Towards the end of my tour on the Northern Frontier, I took on a driver who was from the primitive Turkana tribe. The Turkana were neighbours of both the Gelubba and the Merilli and had many similarities to both. The driver's name was Moru and he was a cocky fellow with a particularly gruesome habit. Every few hours he would start laughing to himself and it appeared that his laughter was prompted by thoughts of the corpses he had seen at various times in the past. The more mutilated the corpse, the louder was his laughter, particularly if they had their vital organs removed. I found the laughter quite irritating and his morbid turn of mind very disturbing.

One day at a camp, he had the lorry bonnet open and the engine ticking over while he adjusted the carburettor. Nearby, an old, nearly naked tribesman was eyeing him curiously and, after a few moments, came over and stood beside him peering at the engine. Moru instantly saw an opportunity for amusement; he took hold of one of the spark plugs then grabbed the old man by the testicles. The reaction was amazing, the old fellow leapt three feet in the air and took off like an Olympic sprinter leaving Moru splitting his sides with laughter.

Although Moru was generally a good driver, there were odd occasions when he could demonstrate a particular lack of attention to the job in hand. Once, while driving a lorry load of Police across the Chalbi desert by a new route, he spotted a lone thorn tree and decided to pull up beneath it for some shelter and a rest. At this point, the Chalbi is flat and empty and there was nothing for many miles around them but this one isolated thorn tree. He drove towards it, but, instead of parking neatly along side it as he had intended, he managed to hit it, head-on. Policemen, who were flung out in all directions by the impact, rushed at him swearing and cursing but

Moru just laughed seeing it as just another in a long chain of amusing incidents.

On a safari to the south of the region with a party of Police, I was driving with Moru beside me when we encountered a densely wooded belt of trees which stretched for many miles in both directions. It looked to be about a mile thick and I decided that for strategic reasons, we should pitch camp on the far side. I drove into the trees and, apart from having to twist and turn and reverse a few times, we had little trouble traversing the wood and there, we set up camp for the night.

We broke camp at dawn and set off to trace our tracks back through the wood to the original route of our safari but, try as we may, we could not penetrate the wood further than about fifty yards. We went back and entered at a different place but, no go, wherever we entered, we could make no headway beyond fifty yards.

We wasted the whole of that day trying to break through but without success and had to camp down again for another night. Next morning we set about hacking our way through but, with many trees to fell and only machete's to fell them with, it took us yet another day before we regained our original trail.

After a year in the desert, I took three weeks leave and had my old Ford roadster towed into Marsabit from the Kaisut Desert where it had stood by the roadside since I had abandoned it a year ago. I consulted our Police mechanic, an Italian by birth, (he so resembled the Italian dictator that he had earned the nickname, 'Musso'), who nodded, rubbed his broad chin and told me to come back in two days.

When I returned, I found that he had replaced the whole engine with one he'd rescued from an old Army salvage dump and it ran beautifully. Immediately, I set off south towards Isiolo then turned east through the Karisima Hills, across the Rift Valley, climbed the Elgeyo Escarpment, and drove on, full speed, to Eldoret and Josephine.

Separation had not dimmed our passion and that first night together was a long and delightful one. I stayed with her for the next three weeks and I confess that I have never come across anything since that we did not indulge in during that wonderful time.

On my return to Marsabit, I stayed the night with Mickey in his old wood and iron house. As we wandered at dusk in the garden we saw a large skunk disappearing down a hole between the roots of a giant hardwood tree which stood some one hundred and twenty feet high and had a trunk at least eight feet diameter at the base. The tree was only about ten yards away from the house and the Mickey expressed the opinion that having such a stinky neighbour so close was not a good idea, so we decided to smoke it out.

The servants were called to light a fire at the entrance to the burrow and for half an hour, nothing happened. Suddenly, the Superintendent looked up.

"Good God!", he exclaimed, pointing upwards. "The bloody thing's on fire".

About sixty feet from the ground, smoke and flames belched from a hole in the trunk looking for all the world like a blast furnace chimney. Apparently the tree was hollow and our small fire had ignited the dry, rotten lining inside the trunk. We poured gallons of water on the fire at the base of the tree but it was too late and soon, the whole tree was ablaze.

By midnight, clouds of smoke and vast showers of sparks were pouring from the upper levels of the tree and we decided that there was nothing we could do but go to bed. The tree was almost vertical, with just a slight lean in the direction of the house but we judged that, when it fell, it should miss by miles. Before we turned in, we had a bet as to what time the whole tree would fall and whether or not it would hit the house.

About dawn, we were awakened by a loud creaking and snapping followed by a mighty whoosh and a ground-shaking thump. The tree had fallen missing the house by six feet.

On a later visit to Marsabit, Mickey and I shot a crop raiding elephant and, not wanting to cut the tusks out with an axe, we left it so that the gums would putrefy. This takes about forty-eight hours and then, the tusks can simply be pulled out of the animal's head. The usual procedure under these circumstances was to cut off the tail to proclaim to anyone finding it that this was a claimed elephant and it should be left alone.

Mind you, this had not always worked, and occasionally, a hunter had brain shot an elephant and cut off its tail to register his claim only to come back later to recover the ivory and find the shot had narrowly missed the brain and only stunned the beast which had recovered and gone on its way. This explains why quite a few elephants were to be encountered without tails.

When Mickey and I returned to the elephant forty-eight hours later, we found that hyenas had discovered the carcass, torn open its stomach and started to devour it. We could see a number of hyena some distance away and before removing the tusks we climbed onto the elephant's back and sat for a while chatting.

Word must have gone around and suddenly, we noticed hyena approaching the corpse from every point of the compass. We were surrounded and in some danger from these ravenous beasts. Having no alternative, we decided to remain where we were on top of the elephant and try to shoot our way out of trouble. We shot sixteen of them before running short of ammunition then, in the ensuing lull, we saw our opportunity and retreated to safety to return the following day for the ivory.

Rabies was rampant in Marsabit as it is throughout East Africa, so some sort of control of the local stray dog population was necessary to try to keep the disease in check. On each of my visits, I would field a force of Police rank and file and, after due warning to the locals, we would tour the trading centre shooting any dogs we could find. The first two or three fell easily but once the rest were wise to what was happening it became much harder. All you saw was a dog's head peeping from behind cover or fleeing out of range with its tail between its legs.

Once, when I arrived in Marsabit, I was told fantastic tales by my men and by locals that there was a huge elephant somewhere in the surrounding forests who's tusks were so large they touched the ground so that, when going uphill, it had to walk backwards. I found this hard to believe but, just in case it was true, I started to hunt it. From then on, some part of every visit was spent tracking the animal until eventually, it became almost a religion to me.

Despite exhaustive efforts, I never did come within sight of the animal although, on occasions, I found tracks which, believe it or not, indicated that it did in fact move backwards up steep slopes. So I was convinced, it really did exist and it wasn't, after all, an African exaggeration.

To give him due credit, Jomo Kenyatta, independent Kenya's first President, accorded this elephant Government protection and assigned to it a full-time game warden to ensure that no poachers would get it. After it died, (of natural causes), the animal, known as Mohammed, was skinned and mounted and now has pride of place in the grounds of Coryndon Museum in Nairobi. Indeed, its tusks do reach down to the ground and would certainly have caused it great difficulty going uphill.

Elephant in those days were very abundant in certain areas and could decimate whole farms in a single night's crop raiding and I was witness to one such herd while hunting with George Adamson, the 'Born Free' Game Warden.

We had camped for the night in a well wooded area on the banks of a small, clear stream in the bottom of a mountain valley. Since we intended to be off at dawn, we turned in early and, for most of the night, slept soundly. About 1.00 am, I was wakened by the noise of elephant feeding nearby and found that George too, had been roused. Gradually, the noise grew louder as more and more elephant approached the campsite and we could hear behind them the sounds echoing down the valley of what must have been a vast herd. The herd split and passed by either side of our camp, some too close for comfort.

"We'd better stand to," said George. "Ready to blot one if they get too near".

Their slow, noisy passage by us lasted for hours and we estimated that the herd must have been about three hundred strong. I must confess that I don't know what would have happened had we found it necessary to shoot, we would probably have been trampled to death in the resulting stampede. It just shows how near to death you can get even if you're extremely careful and, if you're not, it can be even more hazardous like the night I camped by a water-hole and approached a group of elephant unarmed.

I had arrived with my party of Police and at the water-hole in the late afternoon and found that it was just a mass of mud, stirred up, I assumed, by elephant drinking and bathing there sometime before we arrived. We were in need of water so we decided to wait until it had settled and cleared a little, in the meantime, driving away any beasts that came to disturb it again. An hour after dark the elephants arrived so I decided to drive them off. 'I know,' I thought. 'A flare will get rid of them.' And loaded one into the Very Pistol I always carried with me.

I approached the water-hole quite close, armed only with the Very Pistol and fired a white flare into the air. Before firing, I had given insufficient thought as to where the flare would go and unfortunately for me, it came down on the far side of the group and stampeded them straight towards me. I dropped the pistol, took of like a bullet out of a gun and didn't stop running until I was sure the danger was past.

I had noticed, while hunting elephant, that some of them had three toe nails on their forefeet while others had four and I asked George why this was. He, with a lifetime's tracking behind him, confessed that he had never noticed and he didn't have a clue. Later, I asked five other professional hunters the same question and got the same answer from each. Frustrated, I wrote to Archie Richy, the Colony's long time chief

Game Warden, who replied six months later, apologising for the delay, and saying that he didn't know the answer either. However, intrigued by the question, he had written to his opposite number in India who had replied with a short note which read, 'For reasons unknown, some have three toe nails and some have four'. Apparently the phenomenon occurred amongst Indian elephants too and nobody there knew the reason why. I never did find a satisfactory explanation.

On a down-country visit from the Northern Frontier District, I decided to exchange my .577 rifle for another more efficient weapon and in its place I obtained a Jeffries double barrelled .450 No. 2 Magnum.

This gun had relatively short barrels and weighed a good four pounds less than the massive .577. It used bottle-necked instead of straight bullet cases and had a classic performance which could be relied upon to deliver a bullet which was unlikely to break up or deviate when it encountered bone. The bullets weighed 450 grams which were propelled by 80 grams of Cordite producing a striking energy of almost two tons. It handled like a small shotgun and, being perfectly balanced with a good power to weigh ratio, it passed on very little recoil.

Arriving back at Mickey Walker's house in Marsabit, I was anxious to test the new rifle and asked him where I might set up a target. He led me to a large tree to which I pinned a target about six feet above ground level and set off to pace out fifty yards.

"I'll stay here behind the tree," said Mickey. "And let you know where the shots have hit." Suddenly, a red light flashed in my brain.

"No," I said. "Let's be safe. Come back here with me."

After three shots, we walked over to the target and, sure enough, the weapon was spot on but, when we went round the back of the tree, we found three large holes punched out of the trunk where the bullets had passed straight through. At the thought of what could have happened to him, Mickey went pale and I gulped.

"My god," I said. "That was a close run thing." And, for certain, if he'd remained there behind the tree, He'd have been cut to pieces.

My first kill with the new rifle was a marauding bull buffalo. It had been terrorising a native settlement and they called me out to get rid of it so I set up ambush in a patch of trees where it had been known to feed, and waited. Just after dark, I heard the buffalo slowly approaching where I lay, pausing every few seconds to munch the vegetation. It was too dark by now to aim properly so, as it drew nearer, I lit an inch of cigarette and fastened it to the foresight with a rubber band. Slowly, it came towards me and, when I was able to discern its full outline, I raised the rifle and, positioning the red glow over its heart, I fired. It dropped, stone dead.

On full moonlit nights, while I was staying at Marsabit, Mickey Walker and I would often take a party of men just before dusk and entrench ourselves on the crest of a hill a few miles from the settlement. This hill was the roosting ground for vast numbers of guinea fowl who, by day, fed on the plains below but in the evening would return to the hill to spend the night in the low scrub trees which covered its summit and upper slopes.

As huge, spectacular blue lines, consisting of many thousands of birds, rose up the hill making for their roosts, we would snipe them with .22 rifles until they settled in the trees and the light faded. Then, after dark and when the full moon was sufficiently high in the sky, we would send the men to drive them out of the trees. Large clouds of birds in ever changing shapes would flow over the contours of the hill seeking new shelter, while we bagged them with shotguns. This was great sport and the men were delighted at the new and almost unlimited supply of fresh meat they provided.

Quite early in my career in the bush, I had learned never to pitch camp across a Rhino's tracks to water because they had a disconcerting habit of lowering their heads and charging anything which impeded their progress in that direction. Otherwise they, and elephants too, if left alone, were generally considered to be harmless. They would scout around a camp and, unless startled or threatened in any way, would pose no danger to the occupants. Lions however were a different kettle of fish.

One night we were camped by a waterhole two hundred miles south of the border and, since we were in no danger from raiding tribesmen, we had posted no sentries. There was no camp fire and we just slept on the ground in a rough circle.

I woke at dawn to see my Orderly pointing to the ground close by me and chuckling. I turned to see what was amusing him and there, not many feet away were pug marks - lion tracks, heading straight for where I had been peacefully sleeping. I shuddered.

Unseen, the beast had approached to within fifteen feet of me before, thank god, turning and making off. I concluded that my mosquito net must have deterred him from seizing me and dragging me off into the bush for his night-time meal.

I had to make a trip to Nairobi to report to Police Headquarters on my doings in the Northern Frontier District and was forced to stay there for a few days. On my way, I stopped of in Isiolo and, as a matter of politeness, called on the District Officer.

"Look," he said as I was about to leave. "You could do me a big favour. Would you drop in at the bank in Nyeri and collect £5000 for me for the wages bill?" The journey to Nyeri and back was about 90 miles, but I was in no hurry to get to Nairobi so I said it was no trouble and promptly set off.

When I arrived at the bank, the manager told me that he had had a run of withdrawals and had no notes left, only silver. The silver coin of the time was the shilling and it was about the same size as the old British two shilling piece. The District Officer in Isiolo had been very keen for me to get the money but had not specified in what denominations, so without thinking too much about it I said,

"OK, I'll take it in silver." The bank manager looked doubtful.

"I don't think your car will take the weight," he said.

"Don't worry," I replied, cheerfully. "I've got a lorry."

I got my men to spread a tarpaulin in the back of the lorry, load the 50 bags of 2000 shillings each into the middle then fold the edges of the tarpaulin over them and, with the men sitting on top of the pile, we set off back to Isiolo. The weight we were carrying proved almost too much for the lorry and the return journey was slow and painful.

Arriving back at Isiolo just after dark, I went straight to the District Officer's house. He, very cordially, asked me in and invited me to stay for the night.

"And bring the money in with you," he said, expecting it to be in notes in a small carton.

"I can't," I said. "It's too heavy."

When he saw the pile of money, he was furious. Shouting and spluttering, he called me all the idiots under the sun and nearly passed out with rage. To make matters worse, most of the cotton bags holding the coins had split and we had to mount a quarter guard on the lorry overnight. I left at the crack of dawn without saying goodbye. The next time we met, he displayed a distinct coldness towards me and, needless to say, he never asked me to collect cash for him again.

In Nairobi, I bumped into some Army personnel, male and female, and we met several times for a drink. One evening, we sat and talked but after a while, they gradually drifted away leaving only myself and a young ATS Corporal. She was a jolly, roly-poly girl, quite charming, and full of interesting chatter. In the short time that we had been acquainted, I had come to like her a lot and she seemed quite interested in both me and my adventures up country.

That morning, I had collected some photos which I'd taken on the frontier and which I had just had developed. She said that she'd like to see them so I offered to go to my lodgings nearby and get them.

"No," she said. "let me come with you."

We returned to my room and pretty soon, I discovered that it wasn't only the photos that interested her. She flung her arms round me and kissed me, and before long, we were in bed naked. My experience to date had always been with slender women but she was, to say the least, ample - still carrying a good deal of puppy fat, but she was delightful and she made me muse that this was what a water bed was like.

After I returned to the Northern Frontier, we came into possession of a teenage Turkana boy who had been captured by the Merilli, one of our 'tame' tribes, during one of their raids, and then sold on to the Gelubba. He had escaped from the Gelubba and, luckily for him, had reached one of our patrols before they caught him again. He proved invaluable to me since I was able to obtain from him detailed intelligence concerning the Gelubba and their customs.

Before being captured, he had spent some time in Southern Turkana and, while there, he had become a quite fluent speaker of Swahili which allowed me to communicate with him effectively. The Turkana, from whom he came, speak the same language as the Gelubba - never before recorded - which I was now in a position to understand.

During the next eighteen months, I spent endless hours with him recording the Gelubba language in Swahili and then, myself, translating it into English. This exercise also enabled me to learn the language, being the first European ever to have done so.

Copies of my translations reached the Frontier head-quarter's Administrative Centre and in due course I received a letter from the Colony's Secretariat informing me that it was a very creditable effort, (had my English grammar been better, it would have been more creditable), and that my contribution had been placed in the Colony's Archives.

By this time I had become a crack shot and one of the country's best rifle marksmen, especially on moving targets. I never bothered to alter the sights for range, I just aimed higher or lower and still managed to hit my target. A favourite drunken party trick was to flip into the air, a thin disc, about the thickness of a playing card, and cut it in half edgeways with a rifle shot. Very spectacular, and I seldom failed.

Once, on patrol in bush country, we came upon a party of armed Shangilla and a skirmish broke out. We were getting the better of them and, all of a sudden, my sights fell on the back of one of them who was running away. As I squeezed the trigger, a thorn branch brushed my face and I missed. Instantly, I reloaded, and fired again but as I did so, he stumbled and again I missed him but cut the skin cartridge belt from his waist. At the discharge of my third shot, he jinked sideways and disappeared unharmed into the bush. With my shooting skill, he was up against formidable odds and won. I wish him luck and hope he's still alive to tell the tale.

Shooting a man under pressure or in a state of excitement is, in my opinion a very dicey business at the best of times and I strongly sympathise with UK Police armed marksmen. They are forced to decide in only a split second whether or not to fire, with the conflicting pressures of crime control, their own and the public's safety on the one hand, and the threat of suspension from duty, drawn out public enquiries and possible ruination of their careers, on the other.

In Kenya, in those days, it was different. Police were often recommended for commendation or other award after such actions and the consequent reduction of the stress involved allowed more rational judgement of the situation.

Once, in a skirmish, I shot a criminal in the chest with my Smith and Wesson .45 revolver. Only one shot, I thought, until, after the action, I was amazed to see three bullet holes in him. Checking with my men to be sure none of them had fired at him, I broke my revolver to reload and just couldn't believe my eyes, three discharged rounds when I would have sworn I only fired once.

At intervals on the Frontier, tribal 'confrontations' would develop over cattle thieving, water-hole occupation, a killing or two, or some other small, local disagreement. This would inspire warriors to gather, several hundred on each side, all hurling noisy abuse and threats at each other. War dances would commence and both sides would indicate that they were about to attack the other. Occasionally, this would happen but, more often than not, the threats and dancing would continue for hours and even days, neither side really wanting serious fighting.

Inevitably, a few Police would arrive on the scene and separate them and, after a considerable amount of negotiation, would persuade them to disperse. Both sides would go their way boasting and telling everyone they met that, if the wicked Police hadn't arrived on the scene just in time to stop them, they would have attacked the opposition and annihilated the lot.

In remote districts, the Africans loved a baraza. Parties would trek in to our headquarters from miles away and would sit down under a tree or other cover, patiently awaiting my attention. Whole families would stay for hours, and sometimes days, until I had time to sit down with them and listen to their personal problems and disputes and hand out a determination. They so enjoyed these outings that, more often than not, the last thing they wanted was a quick judgement, or indeed, one at all. However, when a decision on a problem was finally made, it was accepted and acted upon without question.

A few weeks before I left the Frontier District, I was leading a patrol up near Gelubba country and with us was our 'tame' Turkana youth, the one who had translated their language for me. We woke at dawn one morning to find that he had gone, disappeared sometime during the night. We followed his tracks for some way and found that they were heading north by west towards a distant Gelubba settlement. This saddened me because, knowing that if he did manage to make contact with the Gelubba, they would not accept him - they never took back anyone who had left them for any length of time - and they most certainly would have killed him.

Down the Nile to Civilisation

It was 1945 and the war in Europe had ended. So, at least for the time being, had my service on the Northern Frontier and I was given a temporary posting to Mombasa to await a ship back to the UK on home leave. Since the force was short handed, my leave was restricted to a mere three months including travelling time, but that didn't concern me much since there was work to be done and I was keen to get on with it.

I left Banya with Ajuro, my personal servant beside me, heading south towards North Horr and Marsabit, then on to the Administrative Headquarters at Isiolo, and eventually, the coast. I was thrilled at the thought of returning to England and my beloved Norfolk and, after nine long, eventful years away, seeing my family and friends again. But, as I left the desert behind, I felt a deep pang of regret that perhaps I may never see this strange, rough, demanding wilderness again. And if I ever did, it would be under such altered circumstances that, for me it could never be the same.

Where my next permanent posting would be, I hadn't a clue. All I did know was that I was almost certain to lose the, very useful, two shillings a day 'hard living' allowance which I had received while stationed in the Northern Frontier District.

In Marsabit, I came across two British Army Sergeants who were on passage to god knows where and had stopped off in the settlement overnight. Since the hour was late and they had nowhere else to stay, I invited them back to my rondavel and offered to feed them.

197

We had just started the soup course when I spotted a bat hanging from the thatch under the roof. Bats commonly roosted inside the hut and I tended to tolerate them except when they hung themselves above me or the dining table owing to their unpleasant habit of defecating frequently on anything below.

Quick as lightening, but unseen by my guests, I picked up my .22 rifle and shot it. The bat, its guts hanging out, fell straight down and landed right in the soup of one of my startled guests. Instantly, I apologised and excused myself for my sudden, instinctive reaction but each of them looked at the other with raised eyebrows and neither finished his meal.

As I said my goodbyes at Isiolo, I was handed a note. It was from the Administrative Officer and I reproduce it here.

From The Headquarters of the Officer in Charge, Northern Frontier District

Isiolo. Dated 18.7.45

My dear Mills
I was sorry to have missed seeing you before you left. I wanted to thank you for all the help which you gave us, you did a very good job of work in the Marsabit district and will be much missed. One reaction of your departure was as soon as the Gelubba heard you were going they immediately sent over a raiding party!

I hope that you find Mombasa a pleasant change from the lava deserts and gales of the lake shore.
With every good wish,

Yours sincerely
Gerald Reece
Officer in Charge

Once again, Ajuro and I set out for Nairobi and Mombasa, both of us a little older and a little wiser. He, knowing we were heading for a friendly, civilised town rather than the wilderness, was a great deal more cheerful and relaxed than when, three years earlier, we had headed together for the desert. Instead of nervously clutching his bundle, he sat back, arms spread and grinning at the thought of regaling his 'townie' friends with endless tales of adventure and heroism.

On arrival in Mombasa, I learned that I would have to wait some while for a suitable, homeward-bound ship and in the interim, was given the job of prosecutor in a special court that had been set up to clear a backlog of criminal cases. I was also given a free hand otherwise, to help or hinder other officers as I wished.

The special court was placed under the jurisdiction of a District Officer who, like all District Officers at the time, had magisterial powers. His ideas regarding court procedure ran, I'm glad to say, very much on the same lines as my own. Commence at 9.30 am, sit until noon then adjourn until next day to 'study prosecution files and write up judgements' i.e. get pissed and then sleep it off. Saturdays and Sundays were also left free 'in order to catch up with other affairs'.

Speaking of other affairs, I made no attempt to contact any of my former loves Margaret, Arlene or Sandra. I had been away three years and I was a little wiser - or so I thought. In fact, events were to prove that I was no wiser at all.

While awaiting a ship in Mombasa, I fell ill with amoebic dysentery and was immediately hospitalised for three weeks, for a course of Emertine injections.

"Emertine has a cumulative effect on the heart," the doctor had said. "And I don't trust you to take it easy at home." In fact, throughout the treatment, I felt just fine.

Obeying the doctors orders, I entered the European hospital and discovered that there was only one other patient there. He was an old pioneer settler and before 'lights out' we had a long and very interesting chat about the old days in the Colony. When I awoke the following morning, his bed was empty.

"Where's my friend?" I asked one of the nurses.

"Oh dear," she said. "I'm afraid he died during the night." So I was left alone, the only patient in the whole hospital and with three nurses to tend me.

The three nurses, all British, were members of the Queen Alexandra's Royal Nursing Corps and rather than 'nurse', they preferred to be called sister. One of them, Joan, was tall and attractive and had a certain presence. When she walked into the room she, and everyone present, knew who was in charge. I took an immediate liking to her.

My treatment consisted of one injection a day and it was Joan who usually administered it. She would march jauntily into the room carrying her tray of equipment, tell me to turn on my side, whip off the sheet and my kikoi, (a loin cloth, which was all I ever wore in bed), then, without ceremony, jab my buttock with what felt like an extremely long, blunt needle. This torture occurred at about ten each morning and was the only treatment I received.

One morning, I woke quite early then dropped off to sleep again lying flat on my back and when, at ten, Joan swept in, I was still dozing. Apparently, I must have been dreaming something delightful because I had become sexually aroused and the signs were made plain by the prominence beneath the single bed sheet. I was very embarrassed and didn't know what to do but Joan just smiled, whipped of the sheet and my kikoi, and stood, completely unabashed, gazing at the erect organ for a length of time which could be considered less than decent.

Late in the first week of my confinement, Joan came and sat on my bed and we talked, mainly about our lives and our plans for the future and gradually, we became closer than merely nurse and patient.

It seemed that she, like me was waiting for a ship, but while mine was taking me home to the UK, hers was bound for Bombay and the far east where she was to marry her fiancé, a Government Officer on a foreign posting. Due to the fact that the war with Japan was not yet over, no shipping dates were published and she had no idea how long she would be stuck in Mombasa. As she rose to go about her other duties, she bent forward and kissed me.

During the following two weeks, Joan would often sit on my bed and, when no one else was about, we kissed and petted and whispered our yearning in each other's ear. I was totally charmed by her but convinced that the closeness that had developed between us would only last for the duration of my stay in the hospital. However, on my discharge, I asked her to accompany me to a mess party, fully expecting her to refuse. To my utter amazement, she accepted.

For the next few weeks, during off-duty hours, we were constant companions and every minute we spent together was, for me at least and I think for her also, a wonderful time. Joan was attractive in uniform but after work, when she changed into civvies and dolled herself up for an evening out, she was positively stunning.

After each date, I escorted Joan across town back to the hospital and, as we said goodnight, we kissed and petted almost to the brink of love-making, but there it always stopped. Her destiny lay elsewhere and though I was sure she would have loved to go the whole way, she remained steadfast in her determination not to commit herself to me.

One night, after a particularly heavy drinking session, she said she would sleep at my place rather than face the trek across town. Of course, I didn't argue and though she shared my bed and we lay half naked in each other's arms, she declined to make love. Just before dawn, we woke and as we looked at each other in the half-light, nature suddenly took control and we concluded the business we had so often started.

Inevitably, notification arrived for her to board a liner for the far east and, on the appointed day, I escorted her to the docks and went on board to say goodbye. I was miserable to see her go just when our romance was starting to blossom and she, in turn was weeping at our parting. In her cabin, as we kissed and held each other, I suddenly felt the ship begin to tremble.

"Christ!" I yelled. "The bloody thing's sailed." And, sure enough the vessel had slipped her moorings and was picking up speed across the harbour with the next stop Bombay.

Thank heaven I was in uniform. I dashed to the Purser's office and told him that I had come on board to make a few enquiries and hadn't heard the warnings of imminent departure. It was vital, I said, that I return ashore by the pilot cutter. The Purser rushed me to the Captain who laughed his head off and gave me permission to disembark on condition that I wrote a note accepting full responsibility for any harm that may befall me in doing so.

The cutter was bouncing along beside the ship at what seemed to me like full speed but the Pilot nimbly threw his leg over the gunwale and clambered down the rope ladder which hung precariously over the side near the bow. Just before he jumped into the cutter he looked up at me, "Wait 'til the bow swerves in and starts to lift on a wave," he shouted. "Then just leave the rope ladder without any hesitation." I watched as he jumped, 'piece of cake,' I thought. And sure enough, he was right. How long it took for Joan to find out what had happened to me, I don't know because, after dashing from her cabin, I never saw her again.

I went ashore from the pilot boat at 2 p.m. and since I was in some need of consolation, I stopped of at an hotel en route to my quarters for a few beers. At the bar, I bumped in to an old acquaintance and his wife who were in the company of a young woman I'd never met before and who was apparently staying in the hotel. Her name was Rosemary and she seemed sad and on the verge of tears because, as she explained, she had just been parted from her new husband.

She had been in the forces stationed in Mombasa and had met and fallen in love with the officer of a cargo ship which had been berthed in the harbour for some months awaiting the shipment of spares from the UK. His ship had sailed two days before and she was anxious to return to the UK where she hoped, before too long, to meet up with him again.

I sympathised with her and told her of my recent parting and, for a while, the four of us drank and talked about the current uncertainties thrust upon us by the recent war.

After an hour or so, my friends said goodbye and departed, leaving Rosemary and I to our mutual commiseration's, in the process of which, we got ourselves fairly lubricated. On parting, we arranged to meet for a drink the next evening, following which, we became regular companions, but on a purely platonic basis.

We did the usual round of bars and parties and one night, after a particularly rowdy and drunken Army mess party at which we got well and truly plastered, we both pitched up in her hotel room for the night. With nothing said by either of us, we lay on the bed and started to make love. I say 'started' because neither of us ever finished the job. In her drunken stupor, she either fell asleep or passed out, while I, equally inebriated, applied myself vigorously to the task in hand, ultimately without success.

Next morning we awoke with mighty hangovers and little recollection of anything that had taken place between us. But this was the start of a very close friendship which lasted until I left for the UK.

I was beginning to despair of ever finding a passage home from Mombasa so, after considerable thought, I decided to apply to headquarters for permission to travel overland to Alexandria in Egypt. There, it was rumoured, troop ships were constantly passing through heading for the UK. To my surprise, permission was granted but with a condition that my absence would be restricted to three months in total.

The journey was to take me from Mombasa to the source of the Nile then all the way down the river until I reached the delta on the Mediterranean. It proved to be a fascinating journey, too much to tell at the present but who knows? It may later be the subject of another volume.

Once I had planned the route and gained the necessary permissions, I needed currency for the various countries through which I would pass, particularly Egypt. The only source I could locate was a military unit which was under the charge of a British Captain.

"Yes, we can accommodate you," he said. Then, pointing to an adjacent office. "Go through there. The girl will sort you out." Imagine my surprise when, as I entered the office I recognised the girl was Sandra who I had jilted three years earlier at the threat of marriage.

"Oh, hello," she said smiling. "You've been gone a long time. Nice to see you again." She sorted out the money for me and for a few minutes, we chatted pleasantly about our lives since last we met. It seems that, not long after my sudden departure for the Frontier, she had met and fallen in love with a British resident in Mombasa. They had been happily married now for over two years and I gathered, to my relief that my treatment of her had left no lasting scars.

Once again, I left my car, my weapons and most of my few possessions in storage and said farewell for the time being to Ajuro. He would miss me, he said, and I believed him, but also I was sure that he was secretly pleased that, for a while, I would not be forcing him into adventures he didn't wholly relish and that my absence would give him more leisure time to hang about with his cronies.

The first phase of the trip was by train from the Kenya coast to Uganda and I drove Rosemary and myself to the railway station, leaving her to drive the police fifteen hundred-weight pick-up back to headquarters. As I boarded the train, we embraced and agreeing, for proprieties sake, not to make contact when we both reached the UK, we wished each other god speed on our separate journeys and parted. I looked back for a last glimpse of her as the train pulled slowly out of the station. Rosemary waved and, as she disappeared from view, she blew me one final kiss.

So, once again, I left the coast for the unknown taking with me the minimum amount of possessions, (but I did include my .45 revolver), and commenced my three months restricted leave.

For the first leg of the journey, I spent a day and two nights confined to a compartment of the up-country train and, for company, only three young catholic priests, who were bound for a missionary station in the Belgian Congo. What a pious trio. All their time was spent reading the bible and asking each other questions about it as if they were preparing for some examination or other. Their constant righteous patter began to get up my nose, so every now and then, I would ask them,

"How about a game of Poker, or Liar Dice?" Or again, "There's a dak bungalow at the next stop. We'll be able to sink a few beers." They didn't take kindly to my interruption to their virtuous discourse and tried their best to ignore me. I pitied the poor Africans in the Congo who were about to be corrupted by them.

The train rumbled slowly westward past Nairobi, Nakuru and Eldoret, where I had served a tour before the Northern Frontier. We crossed the Kenya/Uganda border at Malaba then on to the end of the line at Namagasa. From here I caught an ancient steamer across Lake Kyoga then travelled by land to Butiabi on the eastern shore of Lake Albert.

I rested for half a day in Butiabi waiting for the small East Africa Railways and Harbours steamer which took me across the Lake and then north to Nimule, a small settlement on the west bank of the Nile where it leaves Lake Albert and heads for the Med. Of course nothing happened very quickly and I was beginning to lose track of time. How long it had taken me to reach this point in my journey, I hadn't a clue, but I had ceased to worry - there was after all, little that I could do to speed my progress.

From Nimule, came a succession of native buses, old estate cars and anything that would carry me onward but, as ever, there were delays. Progress was constantly thwarted by break-downs, shortages of fuel, missing drivers, waiting for days at a time for some fellow passenger to turn up, who seldom did. Eventually, I was delivered to a place on the river which was navigable and I boarded a marvellous old stern-wheel paddle steamer.

She was small and rectangular and around her hull were lashed a series of open steel barges of a similar size to herself; one each side, six in two rows of three at the prow and more astern. The barges were intended for carrying cargo but also served to keep the steamer afloat when she hit one of the many sand or mud banks which she encountered every few miles. When this huge 'raft' was assembled, she would be aimed down river and with its paddle thundering and thrashing the water, it could eventually achieve two or three miles an hour.

The boat carried a variety of passenger, men, women and children, some of whom were encamped around her decks with yet more on the barges, where they cooked and chattered, ate and slept surrounded by their multi-coloured possessions. Some had animals - chickens, sheep, goats and even the odd vociferous pig. The whole thing was a colourful rag-bag of noise and heat and smells like a deranged circus on the move.

The vessel was virtually unsteerable and when it came to a bend, it simply hit the bank and ground to a halt with a colossal racket as the barges bashed into one another. Immediately, a dingy would be lowered and a party put ashore to attach ropes to the forward barges and, using trees as anchors for a small hand winch, would drag the whole raft away from the bank and point it down river again. Throughout the whole manoeuvre, the shore party would be shouting, singing, leaping about, cheering and thoroughly enjoying the whole procedure.

On the second day, I ventured onto the bridge and introduced myself to the Captain. He was a Sudanese from Khartoum and told me proudly that, before one could become Skipper of such a paddle steamer, one had to have fifteen years experience on the Nile. The river, he said, was treacherous, full of mud and sand banks which were forever changing position and were impossible to detect in the muddy waters and it took a man of his experience to know the moods of the great river and pilot the vessel safely to her destination. In the event, we hit many of the banks and each time, the shore party set forth in their well practised routine to winch us clear.

Frequent stops were made to pick up the large quantities of firewood needed by the vessel, from stacks of logs which had been previously cut by unseen hands and piled on the bank. All along the river, crocodile basked on the muddy fringes and were notorious for grabbing people who came down to wash or to draw water. The Skipper possessed an old .303 rifle which he kept in the wheel-house and with his permission, I shot a number of these crocodiles in the hope that at least a few of the locals would be spared the agony of providing a meal for the beasts.

Where vegetation and swamps bordered the river, we saw vast herds of elephant and buffalo and quite a few rhino, not to mention huge numbers of various breeds of plains game. In places, hippo were plentiful but there was little sign of human habitation and the greenery soon gave way to semi-desert supporting only thinly scattered thorn bush.

For many days we passed through the vast El Sudd swamp. Through this region, larger than Wales, we followed a bewildering series of narrow and ever changing channels amid a vast sea of giant papyrus, proving the Captains word that great experience was necessary to navigate the river.

From time to time, we would spot a few naked Dinka tribesmen and women in the clearings or foot tracks through the vegetation but otherwise, we saw, from horizon to horizon, only papyrus.

It was during our passage through El Sudd that I came down with a bad dose of Malaria. I took to my bed for three days while the fever raged and I sweated gallons. I felt so ill, I thought I would die, but when the fever broke, I emerged from my cramped little cabin, weak but, thank god, still alive.

Occasionally, we halted and went ashore to view the ruins of ancient temples which had stood the test of countless centuries on the banks of the mighty Nile. Most of them had stone slip-ways which ran down to the river and upon which were carved a series of marks to calibrate the height of the seasonal flood waters. In ancient days, the priest would levy taxes on local farmers in proportion to the flood height which controlled the amount of cultivation that was possible after the floods had subsided.

We passed through Southern Sudan and eventually arrived in Khartoum where I booked myself for a week into the famous Nile Hotel. The Nile had every facility for the gratification of its guests and I decided that, after the discomforts and privations I had suffered so far on my journey, I would spoil myself in its luxurious accommodations. The stay would also give me the opportunity to recover completely from my recent debilitating bout of Malaria.

One day I travelled the mile or so into the centre of the town by taxi and as we were negotiating a roundabout, rather too fast, the vehicle left the road and ploughed into a large shop window. The police were called and, for some unknown reason, decided that the accident was my fault. They jabbered away in language I hardly understood, expressing the firm conviction that I had caused the accident - though quite how, they negelcted to explain - and would be immediately arrested. To my relief, the driver suddenly chirped up and told them that he was to blame because he had fallen asleep and they let me go.

After the week, in which very little of interest happened except for two days of strong winds called a 'Khamsin', I returned to the paddle steamer, much rested for the next leg of my journey. The 'Khamsin' is a hot, oppressive wind from the south or south-east which brings with it swirling clouds of sand and brown dust which penetrates everything and causes considerable discomfort throughout the early months of the year.

I left the steamer at Wadi Halfa and boarded an Egyptian train bound for Alexandria. I was on the train for two nights and I was impressed no end by its cleanliness and the efficiency of the railway staff.

We halted occasionally to drop off passengers and pick up others, and at some, to take on fuel and water. At one such halt where the low, stone buildings apparently doubled as a Police or military outpost, I sat and watched as an Egyptian labourer applied a liberal coat of whitewash to the walls. He worked meticulously with his brush, missing nothing as he proceeded along the building. When he reached the porch with its rack into which was chained a row of old rifles - the total armament of the Police Station - I stared in amazement as he carefully whitewashed everything - rifles and all. I howled with laughter and would dearly have loved to stay and see the NCO's reaction when he inspected the work but, unfortunately, we passed on our way.

By the time the train reached Alexandria, the journey had taken a long time but, since it was beyond my control, just how long it had been, I didn't bother to calculate.

I was directed by a Government transit agent to proceed back to Cairo to await instructions to board a ship to the UK and there I found accommodation on a floating hotel opposite the main entrance to the Gezeira Country Club. The hotel accommodated about thirty guests and, going in to breakfast on my first morning, who should I meet but two of my old UK pals. One was now an Army Captain and the other a RAF Squadron Leader and they were there killing time awaiting further posting. We exchanged news of home, related to each other tales of our experiences since last we had met, and breakfasted together until eventually, they were called to leave. By now the war with Japan was over and there was an air of relief and celebration about the place.

For several weeks I waited for news of an available berth and spent most of my time in the Gezeira Club which, together with Shepped's Hotel, was razed to the ground by anti-British mobs soon after I left Cairo.

Not long after I moved into the floating Hotel, there arrived on board, the daughter of the General manager of the East African Railways and Harbours Company. She was small and very attractive and I quickly introduced myself. She was in transit, waiting for a ship to take her to Kenya so we had plenty to talk about and, for some weeks, we had a very pleasant friendship. Several times, I took her to dinner at Shepped's Hotel and to a few of Cairo's excellent cabaret spots but we remained just friends - no impropriety whatsoever.

There were several British wives with their children aboard the floating hotel and, although inviting looks and hints within their chatter, indicated a willingness to form a closer relationship than mere shipmates, I resisted. An absent husband is one thing, but a wife with children - definitely not.

My hotel and my drinks bills together were costing me twenty-two shillings a day, but since I was drawing a Government retention allowance of twenty-eight shillings a day, I was in profit so I was perfectly happy and in no hurry to move on. The desire to stay was made additionally attractive since my encounter with a couple of Egyptian gunsmiths. We had talked guns and shooting for a while, then they invited me to accompany them for a couple of day's shooting when their duck season opened. They told of countless thousands of ducks on lakes and irrigated land, and what marvellous sport was to be had. I looked forward with eager anticipation to the day.

To my utter dismay, I was allocated a berth three days prior to the start of their duck season and made my way, reluctantly, to the ship that would carry me home.

My passage was on a large, old liner called the Mooltan which had been commandeered as a troop ship. After leaving Cairo, she called at Port Said where literally thousands of military personnel, who were heading for home and de-mobilisation, embarked and it seemed that the ship was packed to the gunwales with heaving humanity. Luckily for me, I was allocated a berth in a cabin with three officers and was able to use the ship's dining room instead of the rougher messing facilities shared by NCO's and other ranks.

The voyage through the Mediterranean and the Bay of Biscay was uneventful and, early one grey, wet afternoon, I landed in Liverpool.

The U.K., Marriage, and Return to Kenya

I had been away from England for nearly nine years and as I came ashore, my first reaction to what I saw was one of profound shock and anger at the devastation wrought by the recent war. I witnessed the bomb damaged docks and the shattered shell that had once been Liverpool and boiled with frustration at the thought that I had not been here in Europe to do my bit in the struggle and the eventual destruction of that vile enemy.

I walked into the crowded bar at Lime Street station and jostled with a mixed throng of servicemen and civilians who, despite the ruination that surrounded them seemed to have lost little of their vivacity and optimism and, as always in Liverpool, the wit flowed unchecked amongst them. My second shock hit me when I got to the bar - 'Bloody hell,' I thought. 'The beer's gone up.'

My train took me through the heart of England and although, while still in Africa, I had seen odd newspaper reports and pictures, they had ill-prepared me for the total extent of the bomb damage that met my saddened eyes. But between the blackened, ruined cities, I could still recognise patches of that green and pleasant land I had left before the conflagration started.

We pulled into Norwich, not as I had expected, at the City Station - that was now a flattened ruin, but across town at Thorpe Station quite close to where Betty, my elder sister and my brother-in-law, a retired Army

Officer, lived. "You'd better stay here for a few days," Betty said. "Give Mother and Father a chance to get used to you first." It seems that my parents had expressed some apprehension as to how I may have turned out and were wary of what their, once wild, son had become after so long in the wilderness. This fear was understandable, I suppose, after all I was only a raw youth when last they saw me and since then, I had hardly been constrained to learn the finer points of English polite society.

By now, Father had retired and, since there were only the two of them at home, my parents kept no servants other than a casual cleaning lady. "Mother even does her own cooking," Betty reported.

I gladly accepted my sister's invitation and while I was with them, I searched the city to find myself a suitable vehicle. After a couple of days, I lit upon a 1927 Austin eighteen-six, a rare old bus, not too steady on her legs and somewhat akin to a motorised greenhouse. She'll do me fine, I thought, and promptly bought her.

After a few days with my sister, I moved in with my parents, who seemed satisfied by now that I was not as savage a creature as they feared I might have become, and they welcomed me with open arms. Father, a keen shot himself, as I have said, was enthralled by my tales of hunting and safari and for a second, I fancied I saw a glint of envy in his eyes.

One of my first journeys in the old Austin was to Ranworth, where I met up in the pub with our old gardener who brought me up to date with events since I had left. After leaving him, I took a walk past the country house, now no longer in my father's possession, and renewed my vow that one day, I would return to this place, the scene of so much of my childhood happiness.

I soon ventured into the social round and renewed my acquaintance with Norwich's premier dance hall, the Samson and Hercules. It was here that, one night during the winter, I met Betty, who was to become my first wife. She was a pretty, twenty-two year old, brunette and petite, and full of confidence and fun. I fell for her immediately and dated her as often as I could in the ensuing few weeks. From the outset, we got on like a house on fire and, before too long, I invited her home to stay with me and my parent and she accepted.

My mother gave Betty a room at the back of the house, some way apart from mine, but, since the house had no heating, it was too cold for her. However, we soon made moves to remedy that particular problem.

After only a few short weeks of courtship, it became clear in my mind regarding my relationship with Betty and, after a romantic evening out, to my great joy, she accepted my proposal of marriage. Mother and Father were delighted, if a little cautious about the poor girl's future in the colonies.

A licence had to be obtained and, when asked for her prospective husband's full name, Betty was stumped. She had never heard me called by anything other than my nickname, 'Peter' and the names with which I was christened were a mystery to her. The elderly clerk who was processing the application was dumbfounded. But then, he shrugged and concluded that the events of the recent war had thrown up many unlikely circumstances.

Soon after the wedding, Betty and I were offered temporary accommodation in my Aunt's cottage close by our old country house at Ranworth. The place had been empty for some time but we were delighted to accept and promptly moved in.

By this time, I had over-shot my three month's restricted leave and had made no contact with my force's headquarters since leaving Kenya. I was worried in case they had abandoned me due to my silence, so I made the decision to remedy the situation forthwith. Before I could make contact however, I started to feel unwell from what I thought was probably a tropical 'low fever' and I immediately reported this to the Colonial Medical Department. I was given an appointment to see one of their doctors in London who checked me over and asked me where I'd been and what I'd been up to. "Oh, Kenya's Northern Frontier," he said. "I spent a couple of years in British Somaliland. Do you know old so-and-so...?

We chatted for some while after which he said, "Three years on the Northern Frontier, then three months on the Nile, eh?" He nodded his head. "You can't go back yet. Come and see me in six week's time." He thought for a moment then quickly amended his advice. "Go back home," he said, "And wait until I send for you for another check-up." The fever slipped away unnoticed while Betty and I lost ourselves in the dream world of early marriage.

In fact, it was getting on for three months later, when I awoke from the dream and decided that it was time I returned to Kenya, so I contacted the doctor again.

"OK, come up and see me," he said. "I'd forgotten all about you."

This time, he gave me immediate clearance and I set about finding passage for my wife and myself, but this proved to be a fruitless exercise. The war was only just over and, as yet, passenger ships to the colonies had not yet been restored to their regular duties. I was lost for a solution.

211

After some telephoning, I discovered that there was an American built, 'lease lend' aircraft carrier about to sail for Bombay via Kenya and then to the States to be broken up. On this, her last voyage, she would carry some passengers - but, alas, no women. I saw no option and booked myself a berth. With a heavy heart, I bid farewell to my new wife, who promised to take passage to Kenya as soon as a ship could be found, and headed for the docks.

Having seen some action, the ship was, to say the least of it, war-weary and was clearly on her last legs so the voyage was fraught with problems and delays. Being American, she was full of gadgets which the Royal Navy crew found great difficulty in getting to function. We passed through the Suez Canal but, in one of the Bitter Lakes, she broke down and for some time, we were left without power. Then in the Gulf of Aden, she started to take in water and again we were delayed.

By now, I was very concerned because my three month's restricted leave had extended itself to nearly a year and I would be in desperate trouble with my superiors once I landed in Kenya. At the start of the voyage, I had been given access to the ward room so, being rather worried and with little else to do, I made regular use of the facility and, I dare say, drank even more than any of the officers did.

Eventually, we made port in Mombasa and I booked in for the night at the Manor Hotel. I went immediately and retrieved my car, my weapons and my possessions from storage so that I would be ready for action the instant I received orders, then, at sundowner time, I strolled into the hotel bar.

To my amazement and horror, who should be seated at the bar with their backs to me, but the Commissioner of Police and his Personal Staff Officer - I froze. Almost the last activities I had performed before leaving the Northern Frontier District was, with a party of fifty of my men, to escort the Commissioner on a tour of inspection of all the frontier forts so, in a way, I supposed, I was fresh in his mind.

Of all the people I could have bumped into before I had chance to make my excuses to lower mortals, it had to be the Commissioner. I turned and was just about to creep out, unseen, when the Commissioner swung round.

"Ah, Mills,." he called. "You just going on leave? Come and join us for a drink." Caught red-handed, I sidled nervously up to the bar.

"Actually, Sir," I said, sheepishly. "Not going - I'm just returning from leave."

He ordered my drink and asked me where I'd been posted to next. Of course, I had no idea, so I shrugged my shoulders and smiled inanely.

"Where will you send him?" the Commissioner said to his Staff Officer. I waited with bated breath while the Staff Officer pondered the question.

"We'll send him to Masai," he said at length. "But he'll have to wait a few weeks. The chap there's been posted to Somaliland but has been held up for a passage." The Masai! I was overjoyed. "Meanwhile," the Staff Officer continued. "He can take temporary charge of Nairobi Traffic Department." I finished my drink, made my excuses and left feeling not a little relieved that I had managed to sneak back in after all this time and not be caught out.

The following day, I packed the car, collected Ajuro from where he'd been staying during my absence and set off for Nairobi.

The Force was responsible for conducting all driving tests and, amongst my other duties as Officer-in-Charge of the Traffic Department, I was the test examiner. My testing ground was on open land beside Traffic HQ and consisted of a figure of eight course laid out in large boulders placed just far enough apart for a vehicle to pass between them. Beside it was a length of corrugated iron fence, eight feet high, supported on two flimsy wooden posts.

My test procedure was first, to ask the applicant a few highway code questions then, if the answers satisfied me, ask them to drive, unaccompanied round and round the figure of eight course until I told them to stop. I was constantly amazed at how many of them almost up-ended the vehicle by climbing up the boulders. Those who had succeeded so far, were then asked to reverse to within a foot of the fence. It was surprising how much din that fence made when it was knocked down.

All being well, I accompanied them on a run through the busiest of the city streets.

On one occasion, I sat beside a lady applicant and all was going well until we turned a corner and started to climb a hill. Suddenly, I saw a wisp of smoke rise up beside me from somewhere under the floor of the ancient vehicle.

"I think your car's overheating," I said.

"Oh, don't worry," she replied. "It goes better when it gets hot." Half a minute later, it burst into flames and pretty soon had burned itself out completely. Up to then, she'd been doing all right and besides, she was very good looking, so I passed her.

After three weeks in temporary command of the Traffic Department in Nairobi, I learned that my predecessor in Masai had been allocated passage to his new posting and I was ordered to leave for Narok forthwith.

I had changed my old 1934 Ford for an English built Ford, 22 hp V8 which was far better suited, I thought, for the territory I was about to command. Again, Ajuro and I loaded up and took to the road.

Masai was an independent Police Detachment forming no part of any Province and coming under the direct command of the Commissioner. its Administrative Centre in Narok, lay some ninety miles over appalling roads to the west of Nairobi and was seldom visited by the Headquarters staff. Some time after I took command, headquarters contacted me and asked what the road to Narok was like. Suspecting an impending inspection by the Commissioner, and dearly wishing to keep my independence of operation, I replied, "Impassable and, in parts, positively dangerous." That was enough for them and they stayed away.

At this time, my wife, Betty, was still in the UK awaiting passage to Kenya and I began to worry about how she would take to living out in the wilds when, eventually, she did arrive.

As everyone who watches TV is aware, Masai and Masai Mara are now game reserves but, in those days, there were no game reserves or game parks and no tourist lodges or even roads. However, the area teemed with game of every description. There was little crime in the area, save for the odd murder, some stock rustling and, occasionally, a border incident when the Masai would raid neighbouring reserves.

On one safari to the Masai/Kikuyu border, intended to discourage a group of Masai from carrying out a reprisal attack upon Kikuyu who had stolen some of their cattle, my party climbed to the top of an escarpment overlooking the border. Down below us, we spotted a party of Kikuyu herders. I trained my binoculars on them and could hardly believe what I saw. The herders, a group of young boys, were sat on the ground in a tight circle in the centre of which was a stick, and it seemed to me that each of the youngsters was masturbating. I turned to my Sergeant for verification.

"Oh, yes," he said, casually. "It's a competition and the one who shoots nearest to the stick, wins." I was astounded.

The Masai region was to me a paradise. I had a three-ton lorry in which I could travel about wherever I pleased throughout its abundant game areas, most of which were infested with tsetse fly and so, were devoid of stock and tribesmen.

Narok, which sat along an elevated ridge, boasted a British District Commissioner, a District Officer, a Police Doctor, a British Nurse and a Veterinary Officer. Wives and families of serving officers were permitted to reside there.

My first action after setting up home in Narok was to take a prolonged safari around my command to ascertain the lie of the land and learn, first hand, some of its problems. When I returned, I received a message telling me that Betty, who was by now heavily pregnant, was on her way heading for Mombasa in an old British India ship called the Modassa. I quickly obtained permission to leave my command and drove down to Mombasa to meet her.

The voyage had been quite good and Betty looked well, and even prettier that when I'd last seen her. I was, however, concerned about the forthcoming journey; over rough, unmade roads and in the prevailing heat, I wasn't certain how she would stand up to it. "I'll be fine," she said, but even so, I decided to take it in easy stages.

We left Mombasa rather late in the evening and stopped halfway to Nairobi at Mac's Inn in Mtito Ndei, then just a few rondavels, a bar and a dining room. Our room was furnished with two camp beds and, of course, we both climbed into one of them.

Shortly afterwards, it collapsed.

We continued the following morning on the second stage and booked in at the Avenue Hotel in Nairobi. Betty was tired and soon after dinner, at about nine o'clock, we decided to turn in. Suddenly, a knock came at the door and I was handed a message from the Force's Signals Officer. He said that he had just received a signal from Narok who told him that the Masai had killed Hugh Grant, the District Commissioner, but before they could continue, the set had gone off the air so he had no more information as to what was happening.

The force had recently acquired a number of ex army No. 22 Morse transmitters and these had been installed at most of the outlying stations but they were not very reliable and the Signals Officer could no longer make contact with Narok. The Commissioner had been informed of the situation and, as soon as I contacted him, he said, "Get up there straight away. Take the Signals Officer with you, and a spare set, and report to me as soon as you can."

I told Betty what had happened and said that I would have to leave her at the hotel and return for her as soon as I was able. "No!" she said immediately. "I'm coming with you." I didn't know what trouble we might be walking into but I was sure it would not be the place for a heavily pregnant lady, however, she was adamant and my efforts to dissuade her were in vain.

Just before midnight, she, I and the Signals Officer set off towards, heaven knows what, and our only weapons, a .45 revolver each. For once, I hadn't packed a rifle nor did I bring my Orderly with his weapons. For all we knew then, it could have been a full Masai uprising with many more killings.

Anxious to get there as soon as I could, I left the track some thirty miles short of Narok and took a short cut across a trackless plain. To me, this was routine, but the Signals Officer was not of the warrior breed and kept telling me it would be wiser to wait till daylight. Betty was quiet but I couldn't help wondering what she, a twenty-two year old pregnant woman fresh out from Europe, thought about the whole fiasco. All she could see in the glare of the headlights was tall grass and light scrub being bulldozed by the front of the car and the gleaming eyes of unidentified animal staring out of the darkness as we bounced and lurched at full speed across this unknown land. She must have been scared stiff. But worse was to follow.

We reached Narok about an hour before dawn and, for the last two miles, I slowed and turned off the headlights. A couple of hundred yards from my Police headquarters, I stopped, turned off the engine and, telling Betty to hold tight, the Signals Officer and I walked quietly to towards the HQ. Poor girl, god knows, she must have been terrified.

Just short of the building we were halted by the night sentry. To my great relief, there seemed to be nothing amiss at my head quarters so, after identification, I went back for Betty then asked for a report from the Sergeant in charge.

It appeared that the incident that had sparked off the panic in Nairobi had taken place, not in Narok, but a hundred miles away and it was not, as had been feared, the start of a general uprising but merely an isolated incident. The news had been transmitted from the radio set at Narok but, before the message could be completed, the set had failed leaving Nairobi in the dark regarding the full details of the incident

It seems that Hugh Grant, the District Commissioner had been camped down with a Government Stock Officer on a mission to enforce the compulsory purchase of some Masai cattle. An agreement was in force that, if the Masai had surplus cattle, they were to sell an agreed quota to the Government to help fulfil the colony's general requirement for meat.

The surplus existed but the Masai concerned had failed to abide by the agreement so Hugh Grant and the Stock Control Officer, together with a handful of tribal police had raided the Masai and confiscated a large number of their stock.

To the Masai, cattle mean everything; their whole lives revolve around their stock and ownership of cattle is their wealth and their pride. To a great extent, the Masai live off milk mixed with blood drawn from the cattle which they obtain by shooting a hollow arrow into the cows jugular vein and collecting the blood as it spurts out. The blood is then mixed with the milk and drunk providing a very rich part of their diet. The cows are milked into a gourd which, after use, has to be cleaned and to do this, the women piss into the gourd and swill it round in order to get rid of the stale milk.

The confiscated stock of one young Masai Moran (Warrior), were being put through a temporary cattle crush erected by the Stock Control Officer and the price to be paid for each one was noted. Hugh Grant was leaning on the crush rail talking to the Stock Officer when the young Moran came up and begged him to release to him one of the beasts which happened to be his particular pet. The Masai usually had one special beast on which they lavished particular affection; it was their proudest possession and they would continually sing its praises. The Moran offered to replace his pet with another beast, or even two but Hugh Grant was adamant. "No!" he said. "You've refused to produce your quota, so those I've rounded up are going for sale."

The Moran walked away but, unnoticed by Hugh, returned a few minutes later carrying his spear.

The Masai spear is a very heavy and formidable weapon used for both throwing and stabbing. It consists of a three foot long razor sharp iron blade, a short wooden grip and a four to five feet long iron shaft and, hurled with some power has a devastating effect. The Moran stopped some distance behind Hugh and hurled his heavy, greased spear which penetrated Hugh's back between the shoulder blades, went straight through him and dug itself into the ground, a measured twenty-two feet the other side.

Only five hours after arriving at Narok, I placed Betty in the care of my staff and an armed Police guard and left for the scene of the crime to conduct my investigation. Poor girl, she was exhausted, frightened and not a little dusty from the journey so, soon after I left, she asked the servants to run her a bath. "Running a bath", however was not quite the procedure we followed at Narok; the bath was a simple galvanised tin affair which had to be filled with water heated over the kitchen fire. This was done, the bath was filled and Betty proceeded to lower herself into the soothing hot water. A sudden unidentifiable noise nearly made her jump out of her skin. A giant bull-frog which was hanging round near the improvised drainage hole, let out an almighty croak and, as Betty said later, she nearly had the baby on the spot.

As if this wasn't bad enough she had another fright that same night. My house was furnished with a primitive outside bucket loo which was emptied every night by one of the servants. Betty was unaware of the procedure and, after dark that night went to use the loo. Just as she had settled down, the flap at the rear of the loo was suddenly lifted and the bucket whipped out from under her. The shock, again, nearly made her give birth.

I completed my investigation and prosecuted the young Masai Moran for murder and in due course, a circuit judge came up from Nairobi to try the case. I had sorted out the best building I could find for use as the 'High Court' and, after we had inspected the guard of honour I had laid on specially for the occasion, I conducted the judge to the court house. Unfortunately, between he and the steps ran a trench carrying water to the settlement into which, dressed in full regalia, he stumbled up to his knees. The spectacle caused a great deal of merriment amongst the onlookers including the witnesses waiting to attend the trial and somewhat delayed the opening of the proceedings.

What transpired enraged me. While I was conducting my investigations into the crime, Government officials, unknown to me, had persuaded the particular Masai clan to which the accused belonged, the Ngidongi, to hand over five hundred head of cattle to Hugh Grant's wife as compensation for the loss of her husband. Tribal custom among the Masai dictated that blood money, usually in the form of cattle, should be handed over to the victim's family to settle the affair after a killing and, believing this to have been accomplished, the accused pleaded guilty. However, guilty pleas were not accepted by the court and the trial had to run its course. I completed the prosecution case whereupon the judge found him guilty then sentenced him to death and he was duly hanged. This, I considered, represented an unacceptable level of hypocrisy and sharp practice to be carried out on relatively untutored natives by a supposedly civilised white Government, and I said so.

This case had taken me away from Narok for ten days and when I returned I found that the District Officer's wife, a kind and friendly lady, had moved my wife into their house pending my return. All in all, it had been a fine introduction for her to Kenya and its Police.

There was yet another shock in store for my poor wife who, by now, I thought, must be getting weary of the primitive conditions she was having to endure. The houses of we Europeans in Narok lay in two lines either side of an elevated ridge which climbed steadily for several miles until it reached the forested levels. Household water was channelled down this ridge in an open furrow fed by a spring a mile or two above the settlement and secondary furrows led from it into each of the dwellings. The water, when it arrived at the house, was not of the consistently pure quality she was used to in the UK. In fact it varied from being merely cloudy to a thick glutinous mud depending whether buffalo, forest hog, water buck, baboon or other animals had availed themselves of the facility and trampled in it on its way down the ridge. Each day, an African labourer had to walk the length of the furrow and repair its banks wherever the animals had been bathing and consequently, our own washing and bathing had to be delayed until the water ran a bit clearer. Drinking and cooking water were however less of a problem since we collected it in tanks from the house roofs. None of the water was ever boiled or filtered, we just used it as it arrived.

I received a message one day while I was still at home, that a small herd of elephants were raiding an area of precious crops some way along the ridge so in company with Myles Turner, a game warden, I prepared to set off to drive them away. "I'll come with you," said Betty, and heavily pregnant though she was, she came along too.

We soon came upon the herd in a forested area of the ridge and after attempts to shoo them away had failed, I selected one, aimed and fired. Immediately it turned, bellowed and charged straight for us. Betty squealed and froze with terror. Myles and I wasted no time and, both firing together, brought it down at a distance from us, far too close for Betty's comfort.

Since the time for Betty to give birth was fast approaching, I gave some thought as to where this should take place. I wanted to make sure that the risk to her and the baby were minimised so the hospital in Narok didn't look to me like the best proposition. It was an African hospital staffed by a British doctor and a British nurse but maternity, particularly, European style, was not its speciality. Most of its patients had dragged themselves in there having reached a stage well beyond help and soon died, whereupon they were instantly buried. I happened to notice that the hospital had only one or two graves, quite inconsistent with the number of deaths that occurred there so I asked the reason for this. Apparently, the body would be buried during the day but, at night, hyenas would come and dig up the corpse, leaving the grave open ready for the next one. I decided that when the time drew near, Betty would go to Nairobi.

The British doctor from the hospital would often drop in for a chat and a bottle of beer and since the temperature was often too high for comfort, he and I would sit on the front verandah wearing very short shorts and no underpants, as was the custom in such a climate. I, being conscious of the rules of modesty in polite society, would take care when ladies passed by. However, the good doctor was neglectful of such decorum and consistently failed to conceal his manhood from the amazed onlookers who were usually too embarrassed to say anything.

The Masai, being stock herders found it necessary on occasions to control lions which raided their cattle and, for this they employed very effective tactics. They would turn out in large numbers, track down the culprit and surround it in a very wide circle. Each would be armed with a heavy iron spear, (like the one used to kill Hugh Grant), and a man-sized buffalo hide shield upon which was painted the warrior's particular 'coat of arms' in a fashion similar to our knights of ages past. Slowly, the circle would close until, eventually, the warriors would stand shoulder-to-shoulder, leaving the beast no other alternative but to charge. It was anybody's guess which way the lion would leap so excitement amongst the throng reached fever pitch until, at last, the trapped animal made its bid for freedom. At the last second, the Masai at whom the charge was directed, would plant the spiked butt of his spear in the ground and, kneeling down behind his shield, would try to impale the lion as it landed on him. A general hullabaloo would ensue as the rest of the warriors hurled their spears at the lion and, as a rule, it would meet its end with little injury to the Masai. Occasionally, however, one would be killed or badly mauled.

Masai showed great respect for their fellows and custom demanded that hospitality be shown to any Masai male travelling through their territory. He would be wined and dined then would be invited to select any woman or girl he desired to sleep with. The couple would be shown to a skin hut where the male would plant his spear at the entrance and as long as it stood there, they would remain undisturbed. If this custom were introduced into Europe, some enterprising iron worker would make a fortune out of spears.

In the 1880's, European explorers found that the Masai knew that mosquitos caused Malaria and that the bark from a local tree cured it. Many years later, a French doctor distilled a substance from the bark, called it Quinine and claimed that he had discovered it himself.

Safariing, hunting and dealing with crime and uprisings under the grand conditions of the region made time fly and, all too soon, the time came for Betty to give birth. I must admit, it caught me unaware so I had to make some rather hurried arrangements for her transport to the Nursing Home in Nairobi where we had arranged for her confinement. Time was getting short and I was heavily involved in a case which demanded my personal attention, however, I had a lorry heading that way so I detailed the driver to make her comfortable and see that she got there safely. The only trouble was, the lorry was travelling to Nairobi carrying a batch of prisoners who had been convicted of murder and were going there to be hanged. In a couple of days, we were the proud parents of a lovely baby girl whom we named Ann.

Very soon afterwards, I was promoted to full Inspector and posted to take charge of the large station at Nanyuki on the foot-hills of Mount Kenya. This district was an up-country, all white settled area consisting mostly of vast dairy and ranching estates, some of which exceeded fifty-thousand acres. It was comparatively sparsely populated but held masses of game and, at higher levels, in the foot-hills and forested regions there were abundant elephant, buffalo and rhino so I was able to keep my hunting skills in good practice.

Under my command, I had three Assistant Inspectors and some fifty rank and file, so, for a change, I was able to stand back and simply direct and supervise operations instead of being involved too closely in the more minor day-to-day problems. Life then, was not too arduous for me. I always preferred to delegate; when you are not in an isolated situation, its the only way to operate and efficient unit.

Nanyuki township had two hotels, one of which was owned and run by a couple who were renowned for being 'characters' - the wife more so than her husband. In the grounds stood a flag pole and, while her husband was away hunting, the wife hoisted a flag at half mast as a signal to her white-hunter boyfriends that she was available. Some even said that, at times, she flew her knickers from it. In any event, the place was lively and we certainly had some wild parties in the poky little bar of the hotel.

Nanyuki was a garrison town where a Company of the King's African Rifles were stationed. This, of course, attracted a bevy of African prostitutes to the town so the Government were obliged to set up a V.D. clinic to which every prostitute had to report weekly for examination. If they were passed fit, the girls would be given a dated card and if any were found with an outdated card or without a card at all, they were picked up by the Police, prosecuted and sent back to their reserves. In East African Law it is an offence not to report the contraction of a Venereal Disease, also an offence for a sufferer not to disclose the source of the disease. We had very little trouble from the girls who always behaved responsibly and also provided the Police with much valuable information.

Personally, I never touched a prostitute, or, for that matter, a coloured woman, but I firmly believe that the former provide a necessary service and, if properly organised, they help to prevent crime and to control disease. I would like to see them licensed in the UK and be subjected to regular medical examination. If you can't prevent it, control it.

One afternoon, Myles Turner and Eric Rundgren, both Game Wardens and professional hunters who are now, sadly, both dead, dashed into my office. "Quick Peter," said Myles. "Elephant are trampling and destroying the maize crop planted just below the forest line. Get your rifle, and hurry." With them was an English speaking Dane who was in Kenya for a short holiday. They had met him in a bar the previous night and he had told them how keen he was to see some game close up so they had brought him along.

We trekked up to the plantation, parts of which were looking pretty battered, and soon spotted elephants - over a hundred of them scattered over a wide area of secondary forest just above the maize crops. We approached the nearest group and each shot one, then, seeing another line of elephants moving off up the slopes, we set off in pursuit telling the Dane to wait here for us.

We soon caught up with the rear of the line and Eric shot one of the elephants driving the rest way off into the higher forest areas. When we returned to where we had left our guest, we found him half way up a tall tree shivering with fright in case the large cow elephant, who was battering the trunk of the tree and screaming with rage, should manage to dislodge him. Myles and Eric thought the whole thing very comical and dallied for some time before shooting the old girl and releasing our friend from his imprisonment. By that time, The Dane had seen enough game to last him a lifetime and positively refused to accompany us again.

A few afternoons later, Myles, Eric and I were called out again to the same location to answer reports that the elephants had returned and were again trampling the maize crop. But, this time, the joke was to be on me.

We found the elephant higher up the slope than on the previous occasion and, as we hurried up a wide game track, we came upon an old cow elephant standing across the track, broadside on. She was some forty yards ahead of us and stood on higher ground. We halted, Eric, who by this time had killed some eight-hundred elephant, was on my right and Myles on my left, obscured by the undergrowth. Just as I was thinking, 'She's a cow, so we'll probably spare her,' Eric's gun exploded in my ear. The elephant dropped only to leap straight up again and, to my amazement, pinned her ears back, stuck out her trunk and charged down hill straight towards us. 'No problem,' I thought as I raised my .45 No. 2 rifle. 'If I miss, with two of the most experienced professional hunters, one on either sight of me, I'll be OK.' And I fired. Fortunately, my bullet found the exact frontal brain shot spot and the elephant dropped dead in front of me. Turning towards Eric to say, 'That's how it should be done.' I caught side of him a hundred yards away, his stumpy legs whirling like flails going flat out for safer ground. He'd had a stoppage while trying to reload for a second shot. I turned to Myles who called out, 'What are you shooting at?' Being in the undergrowth, he had seen nothing of the action. Thank god I didn't miss.

Two days later, I returned to the location in a 15 cwt. pick-up truck, this time bringing Betty with me. Again, I was looking for raiding elephant but this time I drove up the same game track only to get bogged down with wheel spin on the entrails of the beast we'd shot on the last occasion. Hyena had found the carcass and pulled the whole lot out onto the track. It was ages before we got going again.

It is a point of particular interest to hunters that each animal has its own way of signalling aggression when it feels threatened and, if he is to stay alive for long, it's as well that the hunter be aware of these. For instance, the rhino, when suddenly disturbed, will usually paw the ground with its front feet and prick its ears forward in the direction of the threat. This activity indicates that the animal is about to charge. On the other hand, if it waggles its ears in all directions it will most likely turn and make off. Lions will suddenly cease to retreat, lie down, face the threat and attempt to conceal themselves. If the tail suddenly sticks up vertical like a radio aerial, beware, it's a sure sign that a charge is coming.

Eric Rundgren and I set off one day on a buffalo hunt accompanied by several African Game Scouts and Eric's pack of nondescript dogs. Our trail led us up a steep, well wooded valley at the bottom of which ran a small stream. It soon became apparent that a herd of buffalo was browsing some way up ahead of us and proceeding slowly up the valley. "You stay here at the bottom of the valley," said Eric. "And I'll take my party out of the trees, get up ahead of them and drive them back towards you. That way you'll be certain to bag a few."

At first, I thought this a reasonable tactic but, as I watched him and his men climb up out of the valley, I began to realise that, in the dense vegetation of the valley floor, I'd have little chance of a clear shot. I called my scouts together and we slowly climbed to a level where the vegetation was somewhat thinner. No sooner had we reached the higher level and without a warning shot being fired, we saw the whole herd stampeding down the valley at full speed and bulldozing everything in its path. I never got a shot and, to my horror, I realised that, had I remained where Eric had suggested, in the thick vegetation, myself and my scouts would likely as not, have been trampled to death.

Kenya, in its early days had large tracts of land which were uninhabited either by blacks or whites and offered great opportunities for the hunter. So abundant was the game, that it resembled one giant Whipsnade. For the first fifteen years or so of my service there, I combined hunting with game control and with supplying fresh meat for my staff, my men and for local inhabitants. Nothing that was shot was wasted. These days, it may sound obscene to record that, during my service in Africa, I shot over three thousand six hundred animals of all species. Among them were innumerable plains game for meat, buck gazelle, antelope, only two rhino and three lions but many elephant and buffalo. At times, it could be a very hazardous pursuit particularly when attempting to cull a man-eater, an animal that had been wounded or one at bay in thick vegetation, and a saying at the time was, 'Every big animal you shot was one nearer to the one that would kill you.'

I used light magazine rifles for non-dangerous game and heavy short barrelled doubles for the big ones. I never had much time for medium bore rifles since they were too heavy as meat getters and not powerful enough to rely on in times of trouble.

I classified bores of around .303 as light, and bores between .450 magnum and .577 as heavy, though the .416 was a classic heavy, big game rifle. I disliked heavy magazine rifles for two reasons; firstly, bringing another round up from the magazine was a noisy activity; secondly, their rounds had long powder cases and if the bolt was not drawn back that extra distance, the round would bend in the breach and the rifle would jam. Imagine that, when a buffalo, a lion or an elephant is charging straight at you. Daily use of a light magazine rifle using short cased ammunition led one into the habit of drawing the bolt back a short distance, not far enough when it came to using a heavy rifle. After some practice one could easily fire four aimed shots from a double barrelled heavy rifle in the time it took to fire three from a heavy magazine rifle. Heavy game rifles should have short barrels since they are often required to be used in thick bush or dense forest where long barrels would present problems. Also, slings and sling swivels are dangerous appendages since they can catch up on branches or thorns and the like. Telescopic sights were not fashionable then. In any case, how do you deal with a charging animal through telescopic sights in dense vegetation.

Early weapons had low muzzle velocities - around 2000 feet per second - which made the judging of range vitally important and for this, considerable practice was required. I spent every moment while on foot safari estimating the distance to any prominent object ahead of me then pacing it out as I advanced towards it. This practice gave me an excellent faculty for judging distance with a rifle until I could discard the notion of adjusting the sight to suit the range. Instead, I used sights fixed at a hundred yards and simply raised or lower as my instinctive judgement deemed necessary. Similarly, every time I saw an animal, domesticated or wild, I would automatically select the point at which a bullet had to penetrate, having regard to the angle at which the animal presented itself, in order to kill it. Even today, I still find myself doing this.

Each morning, while waiting for breakfast to be served, I would pick up an empty rifle, select a spot on the wall and bring the rifle up rapidly to my shoulder, aimed at the selected spot. I would do this several times, and this practice, coupled with those of judging distance and picking the killing spot, made my shooting very fast, accurate and totally instinctive. Moving targets became no problem to me, in fact, with a rifle, I preferred a moving target to a stationary one and my rate of success was significantly high.

As hand weapons went, I preferred revolvers, such as my .45 1904 pattern Smith and Wesson, to automatic pistols, though the Colt .45 automatic was easy to use, accurate and very powerful. The best way to be sure of hitting your target using a hand weapon is to look at the point you want to hit then bring the weapon up or down as if you are pointing with a finger then fire as soon as the hand and eye coincide, but without sighting the weapon. Pistols are, of course, close range weapons and even at short distances, it's very easy to miss.

One day, a riot broke out in an African township some distance from Nanyuki which resulted in me conducting the prosecution against forty-nine persons, mostly Somali's. Many of the defendants had sufficient means to pay for representation and between them they employed no fewer than nine defence lawyers - of several nationalities.

I could foresee that the case was going to be confusing so, in order to keep track of events I drew up a chart containing forty-nine squares each labelled with the name of one of the accused. I dealt with the accused in the same order as the chart and, as the case progressed, I added the names of witnesses and notes on the evidence to each square so that I could deal with the whole thing in an organised manner when I came to address the Court. The nine lawyers had a whale of a time, cross examining and arguing and contradicting each other. At times I thought the proceeding would break out in a fight. Into the third morning of the trial, I began to have doubts about how well organised I was but the Magistrate suddenly halted proceedings and said words to the effect that, "Look. I think you lot down there are in a bloody muddle and I am too. It's obvious the whole lot are guilty so get them to plead so and I'll give 'em four weeks each and we can all get out of here." I looked around the Court and saw that none of them objected, so I didn't either. They all pleaded guilty and the case ended.

After a year at Nanyuki, during which I re-captured two British prisoners who had escaped from Nairobi prison and who led me on a car chase which, at times reached a hundred miles an hour, I was promoted to Chief Inspector followed, two months later, by promotion to Assistant Superintendent of Police. The time had come when, if I had ambitions to receive further promotion or salary increments, I would have to pass a standard examination in the Swahili language. I put myself forward and was duly called to be examined.

I was the only candidate present and had no trouble at all with the oral part of the exam, but when it came to the written paper, I found that, to me, it was mostly gobbledegook. I sat for a while feeling totally dejected at the thought that I had progressed so far and was about to be tripped up by a few words that I would probably never have to write anyway. The Invigilator, who happened to be a District Officer and also a friend of mine, stared at me for a few seconds and, perceiving my difficulty suddenly said, "Sod off and have a beer. I'll do it for you."

He happened to be a brilliant linguist so when I returned an hour later, I copied what he'd done in my best handwriting and passed with flying colours.

Incidentally, Nanyuki actually had an electricity supply of sorts generated by an ancient steam engine and my wife, Betty, found it quite extraordinary that she had to call a servant to switch the lights on and off.

Return to the Frontier

News filtered through to us at Nanyuki that there had been some trouble at Mandera, a Divisional Headquarters in the extreme north-east of Kenya. Mandera lay right on the border with both Ethiopia and Somalia and was constantly plagued by cross-border raiders but there it was not Gelubba Shangilla, as at Banya, but Somali Shifta.

Not long previously, the British District Officer at Mandera, with a small party of Dubas (armed tribal frontier police), had come into contact with a Shifta raiding party and had engaged them. In the ensuing battle, the Shifta managed to kill him and all his men then escaped across the border. As a result of this action and the constant threat of other raids, the Superintendent of Police in charge of the Mandera Division had succumbed to the stresses of his job and gone completely 'off his trolley'. So anxious was he to get away from the place and its problems that he deliberately shot himself through the hand with a .45 revolver. Pretty soon, a message came through from the Northern Frontier District Headquarters in Isiolo ordering me to get up there and take over - fast.

Leaving my wife and baby daughter in the tender care of the District Officer's wife, I left Nanyuki and drove the sixty miles into Isiolo where a plane had been chartered to fly me to Mandera. I didn't know what to expect but, as I walked out onto the field with the pilot - and ex-RAF fighter pilot - I saw that we were heading for an old, rather battered Tiger Moth biplane. "Mmm." said the pilot. I drew no particular conclusions from this observation but simply put my trust in his undoubted experience of aircraft and flying.

We took off from Isiolo, gradually rose above the low cloud cover and for an hour or so, all seemed well. We passed out of cloud into a clear sky and I was fascinated to watch the world slip slowly by below us. Suddenly, something began to look familiar. I knew that road, and that plateau, and that town. "Hey!" I shouted to the pilot. "Isn't that Laisamis down there."

Sure enough, it was. I had often travelled that road - it was the route from Isiolo to Marsabit and Laisamis lay about half way between the two. Instead of heading north-east we had been travelling due north and were miles off our route.

"My god!" the pilot shouted. "You're right." and promptly laid the plane over on its side. I nearly fell out and almost fainted. "Sorry," he said, after he had steadied the plane onto her new course. "I must have been following the wrong compass heading."

We headed out across a hundred and twenty miles of trackless desert and just made it to Wajir before we ran out of fuel.

Eventually reaching Mandera, we headed for the three-hundred yard sand landing strip but, what at first looked to me like a simple matter of setting the plane down soon turned into an aborted attempt and we powered up into the sky again for another try. Six times we attempted to land, and when finally, we drew to a stop, I concluded that my pilot had never flown a Tiger Moth before.

I spent an interesting six weeks in Mandera and took the opportunity to conduct a safari around the area. The Dawa River, which, at that point, formed the border between Kenya and Ethiopia, ran alongside the Mandera Centre and its banks were flanked for a hundred yards either side by Doum Palms and thick, lush vegetation.

Locals complained to me that baboons resident along the river were constantly raiding their crops and uprooted anything they tried to grow so, one evening I set out with my Orderly in an attempt to remedy the matter. Foolishly, I took with me only an under-lever .22 Hornet Rifle which used long, needle-like, nickel covered bullets of very high velocity but producing very little shocking or stopping power. Bullets would pass straight through an animal and they would hardly feel it at all.

We soon came into contact with baboon and, as soon as I saw them, I recalled that the species in this area were particularly large. A large male showed himself and I shot him through the head, killing him instantly. I soon began to wish I'd left the brutes alone, for then, the whole family group surrounded us roaring and snarling, the bigger males rushing forward in mock attacks, screaming and tearing up vegetation as they came. Nothing was a clear target, only black rushing bodies, half screened by the vegetation. In angry groups like that, they could tear a leopard to pieces, so I got out as fast as I could and never went after them again.

One evening I was camped down beside a dense thicket of Doum Palms and, in the evening, took a stroll down a game track to where I knew there was a small open pool. I sat down beside the pool on a fallen palm trunk and, for ten minutes or so, drifted off into a contemplation of the future. I was suddenly roused from my reverie by the sight of a large Hyena emerging from the undergrowth not fifteen feet from where I sat. The hyena froze, I froze, each I think as frightened as the other. The only weapon I had with me was my .45 revolver and a revolver is hardly the weapon with which a sensible man will engage a Hyena, large or small, so I decided to remain frozen unless the beast made a move to attack me. The Hyena looked at me and I looked at it for what seemed like an hour, but was probably only a minute or so. Finally, it looked down at the water, then back at me, shook its head and wandered off without a backward glance. I waited 'til it was out of sight before daring to breathe again.

While at Mandera, I received news that I had been given a permanent posting to take command of the Isiolo Division. As the Superintendent in charge, I commanded, not only Isiolo Division, itself a large area, but also Wajir and Garissa Divisions which operated as detachments under Isiolo. All together this covered a huge area of some sixty-thousand square miles stretching along the Frontier to the Indian Ocean. Even the old Arab island town of Lamu came under my jurisdiction. This was a considerable step up for me and I was pleased as Punch.

As soon as my relief arrived in Mandera, I handed over and set off back to Isiolo - but this time, by lorry, not by aircraft. It was a four hundred mile journey over atrocious terrain and I drove by day and camped by night arriving in Isiolo in the early hours, exhausted.

During my absence, The Chief Superintendent had organised the removal of my family and our belongings from Nanyuki and I found them securely installed in a large Government owned house. Back on the Frontier, I was as happy as a pig in muck, the only trouble being, there were very few problems from cross-border raiding parties.

Most of the terrain in my command consisted of a fine desert wilderness with vegetation varying from dense bush and forest to none at all. The Garissa Lorian Swamp, to the north of the Tana River basin teemed with game and held the heaviest ivory to be found in Kenya.

A strange phenomenon occurred regularly along the course of the Tana River. Each evening a high wind would blow starting at its mouth on the Indian Ocean coast and continuing for several hundred miles upstream. It extended for only a couple of hundred yards either side of the river and you could set your clock by it. You could hear it approaching, rushing upstream, then it would blow hard for a couple of minutes followed by dead silence. But where it finished, I never found out.

Isiolo itself, contained a number of officials including a Senior Administration Officer designated as Officer in Charge of the Northern Frontier, his opposite number a Police Chief Superintendent, a Game Warden, (George Adamson), a Stock inspector, myself, a British Police Inspector, a District Commissioner and a District Officer. There was, however, no doctor, the Northern Frontier District Medical Officer having his headquarters two hundred and twenty miles to the north-east in Wajir. Families of serving officers were allowed to reside there and altogether, it formed a friendly and very sociable community. The Chief Superintendent of Police at the time was an especially agreeable fellow and was liked by everybody, particularly some of the wives. It was rumoured that he kept them all satisfied while their husbands were away on safari. He and I became great friends and we usually managed to get UK leave at the same time, during which, he and his Swedish wife would often stay with us at Ranworth where he enjoyed the fishing.

It was one day, as I was driving back into Isiolo that I first met Joy Adamson, George's famous wife of 'Born Free' and other literary and artistic works. I saw a lorry approaching me through the bush so I stopped and, as it drew alongside, there, in the driving seat, stripped to the waist, was Joy. Next to her, sat an African, and several more were riding in the back. Now, in those days, in Africa, white women simply didn't go about topless. not even on the coast and I have to confess, I was embarrassed. We chatted for a minute or two and went on our separate ways.

Many years later, George was killed while trying to defend a group of tourists who had landed at an airstrip in the south of the Frontier District and were being shot at by Somali Shifta. Poor George was then over eighty and only lightly armed so he stood little chance.

Some time later, I was sitting at my desk one morning attending to some paperwork when Joy Adamson rushed in, in a right old stew. The Adamson's house was about six miles out of Isiolo and I had been made aware that a military unit was in the area conducting some artillery practice using live ammunition. Joy demanded that I put a stop to it immediately but, since I saw no pressing reason to do so, I declined to interfere.

"But what if zee shells, zay come into zee kitchen?" Joy screamed, so I called up the military and asked them what was going on. A few minutes later, the Officer in charge of the unit rang me back to apologise. Apparently they had miscalculated their grid references and, all morning, had been whistling shells all round the Adamson's property. I insisted that they cease forthwith and the matter was settled.

One evening, just after dark, I was returning to Isiolo, when I suddenly spotted a wide area illuminated by myriad's of fire-flies. A shimmering, cold blue cloud several feet thick hovered a few feet above the ground and stretched away into the distance. I stopped and, for a while, I gazed enchanted at this fascinating phenomenon. After a few minutes, my eyes began to discern a stationary vehicle standing somewhere in the middle of the cloud, so I walked over to investigate. There I found a Police lorry with one of my Inspectors and a few rank and file standing over a small fire upon which sat a frying pan.

"What the hell's going on," I asked.

"Well, sir," the Inspector stuttered. "The lorry petered out and we couldn't get it going again, so I thought, if I heated the plugs it might bring it back to life." We towed the lorry back to base. its condenser had given up the ghost.

The most easterly Division in my command had its headquarters at Wajir and was housed in an Arab style, 'Beau Geste' fort constructed of white-washed stone blocks, as were the rest of the buildings in Wajir. The surrounding terrain consisted mainly of a few, widely scattered thorn trees growing in a whitish, sandy soil which, in full sunlight, gave off an unbearable glare. Close by the buildings were a series of open water holes and soon after dawn, doves and other birds would fly in for water. Since both the ground and the buildings were white, the birds tended to be blinded by the intense glare and many would crash into the walls and die. Regular thuds could be heard, mostly in the early mornings, but at lesser intervals throughout the day. So severe was the problem that the Administration employed two prisoners on a full time basis to collect the corpses of the unfortunate birds and dispose of them.

Early in my second tour on the Northern Frontier, it was decided to build a fort at El Wak which lay halfway between Wajir and Mandera and stood on the border between Kenya and Somalia. This area had long been the happy hunting ground for cross border raiding parties of Somali Shifta and since Wajir was some way inland and Mandera too far north, another strong point nearer to the action was considered necessary.

A sum of five thousand pounds was allocated for the project and a retired Police officer contracted to build the fort. Together, we designed it on the lines of a classic 'Beau Geste' fort - a large square surrounded by battlemented stone walls and large towers at each corner to allow cross-fire to be directed along each side. Building were planned along the inside of the walls for accommodation, stores, armouries etc. and these were to be constructed with flat roofs supported on stone arches, from which the men could gain access to the battlements.

I loaned police lorries and sufficient armed men for protection and for the construction work, the contractor engaged local labour augmented by a sufficient number of prisoners. The site at El Wak was hundreds of miles from the nearest source of supplies and the constant difficulties which the contractor experienced were frustrating in the extreme. But, by one means or another, he overcame them and in the end accomplished a marvellous feat of engineering, and all within the budget

A year or two later, it was deemed necessary to replace my old thorn bush and bully beef 'fort' at Banya because the Gelubba were becoming increasingly aggressive and dangerous and it was decided that a replica of our fort at El Wak would be ideal for the purpose. This time, the Ministry of Works were contracted to do the construction but the budget they were allocated was fifty thousand pound - exactly ten times more than El Wak had cost.

We, the Police, carried out most of our own building and maintenance work ourselves and for this, we were required to submit our annual budgetary proposals. Seldom did we get more than half of the sum required but usually managed, by fair means or foul, to complete our program of works. Activities such as this added spice to the job and since the Force's establishment was increasing at an alarming rate, it was the only possible way to cater for it.

Up country, at around this time, an anti-white sect known as the Deni ya Msambwa began to emerge. They had killed two British Police Inspectors and some Police rank and file and had started to encourage its followers to hold meeting which usually led to violence or to squatting on European owned farms to spread their evil doctrine amongst the otherwise loyal labour force. The Deni ya Msambwa had been proscribed by law and I was detailed to take a force of my Northern Frontier Police to the area and discourage them.

Somalis are a proud, arrogant and courageous people who hated and despised up country tribes believing them to be vastly inferior to themselves - they are truly a race apart and know no fear, believing that fate is pre-ordained and inescapable. I gathered together a hundred men, mostly Somali's from tribes indigenous to the Frontier and transported them to the area where the Deni ya Msambwa were operating.

I selected a camp site then consulted the local Police Divisional Commander as to the state of play. Next, I rounded up a number of locals to act as informers and as guides then commenced an intensive program of night raids and daytime flag waving and displays of force.

African labourers and squatters, some of whom were already members of the Deni ya Msambwa or had been subjected to their indoctrination, were scattered over large areas of uncultivated European owned farm land and these were to be my targets and I made preparations to raid as many of their camps as I could find.

All Africans kept chickens amongst which were always a few cockerels. Cockerels, I had noticed, crow twice in the morning, once a couple of hours before dawn and then again just as dawn starts to break. They - yes, the chickens - I decided, would be our best informers and their crowing would lead us to the camps we sought.

We would enter a suspect area by night and lie concealed until we heard the first outbreak of crowing and this would guide us to the encampment. Just before dawn my men would batter down the doors of the huts and, in their guttural Somali, would bark out orders to the occupants. Any tardiness in responding to an order or any talking back would be met with a kick or the butt of a rifle. If one of the occupants fell, he was kicked and made to stand to attention before his superiors and, if any complained about the rough treatment, they would be knocked to the ground and kicked again. Harsh interrogation and arrest would follow.

A special Court was set up to deal rapidly - in only an hour or two - with any accused, thus freeing us quickly for further forays.

The Somali's in my force acted just as I had expected and their arrogance and brutality were the ideal tool for the reign of terror that I deliberately established in the area and after four weeks, the desired effect was achieved - the cleansing of the area.

Somali Shifta are organised efficient fighters and, if attacked in bush country would rapidly form a circle lying down with their feet touching in the middle and all facing outwards like the numerals on a clock face. Most are excellent rifle shots and in that position, able to see under the thorn trees and fire in all directions they were far more deadly than a machine gun. Ask the Americans who recently, and some would say, foolishly, went into Somalia and then had to pull out when they discovered that they were unable to defeat these magnificent fighters.

The Deni ya Msambwa were certainly purged from the area in which we had conducted the operation but whether they were completely discouraged, or whether the evil face of this or other anti-white groups would show themselves again, only time would tell - but I had an awful feeling that we had not seen the last of them.

Home Leave

In late 1949, I was given foreign leave and so, my family and I returned to the UK for an eight or nine month's holiday. We travelled down to Mombasa and boarded a small passenger ship of the British East India Line called the Mulbera. We were directed to a cabin below decks and settled in for the voyage home, little suspecting at the time that I would soon be responsible for nearly sinking it.

Like all small ships of the day, there was no air conditioning and very little ventilation so cabins could become unbearably hot in the tropical sun. Old liners would never dock at Port Sudan when humidity exceeded a certain level since the captains knew that, if they did, some elderly passengers were certain to die.

To provide some relief, air scoops would be attached to the outside of the portholes to direct a draught into the cabin and though they weren't particularly effective, they were better than nothing and, at least, gave one a chance to sleep.

One night, as we were ploughing through the Red Sea in worsening weather, a crew member came into our cabin, removed the air scoops, closed the portholes and then disappeared without further explanation. Almost immediately, the cabin became like a humid oven and none of us could sleep.

We lay for a while listening to the swish of waves running down the side of the vessel but eventually the heat became so intense that I decided enough was enough, opened the portholes and reattached the scoops. The cabin slowly cooled and after an hour or so, I managed to drop off to sleep.

I had a bottom bunk under one of the portholes and, sometime during the next hour, as the sea became rougher and the ship rolled more, my porthole dipped below the waves. Suddenly, I was awakened by a powerful jet of sea pouring in as if from a twelve inch pressurised fire hose. The water forced open our cabin door, flooded the passageway and all the neighbouring cabins and all hell broke loose. Eventually, between waves, I managed to force the potholes shut again and crew members arrived to clean up the mess. At breakfast the following morning, little was said, but I sensed a degree of coldness towards me from some of the crew and my fellow passengers.

Our stay in England was a glorious rest from the tribulations of Africa. After more than three years away, Betty had the chance to renew family ties and old friendships while, during the season, I enjoyed a few forays into the gentlemanly world of shooting the English way. Our daughter Ann, by then three years old, had never seen her home country or her relatives before and enthralled everyone she met with constant chatter about her life in Africa. All too soon, it was over and I must confess that the old itch to return to Kenya was on me again with a vengeance.

For the return trip, we were booked aboard the Bloemfontein Castle, a brand new Union Castle line ship on her maiden voyage. She was designed as a one class ship, Union Castle's first experiment in this form of travel. The Government paid our fares and, even though I was not at that time a very senior Government Official, we were allocated one of the two most prestigious cabins on the ship, a forward main deck wing cabin, the opposite one being occupied by Union Castle's Managing Director.

We felt very honoured by our selection for this top class accommodation but, unknown to us then, there was a catch. The ship was headed round the Cape stopping at Gibraltar, Las Palmas, St. Helena, Cape Town, Durban, East London, Port Elizabeth, Lorenzo Marques and god knows where else and, for Union Castle, it was a promotional voyage during which they would milk every opportunity for publicity. We had just sighted Gibraltar, our first stop, when the Purser came to me with a strange request. "Sir," he said, smiling. "Would you mind if, when we dock, some of the ship's Officers show a party of guest from ashore around your cabin. We just want to impress them with the magnificent accommodation we have aboard." This seemed a very reasonable request and I saw no harm in it.

"Not at all," I replied, and he went away, still smiling.

Thereafter, on arrival at each of the ports, all the way to Mombasa, we were expected to vacate the cabin, taking all our belongings with us while the stewards cleaned the place from top to bottom and the Officers conducted parties of potential clients around it. I hope it did them some good - it certainly got on my wick.

The voyage was, otherwise, a routine affair except perhaps on three occasions. Each time we docked, I assembled the fishing rod I had brought with me and baited the hook with pieces of raw steak or fish that I had persuaded our table waiter to obtain for me from the galley. I would go down to the lower deck, cast the baited line over the side and catch all manner of colourful fish.

If any meat was left on our plates, I collected it and kept it in the cabin for use later. One day I went into the cabin and my nostrils were assailed by the most awful stench of rotting meat which I picked up and threw out of the porthole. Unfortunately, a Portuguese port official was standing at the foot of the gang plank directly below our cabin and the rotten meat hit him straight in the face. Instantly, he looked up and, spotting a member of the ship's compliment doing security duty at the top of the gang plank, decided that he had thrown it. Without pausing for breath, the Portuguese rushed up the gang plank and set about our man who, of course, knew nothing of the matter. All hell broke loose - screaming and shouting and fists flying, so I quietly closed our portholes and kept a low profile.

We docked in East London, and again, we were asked to vacate our 'show' cabin, much to our irritation. However, as we prepared to 'kick our heels' for a few hours, a message came aboard that a friend of ours was waiting ashore to see us. He was Dr. Dunderdale whom we had first met when he had been in charge of the Government hospital in Nanyuki but who had since taken another job just outside East London. We spent the rest of the day pleasantly with him on a long car trip inland and returned to the ship and our cabin in the evening much better for it.

At the next stop, Durban, we vacated the cabin as usual and, as usual, the Stewards prepared it for their visitors who were due aboard in a couple of hour's time. Our daughter Ann, however, was tired so we put her back in the cabin for a short rest but instead of sleeping, she found a lipstick and with it, painted herself, her bed linen, the cabin walls and everything in sight, a bright red. Inevitably, the party of V.I.P's were shown into the cabin and told, 'This is an example of the Bloemfontein's accommodation.' I was never told what their reaction was.

Later, at Lorenzo Marques, we were delayed for six or seven days by intermittent equatorial rain storms which prevented the shore crew from loading some cargo or other which mustn't get wet. I spent the time fishing from the lower deck. Each time the rain stopped, sea barbel started to bite and, each time I hauled one out of the water, the dock labourers ceased work and scrambled to claim it. Fishing was excellent. After four days of this, the ship's Second Officer came to me with the request that I stop fishing immediately since the hold-up's were costing the company thousands in harbour dues.

While I was on UK leave, unrest had developed in the North Nyanza District of Western Kenya. The pseudo religious sect, the Deni ya Msambwa had emerged again and this time with yet more violent anti-European activity. Already they had killed an Administrative Officer, two British Police Inspectors, wounded a third and killed several Kenya and tribal Police. The threat was considerable and the authorities were deeply concerned.

Soon after landing, I reported to Police Headquarters and was told, 'You know all about the Deni ya Msambwa and are used to this sort of thing. You're posted to the area with immediate effect.'

North Nyanza District carried the heaviest population in Kenya - some two thousand per square mile and the Police Headquarters was at Kakamega which lay two hundred and fifty miles north west of Nairobi and only seventy-five miles from Eldoret, where I had been stationed many years before. Kakamega contained some twelve British families, nearly all of them Government officials and boasted a golf club as well as squash and tennis courts. A couple of miles away was the Rosterman's Gold Mine, a large operation which, at that time, was still active and run by a dozen or so Europeans who lived with their families in a settlement close to the mine. This settlement, too, had its own club with tennis and squash courts.

Later, I became friendly with one or two of the mining families and played tennis several times against one of the mine workers. One day, he was travelling as passenger in his brother's car when he opened the glove compartment and found an automatic pistol. He pulled the pistol out and started to twirl it, cowboy style, around his finger. Unfortunately, the pistol was loaded and went off and the bullet grazed his heart. He was lucky not to be killed and spent several months in hospital.

Not many days after his discharge, this same chap was driving his own car towards the crest of a long, down-hill escarpment road when he stalled the engine and then ran the battery flat trying to re-start it. A passing Asian lorry offered to help and, tying a tow-rope around his front axle, soon had him going again then went on its way. He set off down hill but, after a short distance, he discovered that he had no brakes - the tow rope had severed the hydraulic pipes. The car picked up speed and my friend began to fear that he would leave the road and plunge down the shear fifteen-hundred foot drop to his left. He saw no alternative so, closing his eyes, he swerved the car towards the rocky wall on his right side in an attempt to slow the vehicle, which it did but, in the process rolled over a few times before coming to rest on its side. Back he went to hospital for yet a few more months.

In the late twenties, gold was discovered at several places in the region and sparked a 'Klondyke' type gold rush. White settlers from all over the Colony, many of them near to destitution, left there farms in the hands of their wives and families and flocked to the area to prospect for gold. Overnight, Kakamega became a boom town - five hotels, two banks, garages, hardware companies, domestic housing and a large number of bars rapidly sprung up together with a host of minor support industries and suppliers. Drunken brawls were daily events, some ending in 'wild west' style gun fights.

By the late thirties, gold in workable quantities had petered out, with the exception of the Rosterman's mine, so prospecting ceased and settlers returned to their homes. Hotels, banks and supporting businesses closed down and Kakamega became a virtual ghost town. Rosterman's survived until the late fifties when it too closed, not because of the lack of gold, but because it had become uneconomical to mine it at the depth at which it lay.

I was allocated a house which had been built for the manager of the Barclays Bank and it was quite luxurious. It stood in several acres of grounds in which grew a wide variety of trees including about twenty avocados. The avocados fruited continuously and all one heard, day and night, was the thud, thud, thud of the fruit falling to the ground. Within hours, they started to rot and the rotten fruit attracted millions of flies so I had to employ an African to collect and bury them. It was a full-time job for which I paid him two shillings a month. Later, my successor told me that he couldn't afford this, so he had detailed a prisoner for the job, who did it free of charge. Why I, of all people hadn't thought of this ploy, I cannot imagine.

The first thing I did on take-over, was to appoint one of the Inspectors under my command as Intelligence Officer and sent him off to find out

Mounted Police,
Wajir

Frontier Fort.
Detachment HQ, North Horr

Frontier Fort.
Sounding 'Last Post', Banya

Above: Police Aircraft over Mount Kenya

Below: Police Aircraft. Supply drop

Armed Anti-Mau Mau Policeman

*Elmolo hunter
with crocodile.
At Loiangalani on
the eastern shore of
Lake Rudolf.*

Juma, the Dorobo tracker

Moru, the Turkana driver, with a Nile Perch

Banya. Gelubba elders come to talk

Ready for inspection. Abyssinian irregulars on parade to welcome Peter to their camp

Firing practice, Banya, using Italian Breda light machine guns captured from the Abyssinians

whatever he could about the Deni ya Msambwa, by whatever methods he considered appropriate.

I put my men under orders to allow no spear-carrying rioters to approach within seventy-five yards before opening fire and, when confronting a rioting mob to demarcate a line which, if it were crossed, would result in rifle fire.

One particular disturbance was broken up by my men who charged the mob and jabbed them in the thighs with their bayonets. For months after, we were arresting suspects bearing scars which were accepted as prima facie evidence of having taken part in a riot. I was a bit surprised at the number of young women brought in, and I did wonder how my men came to discover the scars in the first place.

Apart from breaking up a few riots and organising numerous displays of force, life at Kakamega was fairly tame but one incident did brighten up the whole tour of duty - Betty gave birth to our second child, a fine healthy boy and we called him Peter. Mother and baby thrived.

A minister of the prevailing UK Labour Government visited Kenya at this time and decided that the area he wished most to tour was the district under my command at Northern Nyanza, (the one with the densest population). Although the Authorities were aware that this was the heart-land of the Deni ya Msambwa, they seemed oblivious to any danger and ordered that obvious Police escorts and arms were to be kept to a minimum and any incidents which might embarrass the Minister were to be avoided. The Minister himself seemed scared stiff that it might be published at home that he, a Labour Minister, should require armed escorts in 'peaceful' Kenya.

Dressed in plain clothes, I drove the Minister and the Kenya's Attorney General in my own car while ahead and behind I had vehicles containing plain clothed Police carrying concealed arms. Unknown to my passengers I had my .45 concealed about my person while my Inspector in the forward car carried a sub-machine gun which he concealed in a borrowed violin case. Each time we stopped, the Minister and the Attorney General eyed the violin case suspiciously and I doubt whether they were really expecting a recital. Along the route, local dignitaries, organised to appear by the Administration, were introduced to the V.I.P's but nobody plucked up courage to ask what the case contained and I didn't elucidate. Had we been attacked, the Minister would have been amazed at the fire power of apparently unarmed civilian escorts.

At one point on the tour, we descended a steep-sided, wooded valley and came upon a native bus which had broken down and been abandoned. It was on a very narrow track which led down to a ford through the stream at the bottom of the valley. The approaches to and from the stream were dangerously steep, bordered by rough, heavily bushed terrain and presented an ideal location for an ambush which, I considered, was a real possibility. I ordered my men to clear the obstruction, and do so rapidly. Lining up along one side, with a mighty heave-ho, they tipped the bus onto its side, then onto its roof and over the edge down into the stream. The Minister was horrified; he turned white and trembled, no doubt imagining what the opposition in Parliament would make of the affair if it became public in the UK.

This was 1950 and early rumblings of the Mau Mau could be heard, though Western Kenya was apparently not yet affected. But then, we couldn't tell just how far the influence of the Mau Mau had penetrated Kenya's indigenous population.

Mau Mau Rumblings

Incidents of unprecedented trouble were beginning to be reported from all over the Kikuyu tribal lands and from other areas wherever Kikuyu labour was to be found.

Both myself and my wife, although separately, had been subjected to such incidents during the time I commanded the station at Nanyuki. While I was on temporary posting to Mandera on the northern frontier, my wife drove from Nanyuki about ten miles up the slopes of Mount Kenya, taking with her our daughter, Ann, who was then only two years old, on a visit to the wife of the District Forest Officer and her family. There was no road, only a rough track which was often impassable because of rain.

On the return journey, she missed her way and was attempting to turn the car round to get back to the right track, when a party of drunken Kikuyu appeared and gathered around the car. They were mostly men, all armed with machete's, and they were accompanied by a few women. It was obvious that they had just left a secret Mau Mau 'oathing' ceremony and the males clearly indicated that they intended to kill both Betty and our daughter. Fortunately, the females amongst them restrained their menfolk because of our daughter, just long enough for my wife to turn the car and escape. She arrived home trembling with fear at her narrow escape, but why she decided to travel without an armed Police escort, I just don't know.

A short while later, I too was involved in a similar incident. Betty had gone with our daughter to spend a few days in Nairobi and I was travelling with my armed Orderly from Nanyuki to collect her. About half way, just after dark, I got a puncture and, while we were changing the wheel, a gang of about twelve Kikuyu, all carrying machetes, appeared from the bush.

They gathered around the car and started chattering in Kikuyu, a language of which I was almost ignorant but understood enough of to know that they meant us no good. "They're saying they're going to kill us," said the Orderly. Since we were both out of uniform and apparently unarmed we probably looked an easy target. Quickly, I reached into the car, grabbed my rifle, worked a round up the spout and shouted to them to retreat instantly or be shot. They did, and disappeared into the darkness.

This type of incident was becoming increasingly common, caused by the rapid spread of secret Mau Mau 'oathing' ceremonies which were taking place, mostly at night. They heralded a new era for the Kenya Police who, in the earliest days of the uprising, had found the implications of such occurrences, difficult to believe.

One morning, during breakfast, my family and I were disturbed by the sudden outbreak of a great commotion - shouting, crashing and the sound of things breaking - at some distance from the house. No sooner had we first heard it than Arthur Sandford, the British Doctor and our near neighbour, burst in, in a rare panic.

"Quick!" he yelled. "Get your cannon. There's a buffalo and it's gone mad." I leapt up, thrust a .303 sporting rifle into Arthur's hands, grabbed my .450 No. 2 heavy rifle and we set off at a run towards the scene of the excitement.

Owing to the heavy population in the area, no buffalo had been seen within miles of where we were for many years but this one had suddenly appeared out of the blue and, having demolished several fences, chicken runs and the like, had headed in the direction of the African Hospital. As we got nearer, the shouting and screaming got louder until it reached a pitch reminiscent of a football stadium when a goal's been scored.

We arrived panting for breath and found, lying beside a tree at the hospital entrance, an old African with the whole of the skin of his face, complete with hair, nose and most of his lips, round the back of his head and blood was everywhere. He had been sitting against a tree, patiently awaiting treatment, when the buffalo leapt into view and crushed him against the tree. "Leave him," said Arthur. "He's dead."

About a hundred yards away in the hospital grounds was a large banana plantation from which emanated the great commotion created by a large crowd of Africans milling about and shouting. Just visible, was a tribal policeman clinging to the top of one of the trees while below him, was the buffalo pawing the ground and looking distinctly mean.

The buffalo was standing broadside on and I feared that if I fired my .450 the bullet might pass straight through the beast and kill one of the many Africans milling about on the far side. I nodded to Arthur to use the .303. "Aim for the top half of his neck." I said.

He fired, the animal jerked his head up and prodded the tribal policeman's arse with his horn, much to the merriment of the crowd but it also made him slew round and allow me to put a bullet from the .450 into his heart. The buffalo keeled over, dead, but, on examination, we found that the bullet had raked the full length of its body and come out of its rump, fortunately injuring no one in the process.

The job done, Arthur and I returned to the dead African and much to our surprise - and to the doctor's embarrassment - there he was sitting up, re-adjusting his face back round to the front and wondering what the hell had hit him.

From information I received later, it appeared that this buffalo, in company with another, had made its way through forty miles of heavily populated country before it ended up at the hospital. Before reaching us, it had crashed through a line of ramshackle shops in the trading centre, in the process, destroying two Singer sewing machines and tossing the Africans who were working at them, and had also demolished two long stretches of corrugated iron fencing, leaving the Asians at the trading centre in total panic. The second buffalo had apparently parted company some seven miles from the centre and was not heard of again.

This was the last but one big game animal that I ever shot in Kenya. I decided to concentrate on photographing them instead.

The last one I shot was when travelling with some of my men through bush country and we came upon a herd of buffalo. We were in need of meat so I decided that here was an opportunity to obtain it. I nodded to my Orderly who, quick as a flash, drew my .450 No. 2 heavy rifle from its leather case and handed it to me. One buffalo was in a favourable position so I aimed and fired. The recoil nearly broke my shoulder and forced me back a pace. The animals started to move off, so I gave it the second barrel and, again I was nearly floored. Apart from the heavy recoil, the discharges had produced a massive cloud of blue smoke almost obscuring the target but, luckily, the second shot had killed the buffalo. What I had forgotten was that, earlier, I had decided that I wouldn't be using the rifle for some time and had heavily greased the insides of the barrels to preserve them. I was very fortunate that the gun hadn't burst due to the excessive pressure in the barrels that the grease had produced.

Late one night, a signal reached me from one of my outstations saying that a European Agricultural Officer had been shot. He was the only other European living at the centre apart from the young Inspector at the Police outstation, so I went to see that everything necessary was done.

The Agricultural Officer had several Africans working for him and one, who had a small tractor and trailer had been given a contract to supply his boss with firewood. An argument over payment had broken out and for some reason, the Officer had refused to pay the agreed amount. About nine that same night, the Officer and my Inspector were playing chess at the former's house when the African arrived with another load of wood. The Officer went outside to deal with the matter and within seconds, the Inspector heard a shot. He dashed outside and, to his horror, he found the Agricultural Officer lying in a pool of blood dead, with half his head shot away.

The Inspector made straight for the Police station and there he found the African who had walked there after the shooting and simply turned himself in. A few questions elicited that this was not his only crime. Apparently his anger at not being paid had boiled over and, borrowing a shotgun from his neighbour, he had run amok and while travelling the nine miles into the centre to kill the Agricultural Officer, he had stopped off and killed three more people against whom he held a grudge. Africans, like some far-eastern nationalities are prone to running amok, or, as it's called in Swahili, 'Kula Amura'.

Another incident with gruesome similarities occurred at another of my outposts. The Corporal in charge, to all previous knowledge of him, a normal, well balanced individual, arose one morning and set about the daily routine of the station as usual. Then about eight o'clock, he donned his number one uniform, took his rifle and shot dead all the five Constables under his command. No motive could ever be ascribed to the deed. Such matters cropped up occasionally in the course of a day's routine.

At about this time, a friend of mine lived in a nice wood and iron, three bedroomed house which boasted a magnificent view from its windows. It was constructed on piles driven into the ground on a flat ledge one thousand feet up on the side of a steep escarpment. Returning one night from a prolonged drinking session in a local bar, he discovered, to his utter astonishment, that his house has vanished. A high wind had got up while he was at the bar, and had blown up the escarpment, lifted his house off its piles and deposited it a thousand feet below in the valley. Lucky for him he wasn't in it. If he hadn't stayed long enough in the bar to get drunk, he would have been. There must be a moral in there somewhere.

Some while earlier, this same friend had suffered a nasty experience. His house, as most early houses, was furnished with an outside pit latrine which consisted of a deep hole over which was arranged a wooden frame with a seat. On one occasion, he had just settled down on the seat when he felt a sudden stabbing pain in his buttock and found that it was bleeding. He panicked and, believing he had been bitten by a venomous snake, he jumped into his truck and drove like a madman for thirty miles to the nearest doctor. The doctor, seeing that the blood was coming from two small puncture wounds agreed that it was a snake bite and promptly injected him with both nerve and bloodstream anti-venoms. These injections are no joke and they shook him up considerably and, for several days, he felt dreadful. On his return home he investigated the latrine and found, sitting on eggs in a nest under the toilet seat - a chicken, which had evidently pecked him.

A brother officer began to receive complaint about mugging incidents in his district. Apparently, courting couples would frequent an isolated spot where they would park their cars after dark to indulge in a bit of slap and tickle. A gang of local Africans took to creeping up, wrenching open the car door and, wielding machete's, demanding money - or else. He thought about this for a while then decided to consult his local Magistrate. "If we kill a few, will you support us?" he asked. The Magistrate agreed, so my friend dressed himself as a girl, dress, long blonde wig and all, and for a few nights sat in a car in the arms of another officer staking out the place.

On the third night, right on cue, four thugs appeared, smashed the car windows on one side but, boom, that was the last thing they did, as both officers opened up with revolvers, killing three and wounding the fourth. There was no more trouble in that area and, a few days later, the Magistrate simply initialled the Police file as justifiable homicide.

As an armed Police Officer, I quickly learned never to threaten with a gun or even draw one unless you had made up your mind that you were prepared to use it. The very act of drawing a firearm can cause a person to panic and possibly attack you when, without it, they would probably have been prepared to surrender anyway. Some villains, in fact, don't mind facing a hand-gun but point a shot gun at them and their courage quickly leaves them and they collapse.

The best hand arm I ever possessed but, in fact, never had to use in anger, was a brass barrelled Very Pistol. Designed for firing flares, it was perfectly fitted to take a No. 4 shotgun cartridge loaded with four ounces of No.4 shot which came right to the end of the barrel and so, imparted no recoil. The pellets spread out in all directions, even at right angles to the barrel. If you stood in a doorway and fired, you could hit anyone in the room no matter where they were. A long barrelled .45 revolver with the old type of soft lead bullets possesses a great deal of stopping power but, I believe that, these days soft lead bullets are illegal.

Any officer of the Kenya Police, from Constable to Commissioner, could carry any available weapon which he considered necessary for the job in hand. No higher authorisation was needed. In all my experience, the practice was never abused and never lead to complaints.

As Provincial Commander, I would occasionally do a tour of my various Divisional headquarters to keep abreast of events and to offer help should it be needed. At one such headquarters which had become quite a trouble spot with murders, stock theft, burglary and inter-tribal strife, and which returned very low figures for crimes solved, I questioned the Divisional Commander to ascertain what he was doing about it.

"Well, sir," he said, nervously. "I'm keeping the situation fluid and playing it off the cuff." I found this glib, meaningless answer less than satisfactory and obviously, he hadn't a clue what to do so I immediately allocated him a couple of hard-necked Inspectors and a few experienced men to kick-start his failing operation.

While on the move, I pulled in at an abandoned mine and made use of one of the huts as a billet for the night. The windows were simply open holes and I set up my camp bed just below one to take advantage of the cooling night breeze. I soon fell fast asleep but, at about two in the morning, a donkey stuck its head through the window about a foot from my head and brayed, full throat. I leapt almost to the ceiling and, being unable to immediately identify what it was, my heart skipped half a dozen beats. The fear of the unknown, I decided, is the greatest fear of all.

In this same area, I had to escort a VIP on a tour of inspection and, as we skirted a particular high hill, he suddenly imparted to me the information that he was a climbing fanatic and couldn't resist hills.

"Have you ever climbed this one?" he asked.

"No," I replied, hoping to put him off the idea.

"Oh, good," he said. "Let's climb it then."

This wasted several hours and rather put the kibosh on my carefully planned schedule so, over night, I sent runners ahead to alter arrangements for the rest of the tour.

The following day, we skirted another high, and apparently, interesting hill, and again, he enquired if I'd climbed it. This time, I thought - I'm just a little wiser.

"Oh, yes," I replied. "Many times." But, of course, I hadn't.

"Good," he said. "Then you'll know the best route up it." And up we went.

Arriving one day at a swamp, I noticed that there were many duck on areas of open water some way in from the reed fringe edges. We were in need of meat so, taking a 12 bore shotgun, I crawled through the undergrowth and reeds to get near enough to get a shot in when the duck rose. I was almost there when suddenly, just in front of me, in the broken shadows of the reeds, I made out the shape of the rump of a large leopard. My shotgun carried No. 7 shot; all right for duck, but not much use against a leopard, and to run would have been foolish. I was in no position for a confrontation and I didn't know what to do, so, discretion being the best part of valour - I froze.

For minutes the leopard crouched, apparently intent upon some prey other than myself. Had it heard me, or scented me, god knows what would have happened, but gradually, I began to discern the shape of a water buck some way ahead of us both, through the reeds on the edge of the open water. The leopard inched forward. Then, suddenly frightened, the duck leapt from the water in a great whirring of wings and the water buck bounded away. My heart stopped at idea that, next, the leopard would turn and find another meal - me. But when I looked again it had gone, simply melted away into the low, sparse vegetation.

The age old question is often raised as to what is the most dangerous animal to hunt. The answer is simple - the one you have most difficulty in seeing. A lion on flat, well grazed grassland presents little danger but, meet it in three-foot high grass and it's deadly. You can't see it and if it charges, it's doing fifty-five miles an hour after its first spring. If it charges, an elephant in dense forest can smash down everything before it and you can be felled by under-growth and branches before you see the animal itself and have time to deal with it. Put it in light, open, low bush country and it's just a matter of getting close enough and aiming straight. If visibility is adequate, the closer you are to a dangerous animal when you fire, the more likely you are to hit it with a fatal shot and so, the safer you are, the margin of error being reduced as the range decreases. Many an inexperienced hunter has met a gruesome end because, fearing to approach a dangerous animal, has fired from too great a range, wounding or entirely missing the beast and enraging it sufficiently to make it charge.

Talking about margins of error, we once had an acting Commissioner of Police who was a Freemason - a lot of Police are. Personally, I am not and never have been a Freemason and I think they're poison. If they practised what they preached, there'd be no need for them. At a Masonic dinner, he and another senior officer arranged an after-dinner prank. The Commissioner put on a bullet-proof vest under his shirt, and handed a pistol to the other officer. After dinner, the Commissioner stood against a wall and said to his partner in crime, "Shoot me." The Officer did, the Commissioner dropped to the floor and, realising the joke, the rest of the guests applauded. The Commissioner however, didn't get up and blood started to flow. It seems that the pistol was loaded with soft lead bullets not hard, nickel coated ones and the bullet had splintered and passed through the splines of the bullet-proof vest. Splinters missed his heart by only inches he was hospitalised for months.

In those days, whenever an out of town Police Officer visited Nairobi, he was under orders to don his number one uniform, proceed to Government House and sign the visitor's book. Upon reaching Nairobi, often after several day's travelling, covered in dust and sweat, one had to search out a place to wash and change and then go to Government House to sign the bloody book. All one ever saw there was the odd patrolling Police Constable and never saw anyone of any importance. This was the old colonial system so, as often as not, I never bothered with this outdated and pointless ceremony.

It was also expected that we would call at Police Headquarters and enquire whether or not the Commissioner wanted to see us. In my case, none ever did, none that is, until Michael O'Rorke, CBE became Commissioner. He had been Ireland's Chief of Police until just after the war ended when he was seconded to the War Trials Commission.

At that time, I was a Divisional Commander and Divisional Commanders were required to submit a weekly report to the Commissioner to keep him informed of problems encountered and action taken to solve them. Each time, mine came back to me with ticks and comments such as 'Good show' written all over them. On one visit, I was called in and, for the first time, I was presented to him. He seemed quite anxious to meet me and we had a long and very agreeable chat. His comments throughout upon my endeavours were very encouraging and, when I left, I was pleased as Punch. Kenya was then, running into the build-up of the Mau Mau.

The Commissioner had decided to establish Police Districts as an intermediary formation between Divisions and Provinces. The argument was that a District Officer would have no administration to attend to and so, would be free to concentrate on more practical issues. I was vociferous in my opposition to this restructuring on the grounds that Divisional Commanders worked hand-in-hand with Administrative District Commissioners and Police Provincial Commanders along-side the Administrative Provincial Commissioners. Moreover, Police Divisions and Administrative Districts had identical boundaries, as did Police and Administrative Provinces. My argument was that these District Police Officers would be nothing but a pointless interference interposed into an already well established and viable chain of command.

In the event, my arguments were ignored, Districts were set up and I was promoted to full Superintendent to command one. After a couple of years, the formation was found to be too cumbersome and was abandoned.

By this time, the force had grown to some two-hundred British and four-thousand African officers yet we had still not developed any form of effective intelligence network. Operational intelligence is, of course a very different thing from criminal intelligence and, while the Force then had a special branch of sorts, (this consisted of only two men who were stationed at Headquarters), I was, I think, the first to develop a local one. As a District Commander, I took it upon myself to create a Provincial Special Branch Unit.

We had been given powers to call up and appoint full or part-time Kenya Police reserve officers so, for the Special Branch Unit I called up one lady as Secretary, two males as Field Officers and augmented the unit with a few regular officers. This started the ball rolling and as a first step my Secretary began to search the files and archives of every Police Division, opening up a separate file for each mention of sedition, of sect membership or of subversive individuals. As the team developed, I set targets and obtained funds for the payment of intelligence sources and so started to build up a Provincial network of informants.

The Officer in Charge of headquarters special branch knew nothing of my activities in the field until, one day on a tour round, he visited my area and I explained my set-up to him. He was amazed and delighted and, being of considerably senior rank to me, tried to persuade me to allow him to get me transferred into the force's special branch at HQ.

"Not on your life," I said, making it very plain to him that there was nothing on earth that could persuade me. In my opinion, general duty Commanders had by far the best positions; they commanded everything within their area - CID, Special Branch, signals, transport, welfare, prosecutions, buildings, stores and accounts, aircraft, dog sections - you name it we were boss of the lot. Later, I was given other opportunities to specialise but I always declined. Specialist personnel, while being responsible to their own unit commander had a dual and sometimes conflicting responsibility to their own specialist department command structure and this would not have suited my own individualistic way of operating.

The activities of the Mau Mau were beginning to concern the Police, not, however, the higher levels of the Colony's Administration or the UK Government who both thought, or for political reasons were constrained to think, that their beloved African children were loyal, peaceful and contented.

As far back as 1947, we in the Kenya Police had been picking up odd bits of information and rumours, the implications of which were so serious that we couldn't really believe them. Increasingly, we began to swap intelligence and gradually came to the conviction that something pretty nasty indeed was brewing.

By this time I had managed to subdue the anti-white religious sect, the Deni ya Msambwa, the final action being to discover and blow up their religious shrine which they had constructed on the peak of Mount Cherangani, about fifty miles north of Eldoret.

My superior, the Chief Superintendent in charge of the Province was at that point, transferred to Colony Headquarters on his promotion to Assistant Commissioner and, before he left, I asked him if there was any chance of a posting for me to a Mau Mau operational district. I was away at the time of his departure, but he left me a note saying how much he had enjoyed our association and thanking me for the excellent work I had put in, but he gave no answer to my question concerning a transfer. Not long afterwards, I suddenly received the posting I had requested - to take charge of the Nairobi Rural District. as District Superintendent

Nairobi City itself was under the command of another District Superintendent but Nairobi Rural District covered a vast area, bordered on the south by Tanganyika, on the west by the Rift Valley Province, on the north by the Northern Frontier District and on the east by the Coastal Province. It contained all of Masai, both the Machakos and Kitui Wakamba reserves, the white settled districts of Kiambu, Thika and Makuyu. I could travel in a straight line for over four-hundred miles in one direction and well over two hundred in any other direction without leaving my command. Also in the district were parts of the Kikuyu reserve and thousands of Kikuyu were employed in one job or another, but many in white households and it was amongst the Kikuyu that the Mau Mau thrived.

As I said previously, I considered the post of District Superintendent itself to be a farce and my activities consisted mostly of hanging around Provincial Headquarters checking what information came in, then setting forth to become an unwanted, interfering, and bloody unpopular nuisance between District and Provincial commands. But, at least, I was in the right area - where the action would be at its most intense - when it started.

The Mau Mau

Towards the end of 1952, acts of violence, rioting and other incidents attributable to the Mau Mau had become more frequent and the atmosphere had grown so hostile that I, like most officers in similar positions, began at all times to carry a .45 Colt Automatic in a shoulder holster and a sub-machine gun concealed in the boot of my a car.

In late September I was instructed to prepare a list of what emergency legislation should be enacted, what supplies and equipment would be needed and what immediate action should be taken in the province in which I was operational, should a national state of emergency be declared. Then, in company with other officers who had been similarly instructed, I was called to Kenya Police Headquarters in Nairobi for a top level meeting.

Apart from the Commissioner and Senior Police Commanders such as myself, others present included the Attorney General, Chief Secretary and His Excellency the Governor's Representative, also the G.O.C Middle East Military Command and R.A.F. Liaison Officer. The announcement was made that a State of Emergency was to be declared at midnight on 21st October 1952 and we were asked to submit our lists of requirements and demands.

Apart from the usual requests for more men and equipment, the consensus of Police opinion centred upon the following demands:

1. Picking up and detaining without trial, some five-hundred suspected Mau Mau leaders and organisers.

2. The creation of prohibited areas in which the forces would be allowed to shoot on sight.

3.That our Airwing, (by now a few Tripacers), be allowed to conduct aerial bombing.

4.The power to impose curfews.

5.Powers to arrest and detain anyone without trial.

6. Powers to deport anyone of foreign extraction who in any way aided the Mau Mau. (Some Asian lawyers were busy doing just this, knowingly filing false complaints against the Police in the aid of their terrorist clients. Later on, I did manage to get one such lawyer deported.)

The Attorney General and the Chief Secretary were both horrified by the scope of our demands, having regard for the political implications in the U.K., The Attorney General shook his head.

"Regarding the first request," he said. "You can pick up one hundred and twelve. The British Parliament would never accept more." In fact, on the very night that the emergency was declared, we picked up just over eighty, including Jomo Kenyatta, the leader of the Mau Mau movement.

Concerning the question of prohibited areas as 'killing grounds', he said, "Impossible!" However, a few months, or maybe even a few weeks later, I cannot now recall, they were operational.

On aerial bombing he said, "That would entail and Act of Parliament being passed at Westminster." And he doubted that it could be achieved in the short term. In the event, we soon had the necessary authority plus, we were given the last operational squadron of RAF Lincoln heavy bombers, bombing round the clock. In addition, Southern Rhodesia sent up two squadrons of their Harvard fighter bombers to help out.

Before we had time to really bring the new regulations into full effect, we also had powers to impose curfews and full powers of arrest and detention.

The declaration of the state of emergency had the immediate effect that Police intelligence had convinced us it would have, that is, thousands of young Kikuyu took to the forests and were 'oathed up' as members of the Mau Mau. Both the Kenya Government and Westminster were profoundly shocked and dismayed by the news of this eventuality and said to our forces, "Over to you. Do anything you consider necessary. We will provide you with anything you need." The population had truly taken fright.

The Police Commissioner, Michael Sylvester O'Rorke, who for three years had been warning the Kenya Government of impending disaster, had managed against all odds, to add considerably to the Force's facilities and therefore, its effectiveness. He had created the Police Air Wing and formed the Police Emergency Company, a para-military unit, later re-named the Police General Service Unit, which was on offer to any Area Commander who needed its support. He obtained powers for senior Police officers enabling them to conscript any one as full time Reserve Police Officers and already had authorised the supply of arms and a few wireless sets to part- time Reserve Police.

Throughout this period, Commissioner O'Rorke continually issued his warning to the Authorities and, each time, the Kenya and UK Governments told him he must be mad and, by repeating such nonsense, he was acting irresponsibly. In their opinion, the Kikuyu were peaceful and contented.

The facts of the matter were that the Kikuyu were the 'servant' tribe of Kenya and practically every European household employed at least one of them. What's more, the Mau Mau, which arose amongst the Kikuyu had, for some time been conducting a vigorous 'oathing up' campaign amongst the tribe which stipulated that every 'oathee' would, at a given hour, on a given night, rise up and slaughter every white man in the country.

They may very well have succeeded were it not for the increasing weight of evidence which came from Christianised Africans who were being forced against their better judgement by the Mau Mau to take the oath. Their evidence eventually led the Government to declare the state of emergency. It could be said that this was one benefit brought about by missionary activity.

If anybody had brought about the prevention of the Mau Mau's 'night of the long knives' it was Commissioner O'Rorke, but the Kenya Government never forgave him for being right when they were wrong and as a consequence, late on in the conflict, they made him their scapegoat. Despite the fact that he was possibly the best Commissioner we ever had, they forced him into premature retirement and brought out from the UK a metropolitan Commissioner to replace him.

The new Commissioner came accompanied by a 'side-kick', a Chief Superintendent who, like his boss was a London 'street copper' with neither qualifications nor experience for operational command in a colonial civil war situation. How stupid can Governments be?

Allegedly, this couple spent a great deal of their time snooping round behind the backs of hard-pressed, under-staffed, ill-equipped Police commanders searching for reasons to suspend or prosecute them. These commanders, too occupied with the desperate fight against the Mau Mau in this bitter civil war, simply ignored them.

The pair didn't last long. The Commissioner resigned in a huff because the Kenya Government refused to go along with his recommendation that every Kenya Police Officer, right from the top down to the lowest illiterate African Constable fresh from the bush should have the same full legal powers as those afforded the most senior officers. He was replaced by Richard Catling CMG, OBE, (later Sir Richard Catling, Inspector General of the Kenya Police).

Catling was young and very shrewd. He had previous experience, first in Palestine and then in Malaya where, I believe, he had operated close to Sir Gerald Templer in intelligence against the anti-British, Communist terrorists and he was to prove a major influence in the quelling of the Mau Mau. Early on, he showed himself to be an excellent leader of men in troubled times, a leader whom men would respect and follow and one who gained the confidence of the Force the Government and the people.

Fairly rapidly, Catling built up the Force in all of its commands, departments and branches to a total of around seventeen thousand regular Police and twelve to fourteen thousand full time reserve officers. As overall commander, he took full responsibility for all the activities of the Force but did it from the position of Administrator and took virtually no part in the actual operations, preferring to leave that side of things to his Provincial Police Commanders (PPO's), in whom he placed his trust and gave his full backing and support.

The Government opened up its coffers to him and he took full advantage of the changed attitudes and circumstances brought about by the realisation amongst the governments of both Kenya and the UK that here, indeed, was a true emergency.

Catling looked at the force and decided that a better foundation for tackling the emergency should lie, not in the hands of old sweats set in their ways, so he retired them and replaced them with younger, keener commanders. He also realised, no doubt through experience in some of his previous commands, that you can have all the men and equipment in the world but it's all rendered useless if you don't know who the enemy are and where they are hiding at any given time. So, very early on, he made a point of accelerating the expansion and development of our intelligence services, targeting in particular, operational intelligence. His advocacy of the idea that successful engagements are essential if morale is not to suffer, did wonders to boost the enthusiasm of the Force and its determination to stamp our this insidious enemy.

Initially, during the period of build-up for the Mau Mau, a great deal was happening and inadequate Government forces were hard pressed, devoting more of their time and resources to their own defence rather than to the defence of the people.

The Nairobi Rural District, being in the heartland of Mau Mau activity, presented an especially difficult challenge and my Provincial Commander, in particular, was finding the going hard. He was, as events proved, heading rapidly towards a serious nervous breakdown, a malady which became not uncommon amongst both senior Police officers and Administrative Officers as the pace of the conflict hotted up.

Worry is the problem - it is destructive to the worrier and deleterious to his command, and, most of the time no one knows or even cares that about the burden it imposes upon the worrier. Personally, I never did worry. Instead, I simply followed the principle of doing my best under the circumstances and leaving it at that.

In the face of rising pressure, I made the suggestion to my Provincial Commander that I, as District Superintendent, relieve him of all direct responsibility and administration of the rural district. My proposition was to set up a separate headquarters, over which I would have positive and visible command, and channel through it all administration, reports, intelligence and operational command, shifting the burden onto my shoulders and leaving him to deal solely with me.

The idea appealed to him and he passed it on to Commissioner O'Rorke who immediately sent for me to explain to him in detail. The Commissioner listened in silence then asked me if I felt confident that the strategy would be an improvement upon existing arrangements. "Most certainly," I replied.

"Very well then," he said. "On your way. And good luck."

I immediately commandeered an unoccupied block of Government offices and, taking with me a skeleton staff, I set up as a semi-independent command. Of course, I needed a deputy and a chief of administration but, rather than try to draft in regular officers, I turned to the Kenya Police reserve pool. From there I selected a couple of retired army officers, Brigadier Sir Francis Featherstone Godley, (a personal friend of His Excellency The Governor), as my deputy, and Brigadier Henderson as my Staff Officer. Both were then civilians but full time members of the reserve pool.

I was merely a regular Police Superintendent while my deputy, Sir Francis, was a Chief Superintendent in the reserve and he carried higher rank and insignia than I did, nevertheless, we got on fine. In order to keep up appearances in the presence of junior officers, I would salute him and call him 'Sir' - then give him orders but, if we were alone, he would salute me. Brigadier Henderson, my Staff Officer carried the same rank as I did, that of Superintendent, so the problem of protocol didn't arise.

At times, my deputy and my staff officer would fight like alley cats and I would have to 'bang their heads together', but soon they would come into my office together looking sheepish and apologise.

This new command structure didn't at first meet with the approval of my Divisional Commanders but, finding that I was good at wheedling supplies for them from headquarters, and since I didn't interfere unnecessarily with their operations, they soon accepted it.

The battle against the Mau Mau was fought mainly at District and Divisional level, Provinces only stepping in if an operation involved two or more Districts or, perhaps, a neighbouring Province. Although it was, no doubt, an improvement, my new set-up raised some difficulties and proved to be frustrating and still, I was not completely satisfied.

All Masai comprised the Districts of Narok and Kajiado and was under the administrative control of a Senior District Commissioner who was designated Officer in Charge of Masai. His headquarters were in the Ngong Hills, eighteen miles from Nairobi and he was desperate for firstly, the expansion of his area of control, and secondly, for the appointment of a Police opposite number. He and I talked for some while, each expressing his frustration at current arrangements and, eventually we came up with the plan of converting Masai and Nairobi Rural Districts into a new Province. It would cover in total, about seventy thousand square miles and would be called the Southern Province. For the headquarters, he had spare buildings and telephone communications and we Police had, by now, complete radio communications.

The Mau Mau had started to penetrate and to contaminate the Kamba tribes, first into the Machakos area via the railway line and then from the Central Province through into the Kitui Kamba District. Many of the Police and most of the King's African Rifles were recruited from Kamba tribes and this was a strike by the Mau Mau right to the heart of our forces. The Police, the Government, the Military, all were scared stiff.

I discussed the worsening situation and the Southern Province idea with my deputy Sir Francis and we began to plan our requirements for the coming troubles. One morning he arrived at my office earlier than usual, walked in and saluted.

"Sir," he said. "It's all OK. I had dinner with His Excellency the Governor last night at Government House. He likes your proposals and is going to discuss them with the Commissioner and the Chief Secretary."

I was horrified. As yet, I had made no personal approaches to any of my superiors but the Governor was about to descend upon them, out of the blue, to discuss my ideas. This was very much against protocol and would, no doubt, have landed me in extremely hot water so I raced to my Provincial Superintendent to explain the situation before he heard it from elsewhere. As soon as I finished, he picked up the phone and called Commissioner O'Rorke.

"Sir," he said. "I think you should see my Rural District Superintendent. There have been developments."

Commissioner O'Rorke called me in for interview and I explained to him how rapidly things had developed, leading to a massive build up of the Mau Mau and now was the time for drastic action. I put forward to him my recommendation that a new province, the Southern Province should be created and, of course, that I should command it. Two days later, he sent for me again.

"The Government and Colony Emergency Committee have met," he told me. "They have approved the creation of the Southern Province and it is to include everything that you and the Officer in Charge, Masai, think that it ought to include. He will become Provincial Commissioner and you are hereby promoted to the rank of Chief Superintendent to command the Police of the Province." I was pleased and greatly relieved that, at last, we had the go-ahead to set in motion a viable and effective force and I told the Commissioner so.

"You'll need new headquarters, of course," he continued. "But how and where you set them up, I'll leave entirely to you. Just keep me informed." Then he called in the Force's Stores and Accounts Officer and the Assistant Commissioner - Administration and directed them to give me first refusal on any available personnel, equipment, building funds and transport.

I wasted no time in relocating my staff and operations to new offices in Ngong and soon found an available house into which I had my family moved. Regrettably, I had to exchange my Kenya Police Reserve Staff Officers for younger ones since they were getting on in years and didn't fancy either moving out, or travelling daily to, Ngong. The penalty of seniority is that you have to sit back and see your juniors getting all the action and having all the fun. I was now 34 years old.

I now had seven Divisions under my command, three of which were heavily committed to anti Mau Mau operations, and a force totalling over a thousand regular Police augmented by many more reserve officers so good communications were vital. The Ngong Hills, at a maximum elevation of over eight thousand feet provided us with the ideal site for radio transmission.

One of my new staff officers was an old Etonian and an ex RAF fighter pilot who had seen action during the war. He had the reputation of being a 'queer' and had been a member of the 'Happy Valley' set whose behaviour was recently revealed as 'white mischief'. I knew most of that crowd myself but regrettably, I never became involved in any of their orgies. He was a charming fellow and, in Police aircraft, piloted me all over the vast area of my command. The area demanded a lot of flying time and since I considered it advisable for me to be able to bring the plane down in an emergency, he taught me to fly. The planes all had dual controls so, occasionally, he would allow me to fly the aircraft myself until I became sufficiently skilled to attempt take-off and, after a few dummy runs at Amboselli, where there was a long natural runway, to land the plane. In the end, I became a reasonably proficient pilot and, though I was never called to do so, I reckon I would have coped quite well in an emergency.

Although our aircraft were piloted by professionals, mostly ex RAF or ex Rhodesian RAF and flew many thousands of hours in perfect safety, one or two did get into trouble. One was unexpectedly hit by powerful down-draughts from a mountain side and crashed, killing the pilot. Another flew so low along the length of a beach that one of its wheels hit and decapitated an African who was fishing in the shallows but whom the pilot had not seen. Yet another, carrying a Chief Inspector as passenger, was flying low over a newly opened Forest Police post in order to drop a message when it hit a one inch galvanised pipe erected to support a radio aerial. It crashed, though, miraculously, neither the Chief Inspector nor the pilot were killed. In fact, the pilot was soon flying again, though the Chief Inspector had to undergo many operations over several years before he was fit to return to duty. Some while later, I saw the wreck of the Tripacer aircraft and it was just a crumpled ball of metal. One Christmas day morning, one of our aircraft took off carrying the pilot and his wife on a jaunt to flour bomb a nearby military camp. It circled for a second run and hit a power cable killing both the pilot and his unfortunate wife.

I hated to see things stand still and considered that there was always room for improvement so I took every opportunity to develop and expand my command in order to increase its efficiency and its effectiveness. The Machakos Reserve district and the Kitui district, both Wakamba tribal reserves, were considerably under-policed - the Machakos reserve having very few police and the Kitui, none at all. Both these areas had now been penetrated by the Mau Mau so I set about establishing better control.

I was in a position to obtain more than my fair share of personnel and equipment, so I established a Divisional headquarters with four Police stations and eight outposts in the Kitui area. I posted a small hard-core of regular officers to recruit and train, on the job, sufficient full-time reservists, then, supplying them with essential transport, communications and money for building, they were dumped at the selected sites. Their duty now was to recruit local labour, (more precisely, to arrest wrongdoers and make them work), to build themselves quarters and get out patrolling their districts.

All around my command, I reinforced outposts and opened up new ones at strategic places. The Masai still had the reputation of being a warlike tribe so, following reports that terrorist gangs were infiltrating their reserves, the British Game Warden, who was a reserve Police officer, had the idea of raising a fighting force of five hundred Masai warriors for skirmishing. Though, in Masai, the Police strength was adequate, I lent support to this venture by making all the warriors into reserve Police officers and by stiffening the force with a few regular officers. The main body of the Masai force were armed with shield and spear but, by arming a few with rifles, we formed patrolling platoons. In the end, they proved unsuccessful and were disbanded.

In white settled areas I increased establishments and provided unlimited numbers of reserve personnel. One such district, in order to counter Mau Mau successes, were led to form an all white reserve officer group calling themselves 'Dobie' or 'D' Force and they operated under the umbrella of one of my divisions.

They did an excellent job and boosted morale a great deal but, egged on by early successes, they got a bit naughty and, unfortunately, very trigger happy, killing too many people without sufficient explanation. Under the prevailing situation of civil war between black and mainly white, and with the Police and Military forces being black rank and file

262

with white officers, propriety must be observed if loyalty is to be maintained and mutiny avoided. 'D' Force had overstepped the mark and finding the situation intolerable, I conveyed my concerns to the Commissioner who ordered me to disband them immediately.

'D' Force were from a group of fiery white settlers calling themselves the Tigoni Tigers. They and their friends - men, women and children - were being targeted for murder by Mau Mau gangs and, at the time, I was unable to offer them any practical alternative form of defence. I convened a meeting with them and commended them saying that, as a group, they were being slightly wasted but if, as individuals, they were to lead groups of black reservists, their full potential would be unleashed. For a minute or two there was silence amongst them and, at any moment, I expected to be either shot or shown the door but, to my great relief and surprise, they accepted the proposal as a master stroke of strategy and the problem was solved. Of course, I could have pulled rank instead but gentle persuasion, when it works, is always the best way.

The Kenya Police took naturally to their role in anti Mau Mau operations; the high morale, absolute loyalty and blatant confidence which were the hall marks of the force, ideally suited them for the task. Asking for little except for better weapons, public support and emergency powers, we soon developed individual tactics to counter the threat and, despite some UK opposition, got stuck into it. Some officers had Northern Frontier experience but the Mau Mau was an entirely different kettle of fish.

Declaration of the state of emergency by H.E. The Governor Sir Evelyn Baring led to a massive increase in the forces available. Large numbers of reservists were immediately called up, the Lancashire Fusiliers were flown down from Egypt, the King's African Rifles and the Kenya Regiment were stood to. As thousands of young Kikuyu were 'oathed up' and took to the forests forming gangs, An RAF squadron of Lincoln Bombers were flown in to commence aerial bombardment, to be joined later by Rhodesian RAF Harvard fighter bombers and even once, by Meteor jet fighters, though these proved unsuitable for the role. Eventually, forces stood at ten Imperial Infantry Battalions, twenty-thousand Police of all types, including tribal Police, African Home Guard contingents and Ancillaries. From the Kikuyu, the Mau Mau spread insidiously into neighbouring tribes of Embu, Meru and Kamba and they were able eventually to field a force of over twenty-thousand supported by an enormous passive wing running into seven figures.

The scene was set for a bloody conflict, though both sides suffered from a lack of unified direction and command and we, like the Mau Mau, were forced through circumstances to act individually. In due course, the forces became co-ordinated and this, coupled with the villagisation and curfewing of the Kikuyu tribe was what really broke the Mau Mau but not before some fifteen thousand of them had been shot or hung, about thirty eight Europeans killed and four thousand loyal Africans killed or wounded. In all, about twelve hundred Mau Mau were hung and, as I recall it, the hangman was paid different fees for hanging different races. What had started out as a black versus white conflict was manipulated to become a black versus black one.

As far back as the twenties, the Kikuyu, always politically conscious, had formed groups that were beginning to demand the return of their, now white occupied, lands and independence from white rule. Missionaries had antagonised them by trying to ban the ancient custom of circumcision of their young women and by preaching that their god 'Ngai' didn't exist. The Kikuyu were, however, a very religious people whose strict codes of community and family conduct meant that crime was rare and prostitution was unheard of since they practised polygamy. In the early 1900's, Kinyangui, the Kikuyu paramount chief had no fewer than three hundred wives. Prior to white settlement, the Kikuyu lived mainly in the forests to escape attack by neighbouring tribes such as the Masai, the Kamba and the Kalegin who laid claim to ownership of the open plains.

Many tribes practised female circumcision. I think the reason was that by cutting out the girl's clitoris, they knew she would experience diminished sexual pleasure and would be less likely to be unfaithful. Circumcision ceremonies were considered to be important affairs. No anaesthetics were used except that some tribes would immerse the girls for a while in cold water to partially numb their tender areas. An old, and not too sharp knife was used for the operation which must have caused considerable pain and threat to the future health of the victims. Following the circumcision, the girls were painted bright colours and hooded and then kept away from men until they were sufficiently healed and ready for sale into marriage.

Much earlier, during a flare-up caused by missionaries over circumcision, two Kikuyu broke into the house of two elderly white missionary spinster ladies, stripped them, then holding them, down crudely and brutally circumcised them, resulting in the death of them both.

Kikuyu had many 'uncivilised' customs, one of which would be to place the bodies of dead or dying children outside for the night to be taken by Hyenas. Their belief being that if the child died in the house, evil spirits would come in and take over the occupation.

Kikuyu had become the servant tribe of Kenya and they were the most intelligent and politically aware. Europeans had trusted them and this led to an otherwise avoidable number of whites becoming victims of the Mau Mau.

Oathing ceremonies themselves were a traditional practice of the Kikuyu which was exploited by the Mau Mau to bind young Kikuyu to their cause.

At first, the oathings took place at night and in secret. A ceremonial arch of branches and banana leaves would be made and the a noose would be placed around the candidate's neck. The oath itself would include the following affirmations: *'If I become an informer, this oath will kill me. If I object to following Kenyatta, this oath will kill me. If I don't subscribe fees to the Mau Mau, this oath will kill me. If I tell of this organisation, this oath will kill me. If I sell land to a European, this oath will kill me.'*

Gradually, as the Mau Mau grew in strength and numbers, the oaths became more appalling and the ceremonies more gruesome. Those administrating the oaths would use blood, animal's eyes, meat, sodom apples and thorns and the oathee would be smeared with blood and made to eat the meat, eyes would be gauged from live sheep and these and the sodom apples pricked with thorns. Each action would be repeated seven times since the number seven to the Kikuyu, is an evil number, in a way, similar to our number thirteen.

Just prior to the emergency, the oaths became more specific and more demanding and included affirmations any of which, if they were not adhered to, would kill the oathee. They included - to rid Kenya of Europeans, to kill members of their family who was anti Mau Mau, to disobey a Mau Mau order, to declare Kenyatta as my god, to inform on anti Mau Mau persons, to steal from a European when ordered to do so, to kill a European when ordered to do so, to bring in parts of the body of any enemy. Later, the oathing ceremony entailed the drinking of the blood of menstruating virgins who were brought to the ceremony for the purpose. If it was considered necessary, the oath would be forcibly administered and, to these primitives, it was utterly binding.

Six or seven hundred at a time were now being oathed up and instead of the secrecy practised earlier, the ceremonies became blatant. An oath was now introduced heralding a day of doom which averred: 'If I hear a horn blow, I will kill the Europeans I work for.'

Huge meetings were held in the reserves, Mau Mau banners and regalia were flaunted, gangs were formed, crime rose, arson and atrocities on white settler's farms commenced, cattle were mutilated and left to die.

Commissioner O'Rorke officially notified the Kenya Government that a situation had been reached that had all the signs of a imminent mass revolt and it had developed to a level beyond which the Police would be powerless to halt it. The Colony's Acting Governor did nothing and, in fact, was using every opportunity to preach 'peace in our time'. He was replaced and the incoming Governor, Sir Evelyn Baring, who immediately appreciated the situation, decided at once to declare a state of emergency. Senior Kikuyu Chief Wariuhu, loyal to the Government and a staunch opponent of the Mau Mau, was murdered.

Police information told us that Kenya's Member for Law and Order, the Colony's Attorney General, was employing delaying tactics and even prevented the Police from raiding the offices of the Kenya African Union which was now synonymous with Mau Mau leadership. Eventually, emergency powers were introduced, Security Committees set up and the Attorney General lost his position as Member for Law and Order.

So the action, which was to last more than ten years, commenced. Regular army units from the UK arrived in increasing numbers including Yorkshire Light Infantry, Enniskillen Fusiliers, Northumberland Fusiliers, The East Lancs Regiment, the Buffs, Royal Engineers, the Devonshire's, even the Black Watch and the Irish Fusiliers and, of course, there were others. The Kings African Rifles and the Kenya Regiment also became fully operational though later, the Kenya Regiment seconded personnel to other units to act as Guides, Intelligence Officers, Interpreters Scouts and generally to supply local knowledge and information.

By now, forest gangs of Mau Mau were at their maximum strength and were continually supplied by their passive wing with food, weapons, ammunition and all the comforts of home. The vast areas of forest available to them made tracking and engaging them an almost impossible task.

Security committees were established at Colony, Provincial and District levels and these met each morning at about 8 a.m. in, for example the District Police operations room. These meetings, euphemistically referred to as 'Morning Prayers', comprised the Police Officer commanding the district, the Senior Administrative Officer, the Senior

Officer of any military units deployed within the area and again, if they were operational locally, an RAF Liaison Officer. A Police Special Branch Officer was then called in to brief the meeting on any fresh information which had come in over night and to give his assessment of the likely developments. The meeting then discussed events and decided upon appropriate counter operations.

Such operations could be of a few hour's, a few day's or even several week's duration and might involve anything from just a few personnel to all the available forces, amounting to hundreds of men.

Active fighting units were usually the province of District or Divisional commands, while Colony and Provincial headquarters were more concerned with long-term organisation and overall strategy. Overall command of an operation depended on whether the objective was a Police, Military or Administrative one. If it was a Police objective, then the senior Police officer was in command, if Military, then the senior Military officer commanded, and so on however, although the designated commander could brief the combined force on its role and objectives, the performance of that role was still under the direction of that particular force's own senior officers. So used to the system and so skilled in its operation did we become that I could draft an operational order involving several forces and hundreds of men, in only an hour or two.

We also had available to us at District level, the Police General Service unit, by now in five companies with over eight hundred men. As a para-military branch of the force, they carried considerable armament including Bren gun carriers and armoured cars.

Our transport and signals branches fitted these armoured cars with a natty gadget for tackling rioting mobs. They attached a lengthy, flexible metal rod at the end of which was a metal weight suspended from a length of copper wire. The rod was fixed to a swivel mounted on the turret and the copper wire connected to the vehicle's electrical system. They proved very useful in dispersing unlawful assemblies. The car would drive up to a hostile crowd and the commander would call upon them to disperse. If they didn't, the weight would be manoeuvred above the loudest mouthed individual and lowered until the it was only an inch or so above his head. Suddenly, a bright blue spark would flash from the weight to the individual's head and he would drop to the ground, temporarily stunned. A very effective deterrent, but, to UK politicians, it was acceptable to shoot and kill such people but not to temporarily disable or frighten them so, all too soon, orders came through to discontinue its use.

Our anti-riot drill in urban situations developed into a formation, all in riot gear, the first three ranks being armed with shields and pick-axe handles, the fourth with tear gas guns behind which was a rank or two armed with rifles bayonets fixed.

A bugler and a photographer were present wherever possible. Originally our bayonets were the old twelve inch ones but, once again, politicians considered them too intimidating and we had to replace them with eight inch ones.

The Commander called upon the crowd, in the name of the Crown to disperse or face the use of force. Failure to disperse led to the front rank advancing and beating the tar out of the rioters. After a minute or so, a bugle call would recall them to the rear of the formation whereon, the second rank would advance and continue the attack, and so on. Gas would be used if it was still necessary, then a rank of riflemen would advance and usually the gleam of bayonets was sufficient to force the mob into retreat.

If it became necessary as a final resort, the Commander would order the use of firearms. The correct procedure was for the Commander to indicate a particular target and order two men to fire one round each at the rioter's knees. There were occasions when the general use of firearms was called for.

At this time, all our rank and file wore the old 'Tommy's' tin helmet, except they were coloured blue but even these had to be changed to dark blue Stetsons since the military helmet was deemed by politicians to be too intimidating. Eventually, the Stetsons too, had to be withdrawn when Mau Mau gangs started to wear them with the result that, on occasions, Police were exchanging shots with other Police.

Events were moving rapidly and the Force was recruiting hundreds of European 'Contract Inspectors' - white mercenaries who signed on for two or three year contracts. In addition, thousands of Africans were enlisted and put through crash training courses or, in the case of full-time reserves, taught on the job.

We were rapidly opening scores of forest outposts, each manned by two white and twenty black officers. They ran up wattle and mud huts, erected barbed wire defences and dug trenches. In some cases, where bamboo was available, they would make a defensive strip around the perimeter by driving two foot long, sharpened slivers of bamboo into the ground at six inch intervals, pointing upwards and outwards to create a wide 'hedgehog' belt to stop gangsters running over the wire. We called this defensive arrangement 'Panjies'. Heavily armed and carrying radios, it was the job of these units to patrol, track, ambush and kill Mau Mau gangs in their areas.

Very occasionally, a white officer would get trigger happy and, no doubt, there were a few innocents killed who had been unfortunate enough to get in the way of one of their bullets. As soon as any such incident came to light, the officer concerned was immediately posted to a non-operational area. Some units, especially the army, started using score boards to record their kills and, to some these rapidly became excuses for, shall we say, ill-directed and indiscriminate fire. The practice was immediately banned.

The question as to the existence of 'murder squads' has often arisen and I do not know the answer, but I do know that occasionally, a prominent member of the Mau Mau passive wing would disappear to be found later, the victim of a hit and run vehicle or turn up with a knife through his ribs after which, Special Branch Officers would look very pleased.

The Action Intensifies

During the early years of the Mau Mau uprising, I took home leave and was asked, while in the UK, to attend a board of selection who were recruiting 'Contract Inspectors'. The board sat in London and my role was to advise on the suitability or otherwise of the candidates being interviewed. On the first day, a rail delay caused me to arrive late so I said to the girl in the outer office,

"I'm here for the Board."

Misunderstanding me, she replied,

"Yes, yes. Sit over there with the others." I thought, 'Oh, well, I'll wait until the chap under interview comes out', and I joined the queue of candidates.

Immediately I sat down, the chap next to me started to chat, telling me the story of his wasted life, his lack of qualifications and his many misdeeds and ended by saying,

"With my record, I haven't a hope in hell of being taken on. It's a pity 'cos I'd really like to go out there." I rather admired him for his frankness.

In due course, I went through to the interview room and sat down with the rest of the Board. We interviewed one or two more applicants and then eventually, in came my friend. Seeing me seated beside the Chairman, he almost fainted and, presumably because of the shock, he gave a rather poor performance. I helped him with a few easy questions and, after he had withdrawn, I managed to persuade the Board to take him on.

He turned out to be a very good choice and, after his contract had expired, he was taken on as a permanent member of the force. We had a good few laughs over the event when we met up later in Kenya.

On occasions, I was called upon to attend security meetings at Colony level at which H.E. The Governor, the General Officer Commanding and all the top brass would be present. This occurred when a situation in my Province was developing into a serious problem or when my forces were due to be involved in operations along side other Provinces. The first time I attended, I expected just to be given instructions on how to proceed, however, I soon discovered that none of the meeting had any idea of the implications of the problem nor of the action necessary to resolve it and that when I gave them a briefing and suggested a course of action, they all nodded wisely to each other and said,

"Yes, yes, excellent. Get stuck into it straight away." One occasion however, turned out differently.

Sixty miles south of Nairobi and within the area of my command lay Lake Magadi, one of the larger soda lakes. Its surface was composed of a thick crust of soda which was mined by the Magadi Soda Company and the entire production exported to Japan, generating almost half of Kenya's overseas earnings.

The Company had a large workforce composed almost entirely of Kikuyu and my Special Branch gathered information to show that they, every one of them, were members of the Mau Mau. We also learned that they were not only active in aiding forest gangs but were themselves planning a midnight attack on the European company staff.

I quickly drew up an operational plan to pick up and detain the majority but, realising the sensitivity of the situation, I leaked the plan to higher authority before implementing it. Within hours, I was called to a specially convened security meeting at which I was asked - not instructed - to consider alternative action on the grounds that, if I arrested all the workforce, production would be halted and the resulting loss of revenue would prove disastrous. There is always an alternative so, fully appreciating the dilemma, I arranged a continuous series of arrests, of small numbers of Mau Mau at any one time, and so, gradually purged the Company with little loss of production.

Meanwhile, in forest areas, we kept the RAF busy. Police aircraft would spot gang hide-outs and pinpoint them by dropping smoke bombs by day and flares by night to guide in RAF Lincoln bombers which would then swoop down and unload their bombs onto the target. Throughout eight years of continuous day and night bombing, hardly any terrorists were killed because, hearing the sound of approaching aircraft, they would scatter into the forest and be well clear by the time the bombs hit the target. However, practically every tree on Mount Kenya and the Aberdares took shell splinters which were discovered later by shattered blade at the saw millers.

The Kenya Police finished up with a dozen or so Cessna 180 aircraft which, apart from general transport duties and for spotting the enemy, were used for supply drops to outposts and isolated patrols and some were even fitted with racks to carry 20 lb anti-personnel bombs. This was to stop pilots from throwing hand grenades out of the windows, a practice considered by the authorities to be dangerous.

One of my forest outposts, situated at Githunguru, the birthplace of Jomo Kenyatta, suffered a terrible tragedy at the hands of the airforce. The two British Inspectors in charge of the outpost had become friendly with some of the Lincoln bomber crews and, at dawn one morning, the pilot of a Lincoln, which was returning from a night mission, decided to buzz them. The post stood on top of a sugar loaf hill rising some four-hundred feet from the valley floor. Flying down the valley, the pilot underestimated his speed and pulled the stick back too late. The tail of the Lincoln ploughed through the centre of the post, killing several men and then went on to crash half a mile away killing all the crew. A second Lincoln bomber was burned out as it stood on the ground at RAF Eastleigh, Nairobi. Mau Mau terrorists had managed to evade airfield security, then disappear before anyone spotted the burning aircraft.

One night at a place called Lari in my Province, Mau Mau massacred hundreds of loyal Kikuyu. The Kikuyu had been villagised to make their protection by a military force easier but at the time, the military force had been withdrawn for urgent duties elsewhere and protection had been taken over by home guard and tribal police. The Mau Mau had organised a mass meeting nearby and hearing that protection of the loyal Kikuyu had been somewhat diminished, they decided to attack the encampment.

Late one night, they managed to sneak into the camp and while the occupants slept, wired up all the doors and windows then, saturating the place with petrol, they simultaneously set fire to every hut. Anyone who attempted to escape was butchered. Women and children were the main victims since most of their men were home guard, many of whom were out on patrol. Children were sliced up and thrown to their mothers who themselves had their stomachs slashed, their breasts cut off and were left to die. Mau Mau even drank the blood of dying victims. Cattle too were targeted, hundreds being killed or mutilated. The numbers of dead and wounded amounted to over two-hundred and the scene of the carnage was sickening.

At dawn, a running battle commenced with Police, tribal police and home guard all pursuing the fleeing terrorists. In the end, over forty were killed and hundreds detained.

To contain the prisoners, the nearest Police station rapidly ran up a wire compound and constructed sand bag watch towers which were manned by police with Bren guns and paraffin floodlights to illuminate the area at night. Lari, being at an altitude of seven-thousand feet was bitterly cold at night and was subject to heavy rainfall. Since adequate protection against the elements was absent there were many deaths amongst the detainees while they waited for interrogation but, after their atrocities, no one was very keen to protect them, any way.

This was probably the most active period for the Mau Mau and atrocity followed atrocity. The scenes of Mau Mau terrorism were always sickening sights, even to hardened old stagers, so who could really blame our forces if they once or twice overstepped the mark. Feelings were running very high and, in the end, not all the atrocities were the work of the Mau Mau.

Police enquiries following the Lari massacre, over one hundred were arrested and awaited trial so, anticipating a mass hanging, the Government erected a triple gallows on Jomo Kenyatta's own plot of land at Githunguru and tiers of seating were erected to accommodate plenty of witnesses. It was the practice to bring in the relatives of Mau Mau who were to be hanged to watch the execution of their kin. In the end, like so many of our modern prosecution of terrorists, it all collapsed through lack of evidence and these particular gallows were never used.

Through necessity, law enforcement had now reached a high level of speed and efficiency. A suspect could be arrested one day, was tried the next, if convicted could appeal the next and if the appeal was unsuccessful, was hanged only a few days later.

Although Government measures had led to the mass movement of Kikuyu males into the forest areas, it also resulted in much stronger and more open support for the Government by loyal Africans. White conscription was introduced and overall direction and co-ordination at Colony level was streamlined. The Government meant business and it now had the necessary forces, all told over fifty thousand and many lessons had already been learned.

At one place a fifty mile long ditch was dug and manned with armed personnel to cut off the forest gangs from access to supplies and information from their passive wing.

'Drives' involving thousands of 'beaters' and hundreds of forces personnel were organised, very similar to hare shoots in England. The beaters, many of them women, armed with machete's moved forward on a given plan to sweep Mau Mau out of hiding and onto the 'killing grounds' and in a lot of cases the terrorists were more frightened of the women beaters than they were of the troops and many of them rushed to surrender. All in all, the Government and the forces were operating efficiently and as a result were crushing the enemy. It was truly, a dirty conflict.

Prior to the emergency, many Mau Mau had served with the forces and some forest gangs put their military training and experience to good use as was evinced in a number of instances in attacks on Police forest outposts. They used tactics including diversion parties, wire cutters, flank and rear attacks and many other strategies they could only have learned while under military training.

My operations room was kitted out with a large array of radio equipment and my operators could communicate over eight frequencies to my own divisions and stations, to all neighbouring Provinces, to Colony HQ and to military bases. There was a constant chatter from all these sets and the operations room staff, one of whom was Viscount Manderville, then a full time Kenya Police Reserve Officer, was kept extremely busy, day and night.

One evening on returning home, I called in, as usual, to the operations room to keep myself abreast of the latest developments and heard one of the operators talking to an RAF Dakota aircraft which was returning to the airfield at RAF Eastleigh, Nairobi. We heard Eastleigh control say,

"Yeah, OK, we've picked you up. You can come in to land."

"Good," the Dakota replied. "We're on our way." Then the Dakota went silent. Eastleigh control kept calling but there was no further response from the aircraft. My night sentries reported seeing a fire on top of the Ngong Hills and at dawn I sent a party out to investigate. They soon located the burned out wreckage with all but one of the crew dead inside. Searching the surrounding area they came upon the body of the last crew member about two hundred yards from the wreckage. He was dead and had been half eaten by Hyena. He must have survived the crash and

274

crawled away only to be eaten alive. I still have a marching compass found amongst the wreckage.

The RAF at one stage, flew Meteor jet fighters out from the UK but these had little success and were soon withdrawn. One Meteor pilot claimed that, while he was flying low up a narrow valley on the slopes of Mount Kenya, he was nearly 'shot' down by Mau Mau hurling rocks from above at his passing plane.

In heavily forested country, which tended to black out any radio contact between forces at ground level, we used Police aircraft who circled above and acted as radio relay stations.

At dawn one morning, I received information that a Mau Mau gang was making its way across the grassy plains south of Nairobi. They used the route to cross the border into Tanganyika and rest up on the slopes of Mount Meru where, for some time they had been spreading Mau Mau doctrine and preaching sedition amongst the Meru tribe.

Having despatched a party by lorry to chase them on the ground, my pilot and I took off to follow them from the air and soon picked up suspicious tracks in the dew saturated long grass. To see the tracks at all, we had to fly at very low level, forcing the pilot to throw the aircraft about rather violently as the tracks switched left and right following the contours of the land. Very soon my stomach started to churn and, so ill did I feel, that I nearly called off the pursuit. I was greatly relieved when, over a series of low valleys, and with the dew burned off by the rising sun, we lost the tracks and had to return to base.

On such early morning flights, what did surprise and disturb me somewhat, was that the aircraft's carburettors tended to freeze up and ice would form on the wings then break off with a loud bang.

One effective tool against forest gangs of Mau Mau was an army battery of ack ack guns. They had an effective range of fifteen miles or so and would be positioned on the edge of the gang-infested forests of Mount Kenya. Given the map reference of a suspected gang hide-out, they would open up and rapidly saturate the area with a deluge of shells. The shells arrived without warning, and caught the terrorists napping, giving them no time to escape, so inflicting a good number of casualties upon them.

Out of curiosity, I witnessed one hanging and I can tell you, it's not good entertainment. Although I'm said to be emotionally destitute, it disturbed me greatly and I wish that I'd never seen it. Execution by shooting would, I think, be far more humane.

With practice, our forces became expert reading the signs and silently tracking enemy gangs. Police formed pseudo-gangs often guided by Mau Mau prisoners who, as soon as they'd been captured, had immediately turned coat and eagerly guided our forces to hunt down their former confederates. These pseudo-gangs had to learn things the hard way but soon became very proficient, killing many terrorists and going a long way towards destroying overall Mau Mau morale. They would track gangs through the forests and when they eventually came into contact, the terrorists were fooled into thinking that they'd met up with another group of Mau Mau and were immediately mown down. Mau Mau gangs were made so nervous by these activities that they often ended up shooting at each other.

With the exception of a few who had fought in Malaya, Imperial Forces fresh from the UK had little experience of guerrilla activity, and tended to lumber around on noisy patrols, spending much of their time dodging elephant, rhino and buffalo and finding it difficult to achieve results. However, they did perform an excellent role in keeping gangs clear of certain large areas of territory.

Quite late in the emergency, I was commissioned to conduct a Police Court of Enquiry into a disaster which befell one of the Police pseudo-gangs. Two British Inspectors, their faces and all visible flesh blackened to make them appear African, together with a few Police rank and file and couple of ex Mau Mau, camped down for the night on a white farm just below the forest level on Kinangop. By coincidence, a platoon of the Police General Service Unit returning from a forest patrol had arrived on the farm and one of the farm labourer reported to them the position of what he mistakenly thought was a Mau Mau gang. After dark, the platoon crept up on the Police pseudo-gang, opened fire and killed the lot.

On a previous occasion, I had aided the Deputy Commissioner of Police when he conducted an enquiry into the over-running by Mau Mau of the Naivasha Police station. The station's perimeter defences had been demolished to make way for new and stronger ones which had not yet been completed. The Police barracks were a couple of hundred yards from the station but the arms of off-duty personnel were in the armoury in the station itself, so when the Mau Mau attacked they were of little use and the only resistance came from the small armed quarter guard who were forced into retreat by overwhelming numbers of terrorists. The attack resulted in several Police casualties and the loss of over fifty weapons including sub-machine guns and a large quantity of ammunition which, curiously enough, never came to light in future Mau Mau operations. The lesson to be learned was that, in danger areas, weapons should always be kept in the personal possession of the officers themselves.

Mau Mau activity was still on the increase and their oathing ceremonies became ever more obscene. Heads were cut off babies in front of their mothers, pregnant women were slit open and their unborn babies pulled out and killed. Candidates for 'oathing' would be forced to eat human flesh and brains, to drink the urine and menstrual blood of virgins and to have sexual intercourse with animals. One ceremony included the cutting off of genitals which were then pushed into a menstruating girl's vagina or a woman's anus which then had to be eaten by the one being 'oathed'. Defaulting Members were killed to provide ingredients for these depraved and bestial ceremonies. All these foul and contemptible activities were initiated and condoned by those who considered themselves fit to rule the country and, though it may be difficult to believe, there were deluded people in the UK at the time who, quite legally, were busy raising funds in support of the Mau Mau.

Missionaries must carry some of the blame for the deterioration of Kikuyu attitudes and behaviour. They preached Christianity from several different aspects and displayed extreme intolerance towards denominations - Catholic, Methodist, C of E or whatever - other than their own, thus destroying Kikuyu beliefs in their own perfectly adequate gods and replacing them with a vague and confused pantheon. They opposed circumcision and bigamy and set their converts against others. In many instances they bitterly opposed the very customs which had held the tribe together as a loyal and relatively peaceful community. Little wonder then, that with such petty selfishness and intolerance as their examples, the tribe turned, slowly but surely, anti-white and anti-Government.

One Englishman, Doctor Leakey, was captured by the Mau Mau and buried alive, but two African Female nurses had a narrow escape. They were sitting in a cafe when in burst a terrorist gang and 'arrested' them. They were taken to an adjacent building where the gangsters set up a court and tried the girls for giving information to the Police. They were found guilty and sentenced to death by first, having their fingers, toes, breasts and clitoris cut off and then strangled. They were then dragged from the building and taken towards the place of execution. As luck would have it, they were spotted when the girls screamed to a passing pick-up truck full of Police. The Police immediately arrested all the kidnappers and rescued the girls and at the trial the gangsters were found guilty and each given twenty years.

Nairobi became so infested with Mau Mau passive wing supporters, gang recruiters and suppliers of cash, arms and food to the forest gangs that an operation, code-named 'Anvil', was planned to clean it up. It took many months of careful intelligence gathering and preparation before the operation could be implemented; detention camps had to be built, guards recruited and trained, medical facilities provided, food and other supplies organised, communications, transport and go knows what else. Over twenty thousand security forces were involved and when eventually 'A' Day arrived, in one prolong and thorough sweep, we arrested over sixteen thousand suspects.

In the process, we bulldozed two African shanty towns, finding and digging up many Mau Mau murder victims. The process continued and, at one stage we had over one hundred thousand detainees with another hundred thousand arrested and waiting interrogation.

From early on in the campaign, the Kikuyu displayed an unexpected pattern of behaviour. Arrested at, say, midnight, by dawn they would have turned coat and would leading us to gang hide-outs, identifying other members and giving detailed information against all and sundry.

In order to curtail the activities of the Mau Mau passive wing and to protect those loyal to the Government, over a million Kikuyu were 'villagised'. An area would be selected amongst scattered mud hut settlements, and wire-fenced encampments, protected by watch towers and armed guards, would be built. The occupants of the settlements would be given one week to demolish their wattle and mud rondavels and build new ones within the encampment where strict curfews were imposed and the majority of potential Mau Mau members and helpers could be controlled.

Anti Mau Mau forces were placed under the overall control of the Commander in Chief, East Africa, General Erskine and under him, General Hinde who co-ordinated all field operations. Under them, unity of action was developed which boosted morale and this went a long way towards the eventual victory.

One day there was a knock on my office door at my operational headquarters and, to my surprise, in walked General Hinde himself. I leapt to attention and offered him my comfy chair but he motioned me to sit down and himself, sat on a rather less comfortable seat beside me.

He asked me, in a matter-of-fact sort of way, to brief him on how the affair was proceeding in the areas under my jurisdiction. I gave him a quick assessment then, out of the blue, he said "Has villagisation been completed in your area?"

The Administration under the senior Administrative Officer, the Provincial Commissioner, handled the process but, he had sympathised somewhat with the Kikuyu and had been dragging his heels. Although we had gangs operating in the area being supplied by the passive wing, he had neglected to clear large scattered pockets of Kikuyu settlements and my regular intelligence reports had emphasised this fact. Unknown to me at the time, the Provincial Commissioner had submitted a report stating that he had completed the task.

"No, sir," I replied. "Not yet."

"Are you certain?" the General asked, and I confirmed my statement.

"Right," he said. "Can you spare an hour or two?" I nodded so he picked up the phone and ordered an aircraft to stand by for him at RAF Eastleigh. He asked me to show him the situation from the air and, as we took off, I began to sweat in case the Provincial Commissioner was right and he had, in fact, completed the task. I was relieved to be able to point out hundreds of scattered Kikuyu huts which were obviously still occupied. On landing, the General gave me tea in the Army mess.

A few days later, the Provincial Commissioner dropped into my office.

"There's something cooking," he said. I've been called to Government house."

Next morning, after his return, he called into my office again, this time looking very sorrowful "I've been made redundant," he groaned. Later, I learned that he had come under heavy criticism from his own subordinates for failing to give adequate support to important anti Mau Mau matters. In any case, he was nearing the end of his service.

A senior Police Special Branch Officer, who later became a Chief Superintendent in charge of my Special Branch, won fame for his initiative and bravery. He was Bernard Ruck GM & Bar, the first ever holder of two George Medals. He was responsible for organising what became known as 'The Green Branch Mass Surrenders'.

Either alone or accompanied by one or two 'converted' Mau Mau and perhaps an Administrative Officer and another Police Officer, he ventured deep into Mau Mau infested forests, making contact with their leaders and persuading them to surrender along with their gangs. They were to issue from the forest at an agreed place and time, each carrying a green branch, and present themselves for arrest. If any action during the emergency took persistent cold courage, this was it and for his bravery, he received the honour of two George Medals. He is in the Guinness Book of Records as the only person at that time ever to have done so.

On one occasion, large groups of terrorists had gathered and were preparing to surrender when, within earshot, a military unit commenced heavy fire, though not at these particular terrorists. The groups thought that they'd been led into a trap and were about to be massacred so they changed their minds, turned and fled back into the forest.

At the height of the emergency, two UK Labour Government MP's arrived to appease the Kikuyu - Mau Mau supporters or not. They had to be given Police protection against the anger of white settlers who, in the face of recent atrocities, disapproved of their conciliatory stance. One of them was a member of a movement fighting for the freedom of the colonies.

It was rumoured that the other had arrived without socks so, when the two were attending a gathering in the Kikuyu reserve, a Police aircraft flew in very low and, to his eternal embarrassment, dropped him a pair attached to a streamer.

Atrocities kept on increasing and over a short period of time, eight Europeans were hacked to death in their own homes all because they had trusted their Kikuyu servants who had simply opened up their houses at night to admit the Mau Mau gangsters.

One lot, however, got more than they bargained for. Bursting into a house occupied by two lone European women, they were immediately greeted by a hail of pistol and shotgun fire from the ladies and four were killed before the rest fled leaving the ladies unharmed.

Under these conditions, it was useless to have a weapon in a cabinet, leaning against a wall or in a holster, the terrorists didn't waste time. The weapon had to be actually in the hand and cocked ready for immediate action. For years, I slept with a .45 revolver in my hand, loaded with five rounds, set so that the hammer would come down the first time on the empty sixth chamber.

Throughout the emergency, Police and the other forces involved had insufficient strength to offer protection to every individual. Kenya is a large country of very diverse terrain and many scattered and isolated farms and settlements, to protect them all would have needed many times more resources than could possibly have been mustered. We did, however, set up manned watchtowers at vantage points and issue distress rockets to isolated homesteads for use if danger threatened. On balance, people were very brave in the face a threat which could only be described as horrific and many examples exist of their stoicism. For instance, one night, in a wooded area containing many European houses quite close to Nairobi, a gun battle broke out between Police and a gang of Mau Mau terrorists. I just happened to be in my operations room at the time and, amid the chatter of a dozen radios, the telephone rang.

"I'm sorry to trouble you Officer." It was the voice of an elderly lady. "But I thought perhaps you should know, I've got bullets pouring in through my windows. Do you think I should just keep my head down 'til it stops?"

The Mau Mau did achieve quite a lot, but what is surprising is not what they did do but what they could have done and failed to do. Properly lead and co-ordinated they might well have achieved their original objective of driving all the Europeans out of Kenya.

One mid-day, a Mau Mau raiding party was spotted in a heavily wooded valley only five miles from the township of Thika which was within the area of my command. A combined Police and Army party was sent in pursuit and arrived at the valley to be met by sporadic gun-fire. The commander of the Army group, a captain who was the son of an English Lord, but which one, I cannot now recall, stood up on the sky-line on the rim of the valley in an attempt to pinpoint the enemy and was immediately shot dead. At once, his second in command, a lieutenant, stood up to retaliate and he too was shot dead. Reinforcements were sent for and the valley was surrounded, mortared, bombed from the air the swept at bayonet point but, too late, the gang had escaped without casualties.

The northern part of this area was quite arid and it was decided to feed it with an irrigation channel many miles long from the Thika River using Mau Mau detainees as labour. The design of the camp to house the detainees fell to me. My brief had to preclude the possibility of a mass breakout and also to cater for the possibility of attack by Mau Mau from the outside. Here, my experience of the design of defences in the Northern Frontier District was brought to bear and it proved to be an interesting and, ultimately, a successful exercise.

We didn't have it all our own way, however. One cheeky Mau Mau leader, while in transit with his gang, pitched his camp one night close to a Military base and the following morning, as he moved on, he sent a note, via a local African, to the commander of the base thanking him for his hospitality and for providing security for him and his gang.

Morale of the forces was further boosted by the arrival of the cruiser HMS Kenya carrying Royal Marines.

In company with General Hinde, I visited an area of my command in which a contingent of the Kenya Regiment was deployed. I had arranged for a guard of honour to greet the General as we landed and from there, we proceeded to the Kenya Regiment camp where the commanding officer had laid on a demonstration of fire power. The contingent had a strength of three companies, all white, and the fire party consisted of a hundred personnel all lined up at about a thousand yards from a clump of bush in a rocky hollow.

"Now," the commanding officer said. "We'll 'wipe out' any gangsters hiding in it." and he gave the order to open fire.

Every man in the fire party opened up with a variety of weapons including rifles, Bren guns, belt machine guns, mortars and heaven knows what else. Fire rained down on the rocky hollow and for a while, it was blotted out by flames fire, dust and a cloud of black smoke. After a minute or two, the commanding officer shouted the order to cease fire and, to everyone's surprise, slowly, out of the smoke and the inferno, emerged a flock of goats and an aged Masai counting his animals and looking somewhat bewildered.

A few days later I was travelling through the Masai when I came to the Mara River. The Mara River had two bridges, one old bridge and one new one, both miles apart and with no track connecting them. I had emerged at the old bridge which, I found, had one in three of its planks either rotted, broken or missing completely.

The bridge was some thirty yards long and thirty feet above the crododile infested river and it had no side rails. The steel bearers of the bridge were so narrow that the outer wheel of my three ton twin-wheeled lorry overhung the edge, none the less, I decided to cross sincere were in a hurry and I didn't relish the thought of the arduous trek to the new bridge.

I crossed the bridge on foot and planted a stick on the far side to give me a point to aim for then my men prised up good planks and laid them so that I could advance onto the bridge. Lining up the centre frame of the split windscreen with my stick, I moved slowly forward and every ten feet or so, I stopped while my men retrieved the planks from behind the lorry and relayed them ahead of me. Slowly, we inched the vehicle over the bridge but now and again the outer wheels snapped off the ends of the planking and the lorry teetered dangerously on the edge. After what seemed like an age, I made it to the far side and breathed a sigh of relief as I looked down into the swirling waters where I could just make out the nostrils of several large crocodiles waiting patiently for a free meal. A few weeks later, while camped close by, I had my men rip up the remaining planking and throw it into the river. Mine was the last vehicle ever to cross that bridge.

The battle against the Mau Mau started as a fight to save the long-term future of the white settlers who were told that it would be years before consideration would be given to granting independent rule to the Africans. However, after only a few years it had been commonly accepted that the battle had become one to wipe out the forest terrorist gangs and thereby create a peaceful and stable conditions conducive to handing the Colony over to an independent black government. It was merely a repeat of what had happened in other colonies, one after another; a somewhat farcical process by which the forces of law and order were busy killing off the very individuals who were fighting to achieve the self same objective. We knew that black independence would not only see the dispossession and eviction of white settlers but also see the end of orderly progressive development.

Back to the Orthodox

In 1956, when I was aged thirty-eight, I was awarded the Colonial Police Medal for Meritorious Service, ('though, 'Notorious Service' would perhaps be a more apposite description), and in 1961 at the age of forty-two, the Queen's Police Medal for Distinguished Service. I was younger than my Deputies, my Staff Officers and most of my Divisional Commanders. I think that, had her Gracious Majesty, our Queen, been aware of the full facts, it might have been a period of detention at her pleasure rather than the honour of the Queens Police Medal that she would have bestowed on me.

By now, action against the Mau Mau had developed into 'cleaning up' operations and ever widening areas were being swept clean of terrorists and their activities. Operational intelligence poured in, the passive wing gradually ceased to support the forest gangs and terrorists in increasing numbers surrendered to our forces. Women in particular became anti-terrorist and would turn out in large numbers to aid the forces and loyal 'home guards' and, armed with machete's hunt down and kill Mau Mau.

I had just completed the task of establishing and expanding Police formations throughout the new Southern Province - which had entailed a very large buildings and communications programme and had proved a very interesting sideline to anti Mau Mau activities - when I received a letter from His Excellency the Governor of Kenya, which I reproduce here:

Government House,
Kenya,
East Africa.
2nd January, 1956

Dear Mr. Mills,

I am writing to you today to congratulate you on the Honour which Her Majesty the Queen has been graciously pleased to confer upon you.

You have performed excellent work in the Southern Province since you assumed charge and have done much to improve the situation in that district. I am very glad indeed that your services have received this recognition.

Yours sincerely,

E. Baring.

Soon after receiving the Colonial Police Medal, I was promoted to Assistant Commissioner of Police, aged only 38, and posted to take charge of Kenya's Lake (Nyanza) Province. Though geographically much smaller than the Southern Province, Lake Province was Kenya's most densely populated area with all the urban crime patterns that civilisation breeds. In addition, its main tribes were extremely politically minded and since Kenya, in the process of finishing off the Mau Mau, was in no mood to let another rebellion start for lack of intelligence and prompt action, my Special Branch was kept very busy. For me, it was all a very new experience and I settled down to a rather different and mundane existence.

I had been allocated a fine house in the European residential area of Kisumu on what is now called the Winam Gulf, a branch of Lake Victoria, and together with my wife Betty, our two children Ann and Peter and our servants, we moved in. The house was a large, comfortable, colonial style building constructed on a square plan, somewhat in the manner of a Roman villa, and in the centre was a shady, enclosed garden planted with trees.

In order to occupy herself, and because ladies of her status did no housework, Betty took a position as Supervisor in charge of the Province's East African Currency Board. We had always had plenty of servants and Betty had held a number of positions in the past including a full-time Police reserve Inspector, manager of a gift shop, supervisor of a large telephone exchange and, during the war, she had been in the land army.

Ajuro, my personal servant was of the Jaluo people whose native reserve was here in the Lake Province. He had been with me, through thick and through thin, ever since I had been at the Police training depot, twenty years or so ago. He had come full circle and he decided to return to his people in honourable retirement, no doubt to spend the rest of his days regaling them with tales of his extraordinary adventures. We said goodbye with sadness in our hearts.

Most of Kenya's tea was grown in two districts in the Lake Province and all around the fringes of the lake shore were rice fields. The rice fields and lake shore swamps attracted enormous amounts of duck and geese which provided first class shooting and gave me compensation for the dull routine of Provincial command. Despite the very high incidence of bilharzia, a chronic disease caused by infestation with schistosomes - blood flukes - carried by a tiny water snail, I often waded waist deep to find good spots to shoot. Crocodile and hippo abounded and could be a nuisance when, for example, I was secreted in reed beds waiting for duck, one or the other would approach too close for comfort and I was forced to retreat rather rapidly.

One day, I was watching a fellow wildfowler as he waded to an island where he hoped to find good cover when suddenly, his head and shoulders disappeared below the water. All I could see was one arm holding his gun and cartridge bag clear of the surface. A second or two later, he reappeared, then, again disappeared below the surface. I was intrigued and couldn't wait to hear the explanation for his strange behaviour. It transpired that, when part way to the island, he had sneezed and his false teeth had shot out into the lake, and despite many attempts, he never did find them.

One day I was in my office when I heard a commotion in the outer office. An attractive Greek lady aged about forty stormed in past my Deputy, my Staff Officers and my secretary and barged straight into my office. My secretary rushed in to apologise for not stopping the lady so I told her to stay fearing that our enraged visitor might be a nutter about to accuse me of rape or something similar.

"Get him back! Get him back!" the Greek lady screamed. "You must get him back and lock him up."

Eventually, we persuaded her to sit down then, slowly, she became calmer and through her sobs, she managed to explain her predicament. It appears that she was the wife of the Greek owner of a sisal plantation and on their estate was a small open-cast gold mine still producing workable quantities of gold. Some months previously, the couple had brought a young man out from Greece to assist in the management of the estate and she, the wife, had fallen into a passionate affair with the young man. Things between them progressed until eventually, they hatched a plot for him to pilfer the gold, return to Greece with it then, after a while she would join him and they would live happily ever after.

By all accounts, the gold he had stolen was worth some thirty thousand pounds - in those days an awful lot of money - and he had managed to smuggle it out of Kenya and into Greece. Things seemed to be going according to plan and she was almost ready to leave her husband and travel to Greece when she received a letter from her lover saying, "Don't leave Kenya. I've met and married a young Greek girl."

Hell hath no fury like a woman scorned. And, for once, I was glad I wasn't at the receiving end of it. I raged against the iniquity and promised the lady I would do everything I could to help so, feeling content that the lad would eventually be brought to justice, she left. There was, of course, little I could do.

Throughout my Police career, there were a couple of things I always managed to escape - training courses and promotion boards. Our officers were sent to both Hendon and Bramshill when on home leave but I always manage to see to it that my UK leave never coincided with any courses so that I was unfortunately 'prevented' from attending.

Throughout my career I was never a deputy and indeed don't recall ever being ordered or instructed to do anything at any time. From the time I was promoted to Inspector, I was operating continuously in 'acting' rank, that is, one rank ahead of my substantive rank while waiting to be confirmed into an establishment vacancy. At one such stage, I was called to attend, as a candidate, a promotion board for officers seeking the rank of Superintendent. I was the first in and, as soon as he saw me, the Commissioner said, "What are you doing here? Then, seeing that I was a bit puzzled he added, "I promoted you two days ago."

I turned and was about to leave. "Don't go, Mills," he said. "Sit down and tell me which of those waiting outside do you think I should promote."

While I'd been waiting to be called in, I'd been chatting to the Chief Clerk who, unknown to the Commissioner, had shown me the short list. I took my time, apparently to consider the question, then, with the Commissioner watching me attentively over his glasses, I mentioned six of the applicants and deliberately threw in one who was not on the shortlist but had been noted as a border-line case. The Commissioner gazed at me for quite some time in silence.

"Very shrewd," he said at length. "Very Shrewd."

On one particular home leave, I was asked to attend, as umpire, a four week training course at Minsmere Manor - near Camberwell, I think. With recent experiences in Malaya and then in Kenya, and with rumblings of more trouble around the world, the course had been organised with the object of teaching officers of the rank of Major or equivalent from all branches of the services, the niceties of providing aid to civil authorities in times of emergency. As umpire, my decision was final and I was given the honour of a bat-man and unlimited access to their lavish hospitality, and since the working hours were not over-long, I thoroughly enjoyed my stay.

The training centre was under the command of a Brigadier who, at the end of the course, on the eve departure, gave a splendid dinner in the main mess hall. I dressed for the occasion and, presenting myself at the entrance to the hall at the appointed hour, I searched the seating plan to find my place, but in vain. I began to feel embarrassed that perhaps, I wasn't supposed to attend, when a Major whose acquaintance I had made during the course, came alongside.

"What's the trouble, old boy," he said. "Can't find your place?" In my embarrassment, I mumbled something. "There you are," he said jabbing his finger at a seat on the top table next to the Brigadier. I was, it appeared, to be the guest of honour. Immediately, I got a terrible sinking feeling in the pit of my stomach. 'My god,' I thought. 'I'll have to make a speech.' A thing I had always dreaded since childhood and the days of my speech impediment. So nervous was I, that I hardly touched a morsel of the food placed before me and spent the time, as course after delicious course went by, trying hard to think what to say. At last the meal was over and the moment I dreaded had arrived. The Brigadier turned to me and put his hand over mine, I went cold.

"Don't worry old man," he said, smiling. "There'll be no speeches tonight." My relief was only tempered by the thought of all that lovely food I'd just missed.

In the later years of my service, ceremonial became a large part of my duty, for example, when circuit judges toured the Provinces to try capital offences and the like. Protocol demanded that we book them in to the best available accommodation, provide a vehicle and Police driver and a full-time armed guard at the judge's door. At 6.00 pm on the day of their arrival - 'sundowner' time - the most senior Police officer in the area would present himself to enquire whether the judge had everything he required and, usually, an invitation to a glass of sherry followed.

At 9.30 am the following morning, the Provincial Police Commander would collect the judge from his accommodation and conduct him to the court where he would receive a general salute and be invited to inspect the fifty man guard of honour. Then to the judges chambers where a brief discussion of the cases to be heard would take place.

Most judges would be pleased to hear Police opinions of a case, for example, in many murder cases, we Police would start at the top and could, if we thought it appropriate, reduce the charge, and at times were content to accept pleas of guilty to manslaughter. This could simplify matters considerably whereas Solicitors would often advise their clients not to accept this bargaining, resulting in the accused being hanged for murder instead of getting five years for manslaughter. (By giving such advice, Solicitors would prolong the case and of course, obtain extra fees). Between cases, the judge would retire to his chambers, often accompanied by the senior Police officer and usually another glass of sherry would be taken prior to commencing the next session.

High courts used assessors instead of juries when trying Africans for serious crimes. Three assessors, usually tribal elders, sat beside the judge and, when all the evidence had been heard, the judge would ask the assessors whether they considered the accused was innocent or guilty. Invariably, the assessors would ask why they had been kept there for many days when they knew right from the start that the accused was guilty/not guilty.

Up to the rank of Divisional Commander, one always had to command the parades on such ceremonial occasions, but I, being born without a sense of timing or rhythm, was always embarrassed to be shouting out orders to men marching behind me, not knowing whether I was in step with them or not. I made sure that our men were trained to execute the correct movements at the correct time, whatever the order and I am fairly certain that spectators seldom detected any error.

There were many other occasions upon which we were expected to provide a Guard of Honour and on one such occasion I, as Provincial Commander, had to provide one for H.E. The Governor who was due to change planes at the local airport, followed by another half an hour later for a big-wig from the Belgian Congo.

My Divisional Commander took charge of the hundred man parade while I escorted the Governor on his inspection but the Divisional Commander mistakenly ordered a general salute for His Excellency instead of a Royal Salute. The Congo chap was only entitled to a general salute and probably felt very honoured when he was greeted by a royal one. H.E. The Governor didn't bat an eyelid and I breathed a sigh of relief thinking he hadn't noticed.

As His Excellency boarded his plane, he shook my hand and leaned forward in a confidential manner. "By the way," he said. "I usually get a royal salute." And he laughed then complimented me on excellent turnout of the guard.

My Provincial centre at Kisumu had a resident judge, a resident stipendiary magistrate and a Senior Administrative Officer, the latter having magisterial powers under which he would hear cases out in his district.

Early one morning, the judge requested that I call and see him. He sounded a bit put out so, with some trepidation, I hastened over to his chambers where I found him with the magistrate, both white with fury and stammering incoherently. It appeared that the Administrative Officer had publicly accused them both of corruption and they wanted me to take immediate action. I pacified them as much as I could and told them that, as far as the Police were concerned, there had never been even as much as a rumour of corruption and I advised them to take civil action. I never did hear the outcome, though the Administrative Officer was posted else where a few weeks later.

One morning, I received information from headquarters expressing concern about bandits who were operating from several of the islands in Lake Victoria. The problem also worried the Government of Uganda in whose territory most of the northern half of the lake lay. At night, the bandits would venture out from their islands by canoe to reach isolated trading centres on the shore, then ransack them and, without a second thought, kill anyone who dared to oppose them. I was given command of an air, sea and land operation launched to curtail the activities of these bandits.

I had managed to obtain funds which I used to persuade the East African Railways and Harbours local marine branch into converting a 45 ft. diesel engined, steel hulled lighter into a rather nicely proportioned 'gunboat'. The crew consisted of a Police Sergeant and two Constables who between them, had to share the jobs of coxswain, deck crew, gun crew and wireless operator. Fire power comprised rifles and a Bren gun fixed to the forward radio mast on a mount which I designed and had made by our transport branch. The muzzle of the Bren fitted into a swivel and the butt clipped into a slot lower down the mast. The gunner pulled the butt up to his shoulder and could walk all round the mast giving him a 360 degree field of fire but limits were built into the mount so that he couldn't hit any part of the boat.

The islands used by the bandits were quite small and mostly covered in timber and dry bush, and were fringed around their shores with dry reeds and papyrus.

Liaison with the Ugandan Government produced a couple of water-borne parties of their Police and I provided air reconnaissance.

Aircraft located occupied islands and radioed the 'fleet' which would rapidly make for the island where bandits had been spotted. The crews would set fire to the dry undergrowth and wait for the bandits to be flushed out and flee in their canoes. Sound in theory, but, I'm afraid, not many bandits were accounted for. However, it did discourage them and the problem largely ceased. There was an added benefit - the burning did wonders for the regeneration of the islands' vegetation.

The Lake Province had several hundred miles of shoreline on Lake Victoria and, prior to the introduction of the 'gunboat', it was impossible for Police to make surprise visits to lakeside villages and settlements. To get to most of them we had to advance on foot with the 'bush telegraph' busily announcing our progress. But now, we could approach silently at night by water and before dawn, we could have the area surrounded without even waking the inhabitants. Life for lakeside miscreants became far less comfortable.

A couple of my friends had a near disastrous experience while sailing on Lake Victoria. They were in a small dhow-rigged sailing boat crossing from shore to a remote island when they became totally becalmed. They sat motionless for hours until, at mid-day the sun was so hot that they decided to take a dip to cool off. Both went overboard and had been swimming around for a while when, suddenly, a breeze sprang up and the next thing they saw was the dhow shearing off down wind faster than they could swim. The Lake teemed with crocodile and they were miles from land so they just paddled round in circles having abandoned all hope. At about half a mile from them, the dhow suddenly luffed to windward, the breeze dropped and it remained hove-to long enough for one of them to reach it.

While in the Lake Province I would occasionally take to the highlands with a friend for a spot of trout fishing. One day we came across some particularly good fishing but were obliged to take to the water to get near enough to cast so, having no waterproofs, we stripped off our shorts and underpants and waded thigh deep into the stream. The trout were rising and we became thoroughly absorbed that we hardly noticed the mid-day sun until, on the way home that evening, we both began to feel the effects of the sunburn on our delicate parts. Both of us ended up with painfully sunburned and blistered penises - no joking matter, I can assure you.

In addition to imprisonment, Kenya Courts had the power to sentence offenders to corporal punishment which was to be carried out by the Police at their nearest station. An N.C.O. would beat the tar out of the villains who would scream the place down. I considered this to be against the interests of the Police in promoting their public image because members of the public, hearing the din would think we were interrogating suspects in a rather too brutal fashion. I made representations to headquarters and eventually succeeded in getting the practice stopped and floggings carried out in jail by prison officers.

In two other matters, I failed to get my way. At night, our African Police Officers wore long dark coloured greatcoats and, themselves being black were rendered almost invisible, particularly to vehicles. As a consequence, we suffered many casualties some of which were fatal. I proposed that we issue detachable reflectors to be clipped onto the back of the belt to make the men visible to approaching drivers, but every time I mentioned the idea at conferences, it was laughed out of court. Now, in company with forces everywhere, some form of reflective clothing is worn.

Our female Police Officers, like those in the UK carry a handbag on a shoulder strap. In a rough and tumble and in any circumstances where they may be attacked, these form a hindrance and in some instances a positive danger. I accept that a woman needs a bag, but surely it would be safer to have an easily detachable one clipped to the belt allowing them freedom of movement. I proposed this on several occasions. 'How do you quell a riot while safe-guarding a handbag?' I asked, but again, the idea was rejected.

I suppose, throughout my career in Africa, I was fortunate as far as my health was concerned. I suffered very few setbacks - mumps, malaria, a few bumps and bruises but, considering the possibilities of serious wounding from either enemy action or from wild animals and a myriad other mishaps, and the hazards to health of impure water and rotten food, I got away lightly.

I suffered from varicose veins from before the time I left home for Africa but I took good care to conceal the fact by wearing unauthorised items of uniform. Instead of shorts and stockings, I always wore long trousers. For other reasons I wore short sleeved jackets instead of long sleeved tunics and tie and a beret instead of official headgear. I never sought authority from headquarters for this and no one, from Commissioner down, ever queried my choice of clothing. On official and ceremonial occasions however, I reverted to authorised uniform.

A few weeks before I finally left Kenya, I had my varicose veins stripped out and the surgeon who removed them met me one night and he was laughing his head off. Apparently, a couple of Asian males had knocked him up one the night before at his home with a painful problem. One of them had slipped a small gold ring over the end of his penis before having sex with his wife because, he said, he thought it would give her greater pleasure. After the act, his penis wouldn't deflate and he was in great pain. The surgeon set about removing the ring with hot water and plenty of soap and eventually wrenched it off. The Asian gave him a nice shotgun in gratitude but history doesn't record whether or not the wife's enjoyment was at all enhanced by the device.

A medical examination for an insurance policy for school fees for my children disclosed the fact that I possessed only one testicle. I was unaware of this until the doctor commented on the fact and, oddly enough, no lady of my acquaintance had ever drawn my attention to it or, for that matter, ever complained of the deficiency. Nature, I think, must have provided me with compensations which disguised my true condition.

In mid career, one of our officers was very nearly discharged from the force on medical grounds which were only resolved at the eleventh hour. He reported to the doctor that, over a long period, he had been suffering severe bouts of dizziness. The doctor examined him and could find nothing wrong. The Officer felt fine and returned to his headquarters which were situated at high altitude where it was often cold. A few days later he began to suffer the symptoms again. Again, he came to the doctor who again, could find nothing wrong but the officer was obviously unfit for duty, so the wheels were set in motion for his discharge. The next time it happened, the doctor decided to visit the officer at his headquarters and, after a wander round the place, he discovered that, on cold days, the officer used a charcoal brazier to heat his office and was suffering from the effects of the fumes.

One medical problem nearly caused me more trouble than I needed. Not long after I arrived in Kenya, I got a terrible toothache. I lay all night in agony and, by dawn, after a lot of aspirins and a glass or two of brandy, it was no better. I called my driver and travelled sixty miles to the nearest dentist only to discover that he wasn't really a dentist, just a dental mechanic who was allowed to practice in the absence of a qualified dentist. I arrived at his house shortly after dawn and he greeted me half asleep.

"Come to my surgery at 8.00 am," he told me, and I went away feeling very miserable.

Just as we were leaving the driveway, my driver and I spotted a tame chimpanzee which was tethered to a running wire, and he spotted us. He leapt up in the air, turned somersaults, pulled faces and every did trick he could think of. We thought him very entertaining and the more we laughed the more antics he got up to. Suddenly, I realised that my toothache had gone. At 8.00 am I turned up at the surgery.

"Right, let's have a look," said the dental mechanic. "Mmm, you've got a problem; most of your teeth will have to come out. Come back at eleven."

This was only two years after I had left England and just before my departure, I had visited our family dentist who had pronounced my teeth to be in excellent condition. Either the dental mechanic was a fool or, I began to fear, I'd caught some dreadful disease in Africa which was about to destroy my teeth - and maybe, me. I dashed to see the Government Medical Officer and asked for his opinion.

"Well, I'm not a dentist," he said. "But I can't see anything wrong." Then he scribbled me a chit to a qualified dentist ninety miles away. "Go and see him," he said.

The dentist sat me in his chair and peered for a while into my mouth. "I see, I see," he said, tapping my back teeth with a steel instrument. "Your teeth are generally in good order except you've got a wisdom tooth impacting against your molars." And he took it out. Thank god I didn't listen to the dental mechanic.

Years later, I developed toothache in a back tooth and went to a dentist who recommended its extraction, saying I wouldn't miss it. After heaving and tugging, this way and that to no avail he gave up.

"I'm sorry," he said. "You'll have to come back. I've lost the strength in my wrists." I absolutely hate the idea of going away with the job half done and having to return later.

"Have another go," I said. "I'll hold your wrists and whichever way you push or pull, I'll use my strength in the same direction."

This time, we both had a go and, with almost no trouble, out it came. The tooth had an upward curving root which went into a hole in my jaw bone and, once the direction of its extraction had been lined up, it just popped out.

Since then, I have been to the dentists only six times and at the age of eighty-one, I still have all but three of my own teeth and all in good condition.

Suffering from the stress of his command, one of our officers went off his rocker and took up the Mohammadan faith. He was reported to be acting in a strange manner and when we found him, he was standing on his head at the cross-roads in the centre of the town-ship, dressed only in a white sheet. He was certified insane and another officer was detailed to escort him to the Mathari Mental Hospital in Nairobi, four hundred miles away.

During the over-night rail journey, the insane officer threw all the escort's clothing including his uniform out of the carriage window. When they arrived at Nairobi shortly after dawn, he stepped out of the train immaculately dressed, and told the Police who were there to meet them, there's your man, and pointed to the escorting officer who was wrapped only in a blanket.

In Kenya in those days, if a Magistrate and a Commissioned Police Officer, both or singly, but together with a white doctor, decided that a person was insane, then that was it; a paper was signed and the individual concerned was taken immediately to Mathari Mental Hospital. Many were released quite quickly and on leaving Mathari, were given a certificate stating that they were sane. Often in conversation, if you said to someone, 'You must be insane,' they might just say, 'Oh no I'm not,' and pull out their certificate to prove it, followed by, Can you prove you're sane.'

Reports came in that Wakamba witches were killing people and I sent a team to the reservation to investigate. The Wakamba tribe had been cannibals and filed their teeth to a point to publicise the fact. Several wizened old lady witches were pulled in for interrogation and freely admitted the accusation saying that, with their powerful spells and potions, they could kill an enemy for anyone willing to pay them.

Suspecting poison, I had half a dozen bodies exhumed and subjected to autopsy but my suspicions were proved groundless because the corpses had all died of various natural causes. When subjected to further questioning, the witches admitted that they had been claiming to have caused the death of persons they knew were ill and beyond help so that prospective clients would pay more for their services.

For the last year of my service, I was posted to Colony Headquarters in Nairobi as Assistant Commissioner - Administration. This, in my opinion, was a simple, fairly routine job containing little prospect of excitement, or for the chance to contribute further to the improvement of the Force.

Kenya had been granted internal self-government and promised full independence in the very near future, leaving Government officials with the choice of staying on under the new Government, applying for a post in another colony or taking early retirement. I was forty-four years old and, with no wish to serve under an independent black government led by the convicted Mau Mau leader, Jomo Kenyatta, I opted for early retirement.

Kenya had given me a wonderful life but conditions had changed and were continuing to change at an ever increasing rate. Besides I had recently purchased property back in the UK, in fact, most of that same property that my father had owned at Ranworth in Norfolk and where I had spent so many happy years of my childhood. I had visions of developing the property commercially to provide an income and a new life for myself and my family and, in that last year in Nairobi, my thoughts were elsewhere and I looked forward eagerly to my retirement.

Retirement promised to be a considerable financial blow but this was diminished by the fact that I had accumulated one and a half years additional overseas service, so I didn't switch from salary until I was aged forty-six. Every day, my informers in the establishment section of the Government let me know how releases from service were progressing until, eventually, it was my turn.

On leaving the Force, I received a letter from the Commissioner condensing my twenty-five year's service into just seven paragraphs:

296

Office of the Commissioner of Police

Police Headquarters
PO Box 30083
Nairobi
31st May 1963

My Dear Peter,

You are shortly retiring, at your own request, from the Kenya Police under the terms of the General Compensation Scheme.

Your record of service shows that you joined this Force on 18th July, 1938 in the rank of Assistant Inspector. You were promoted to inspector on 1st July, 1947; to Chief Inspector on 1st January, 1948; to Assistant Superintendent on 1st August, 1948; to Superintendent on 1st January 1951; to Senior Superintendent on 1st July, 1954 and to your present rank of Assistant Commissioner of Police on 1st July, 1957.

During your service you have served with distinction in many parts of the Colony as a divisional and provincial commander and on staff duties.

You have been commended for courage, devotion to duty and initiative on four occasions.

In 1956 you were awarded the Colonial Police Medal for Meritorious Service and in 1961 the Queen's Police Medal for Distinguished Service - both awards were well merited recognition of many years excellent service.

Your annual confidential reports have consistently described you as a deliberate, responsible, reliable and efficient police officer of sound judgement and exemplary conduct.

I take this opportunity of thanking you for the long and loyal service you have rendered and of wishing you every success in the future.

Yours sincerely

R.C. Catling
Commissioner of Police.

A little later, I received a further communication:

Colonial Office
Great Smith Street
London. SW1
28th October, 1963
Dear Mr. Mills,

Now that you are on leave pending retirement from public service overseas, the Secretary of State has asked me to let you know of his appreciation of your able service to the Government and people of Kenya for over 25 years.
He sends you his best wishes for the future.

Yours sincerely

N.B.J. Huijsman
Private Secretary

So the adventure, my great adventure, was over - not my life, of course, only the first half of it.

A New Life

At last the great day came when we were to leave Africa for good. We bid farewell to our friends and colleagues and drove down to Mombasa to board the British India ship SS Kenya bound for Southampton. The SS Kenya was a new and luxurious liner and, for this our last trip, we were allocated a large, deck-level, en suite cabin and had a pleasant voyage home on a calm, unruffled sea.

Prior to leaving Nairobi, I had purchased a new estate car for delivery to the docks in time for our arrival and, within three hours of disembarkation, we were back at Ranworth, installed in our own house as UK citizens.

Many years ago, before I left England, I had wandered round my parents' country home at Ranworth, remembering all the joy and excitement I had experienced there throughout my childhood and swearing that, one day I would return. All through my life in Africa, that ambition had stayed with me; often consigned to the nether regions of my mind but never far from my thoughts. In later years, when on home leave, my family and I stayed there in my Aunt's cottage, and I began to take practical steps towards achieving my ambition.

The main house had been sold many years previously but, still within the ownership of an aunt and cousins, was the majority of the land and the buildings which had once been my Grandfather's barley malting business - the manager's house, the maltings itself, a cottage, land to either side, the land fronting the Broad, and a large stretch of marsh which lay between the Broad and the River Bure. All this, I managed to purchase from my relatives, dreaming that one day, after my retirement, I would be able to develop it into a commercial venture sufficient to provide myself and my family with a reasonable income.

In 'retirement', we could have existed on my pension alone but it would have been just that - existence. For anything more, I would need to earn a living and I thought long and hard about what to do but laid down five criteria which would govern my choice:

1. I wouldn't work for anyone else;
2. I wouldn't employ anyone full time;
3. I would do nothing which committed me to set hours of work;
4. I would do nothing which demanded great capital expenditure;
5. I would do nothing that I really didn't want to do.

After a couple of months settling in, renewing old acquaintances and organising adequate shooting for the future I decided it was time to set about earning a living.

In Norfolk, a 'Broad' is an open stretch of water created by mediaeval peat diggings in the marshes alongside the many rivers. Broads, if allowed to do so will slowly silt up, turn to reed beds then after many decades will develop into 'Alder Carr' - marshy land covered in Black Alder trees, willow, reeds and sedges.

For centuries, the Broads and their connecting rivers had formed a major highway for shipping goods, such as barley to my Grandfathers Maltings at Ranworth, by 'Wherry', a sailing barge unique to the area. But, with the arrival of modern road transport, the trade had declined and some of the formerly busy waterways had been neglected and allowed to silt up. Malthouse Broad was one such which, when we moved there, was reduced to a narrow channel between acres of reed beds.

With the post-war increase in the holiday industry, the Norfolk Broads were in greater demand so the authorities decided to dredge Malthouse Broad and open it up into a sizeable lake stretching from the river, past my own land to the public quayside and beyond. Holiday-makers on the Broads then would have somewhere for overnight mooring and for gaining access to facilities ashore.

The dredger arrived and started work but immediately arose the problem of disposing of the dredgings. With a little negotiation, I persuaded the contractor to dump the dredgings on the marsh at the margins of my property and before they had finished I had the makings of a considerable area of dry land along my water frontage.

My plan now was to create permanent moorings for rent to boat owners so, single handed, I set about driving piles and constructing timber quay headings to form a marina. Later I started to take boats out of the water, store them for the winter and carry out repairs and maintenance and, gradually built up a reasonable business which fitted nicely into my original specification.

Not knowing at that stage whether the 'marina' would prove to be a financial success or not, I decided to start importing African wood carvings for sale to UK wholesalers and as my source for these, I remembered an acquaintance in Kenya.

Living within my jurisdiction for the six years prior to my retirement, had been a refugee couple called Konigsberger who had reached Tanganyika after Hitler's attack on Poland. By profession, the husband had been a barrister in his homeland, a doctor of law, but was not allowed to practice in Kenya. I always called him 'doctor'. His wife was a delightful and very attractive woman. At first, he had earned a living shooting crocodile in Lake Victoria, then, while working as a Solicitor's Clerk, he saw a market for wood carvings and opened a shop selling them.

Though I had never come to know them well in Kenya, I had always been impressed by their integrity, ingenuity, energy and willingness to turn their hand to anything to earn a living and I respected them because, against all odds, they were succeeding.

By coincidence, I bumped into the doctor a few days before leaving Kenya. By then, he had a second shop in Mombasa and had just opened a third at Nairobi's Embakasi Airport. In addition, he employed Kamba wood carvers to produce sufficient goods when he couldn't get them elsewhere.

"I'm off out of Kenya," I told him. "I might one day import some of your stuff for sale in the UK."

Well, I did, and that started a very happy and successful business relationship which lasted for many years.

At first, I ordered £400 worth and sold them all to boat owners in my marina. Then I ordered £800 worth which I sold to a wholesaler, followed by more, and yet more. The doctor then wrote to me to suggest a partnership in which he would supply the carvings on a sale or return basis and I would pay him as I sold them.

The business went well and eventually, we opened a shop in Bournmouth called 'Safari' which I had fitted out and for which I employed staff to run it. I started to import hand-craft from other parts of the world including Russia, Italy, France, Poland, India, South Africa, Finland and many more.

I expanded the business by opening gift cabinets in almost thirty hotels giving the hotel a percentage of the profit and the business traded very successfully. After three years, the doctor and his wife sold up in Kenya and bought a property just outside Bournmouth and he took over the running of the business. Eventually, we reached a point where, to make more profit, or even to keep it at a steady level, we would have had to expand but, since by that time, we were both ageing, we sold the business. Happily, the doctor and his wonderful wife are alive and well and living in some comfort.

The Marina proved successful but very hard work, and, too late, I realised that I had been concentrating on the business and taking my wife too much for granted. The children, Ann and Peter had, by now, both flown the nest and relations between Betty and myself had become strained and, after, what to me had been twenty-five years of happy marriage, we decided to part. It was an amicable parting with no animosity; I bought her the house of her choice, a car and she took our capital, while I kept the house, the land and the business. We remained good friends until her sad death in April 1999, often meeting on family and social occasions and, happily she and my second wife were very close friends.

Shortly after our separation, Betty remarried but I, now alone and having no knowledge of cooking or housekeeping and little desire to learn, engaged a housekeeper/secretary. She was very pretty and did her best - what man would complain or see the limitations in one so attractive.

It was always my habit to take a drink at lunchtime and, in the centre of the village, not three hundred yards from my house, stands our village pub called, not surprisingly, The Maltsters. I strolled in one sunny day and was amazed to see behind the bar, the prettiest, liveliest young woman you could imagine. She was petite, blonde, vivacious with a spectacular figure and with a Cockney's vocabulary and sense of humour. For me, the village pub, normally filled with holidaymakers in the summer and just a few locals in the winter-time, had suddenly been transformed and I looked forward with a fresh eagerness to my regular lunch-time visits.

I learned that the young woman, Barbara, had recently retreated from London to stay with friends in a nearby village following the rather harrowing break-up of her marriage and, to earn her keep and for something to fill her day, had found a job behind the bar of The Maltsters.

For me, Cupid's arrow had struck with a vengeance and I began to spend more time than usual in the pub.

Slowly we came to know each other and, between us, grew a bond of sympathy, each for the other's solitary state of existence. To save her the long and difficult trips to and from work - there was no public transport - I offered her accommodation at my house close by, which she accepted. The large old house now echoed with Barbara's laughter and she brought happiness once again into my bachelor existence.

Months went by and friendship slowly turned to love until, one day, I plucked up courage and proposed marriage. I was on tenter hooks like never before, I knew that I could make her happy but, the age difference - she was twenty-three and I, thirty years older. To my great joy, she accepted and soon, we were married.

Our friends said it wouldn't last six months and every six months since then, we have celebrated that fact that it did. So far, we have celebrated fifty-four six months and in the meantime we've had a lot of fun and joy and laughter, and I think I can safely say to our 'friends', Yes! It will last.

Barbara has, over these past twenty-eight years, been my devoted wife, companion, secretary, organiser, cook, housekeeper, dog handler, marsh-person, boat mechanic, lover and friend and I hope, beyond all things, that I have in some way been worthy of her.

Not long after our marriage, I suggested to Barbara that we take a holiday in Kenya. I was keen to show her some of the places I had known and introduce her to some of the friends with whom I still had contact. We flew to Nairobi's Embakasi Airport and set off in a hired Volkswagen Beetle for an eight week tour of Kenya and Tanzania. The tour was a splendid one. Of course we had the odd mishap with tarantulas, rabid dogs, warthogs, elephant dung and the like, but Barbara took it all in her stride and, after that we had many enjoyable holidays over there. However, I began to see a gradual decline in standards which worried me.

Some years later, on a holiday there, we decided that it would be our last visit.

Britain had handed over to independent rule, what was a disciplined, viable, exporting country, free from famine, health hazards, unrest and serious crime but what had now become a ruled by corruption, malad-ministration and noted for famine, civil unrest and the begging bowl.

I loved Kenya; I have seen its wild places, its rugged beauty; I have suffered its heat and its cold; met its people, good and bad, and have borne witness to the magnificence of its fauna and flora, its storms, its peace, its

303